The Global Fight for Climate Justice

Anticapitalist Responses to Global Warming
and Environmental Destruction

edited by Ian Angus

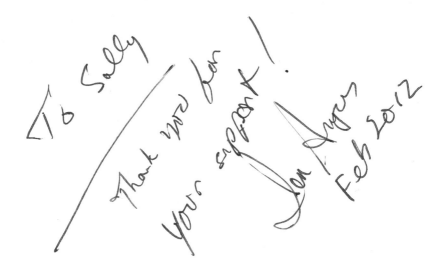

To Sally
Thank you for your support!
Ian Angus
Feb 2012

Resistance Books, London

Resistance Books would be pleased to receive readers'
comments about this book,
and any suggestions you may have for future
publications or wider distribution.

Resistance Books
PO Box 62732 London SW2 9G Britain
Web: socialistresistance.org
email: contact@socialistresistance.org.

Resistance books are available at special quantity
discounts to educational and non-profit organizations,
and to bookstores.

Design by Ian Angus
Published by Resistance Books, June 2009
Printed by Lightning Source

ISBN: 978-0-902869-87-5

EAN: 9780902869875

The Global Fight for Climate Justice

Anticapitalist activists from around the world offer radical answers to two of most important questions of our time:

▸ Why is capitalism destroying the conditions that make life on earth possible?

▸ How can we stop the destruction before it is too late?

The Global Fight for Climate Justice makes the case that saving the world from climate catastrophe will require much more than tinkering with technology or taxes. Only radical social change can prevent irreversible damage to the earth and civilization.

edited by Ian Angus

Ian Angus, who wrote several of the articles in this book and selected the others from a wide range of authors and movements, is one of the world's best-known ecosocialist activists.

He is editor of the online journal *Climate and Capitalism*, which has been described as "the most reliable single source of information and strategic insights for climate justice."

Ian is also Associate Editor of *Socialist Voice*, a founding member of the Ecosocialist International Network, and director of the Socialist History Project. He lives in Ontario, Canada.

To my grandchildren
Abby and Sam
in the hope and conviction
that you will inherit a better world

"From the standpoint of a higher economic form of society, private ownership of the globe by single individuals will appear quite as absurd as private ownership of one man by another. Even a whole society, a nation, or even all simultaneously existing societies taken together, are not the owners of the globe. They are only its possessors, its beneficiaries, and they must hand it down to succeeding generations in an improved condition" —*Karl Marx*

Contents

more...

5: Privatizing The Atmosphere

6: Voices From the Global South

7: Building a Climate Emergency Movement

8: Ecosocialist Responses to Capitalist Ecocide

Red and Green

Robb Johnson

I dreamed the old dream, just last night
    Red and green, and going home
I dreamed of no more wars to fight
    Red and green, and going home.

I dreamed of those, who know no rest
    Red and green, and going home
The refugees, and the dispossessed
    Red and green, and going home.

Submarines ploughshared the sand
    Red and green, and going home
And factories turned to fertile land
    Red and green, and going home.

We healed the sick and the obscene
    Red and green, and going home
The leper and the limousine
    Red and green, and going home.

We sought our likeness in each face
    Red and green, and going home
And with each kindness, added grace
    Red and green, and going home.

So broke the walls of greed and fear
    Red and green, and going home
With love to all things suffering here
    Red and green, and going home.

These are old dreams, nothing new
    Red and green, and going home
And yet to come nonetheless true
    Red and green, and going home.

And yet to come nonetheless true
    Red and green, and going home.

Foreword

Derek Wall

This book brings together some of the most important ecosocialist activists and thinkers on our planet. Editor Ian Angus has argued that the task of ecosocialists is to "make greens redder and reds greener" — *The Global Fight for Climate Justice* will make that task easier.

The publisher, Socialist Resistance, has worked hard to promote ecosocialism, and while I am not a member of their organisation, I would like to thank them for all their efforts. Their non-sectarian approach of working with other ecosocialists is refreshing.

I am particularly pleased to see that this book includes a contribution by my friend and comrade Hugo Blanco, who was one of Che Guevara's contemporaries. Hugo led the peasant uprising in Peru in 1961, and was rescued from execution by a huge international campaign led by Jean Paul Sartre and Bertrand Russell. Today he publishes *Lucha Indígena*, a newspaper that carries news of the fight of indigenous peoples in Latin America for freedom, for social and environmental justice.

Indeed, all the contributors have impressive track records. Joel Kovel's *The Enemy of Nature* is one of the most important ecosocialist texts. John Bellamy Foster's *Marx's Ecology* has revealed to a generation of revolutionary socialists the vital importance of ecology to Marx's thought. Larry Lohmann has done impressive work to expose the carbon trading con. Daniel Tanuro has been a powerful voice for promoting ecological thinking among Marxists. Kevin Smith has researched the role of banks in devastating the environment and is an activist with the climate camp. And I could go on ...

My own introduction to ecosocialism came in the 1980s, when I joined the Ecology Party. My ecosocialist ideas were shaped by Australian writer Alan Roberts, whose 1979 book *The Self-managing Environment* is still essential reading. He was one of the first to write about Marx's concern with the metabolic relationship between humanity and nature, the concept of "commons," and the way that alienation of our labour leads to destructive consumerism. Roberts challenged the inadequacy of the solutions proposed by most environmental writers:

> There now exists a highly valuable store of information and analysis on environmental problems. On the whole, however, the recommendations in the literature do not measure up to the level of their factual exposure and analysis. Some treatments hardly go further than to suggest (often rather quietly) that "something should be done." Many others, after sketching sombre

pictures of the likely future, will startle the alert reader by the inconsistent feebleness of the curative action they recommend: write to your MP or to your congressman — "bring some pressure to bear."

Climate change and other ecological problems are rooted in an economic system that needs continual growth, even though that is often dysfunctional for human beings.

Yet few environmentalists have faced up to the fact that capitalism is incompatible with ecological sustainability. In fact, the current global framework for dealing with climate change is based on carbon trading schemes that do more to benefit bankers than solve the problem.

An essential part of any real solution involves maintaining key ecosystems such the Amazon rainforest that act as carbon sinks and perform other vital biological functions. In 2008, direct action by over 50 indigenous groups in Peru prevented Alan Garcia's government from making it easier for corporations to steal their communal land in the Amazon. They won a huge victory for planetary ecology by preventing logging, oil and gas exploration in the Amazon. Any serious solution to ecological problems must involve indigenous people, who have been at the radical edge of the Latin American left and who have put socialism back on the political agenda globally.

Solutions to climate change must also involve workers. Alan Thornett, a leading member of Socialist Resistance and a former car worker, has argued that instead of producing cars, worker-directed alternative production plans could produce renewable energy systems and other ecological goods.

The Cuban experience of surviving the loss of Soviet oil by introducing ecological policies such as organic permaculture and renewable energy, shows that socialism is a precondition of ecological sustainability.

We need to move beyond capitalism to an ecosocialist system. Creating such a future will demand intense political struggle.

This book is an essential tool for that struggle, and I commend it to all who are serious about creating a liveable future for humanity.

Derek Wall is a founder of the Ecosocialist International Network and a former principal speaker for the Green Party of England and Wales. He has written six books on green politics and blogs at www.another-green-world.blogspot.com/. His most recent book, Babylon and Beyond *(Pluto Press), examines anti-capitalist economics.*

Introduction

Ian Angus

In this book, anticapitalist activists from around the world offer radical answers to two of the most important questions of our time:

▸ Why is capitalism destroying the conditions that make life on earth possible?

▸ How can we stop the destruction before it is too late?

The authors disagree on many things. Some are Marxists, some are not; some proudly call themselves ecosocialists and others see no need for that label; some are members of political parties and some reject traditional forms of political activity. Even among those who consider themselves Marxists or ecosocialists there are differing views on to build a movement, what social forces can change the world, what technologies and policies should be supported or condemned.

But they all agree that solving the climate crisis of the 21st century, saving the world from climate catastrophe, will require much more than tinkering with technology or economic policy, the solutions promoted by capitalist politicians and most of the green establishment.

As John Bellamy Foster wrote in his recent book, *The Ecological Revolution*: "We have reached a turning point in the human relation to the earth: all hope for the future of this relationship is now either revolutionary or it is false."

The climate emergency exposes the present social order's deepest contradictions: unstoppable thirst for wealth and material growth that can only be obtained by condemning billions of people to poverty, while simultaneously undermining of the very conditions of human existence.

This system, as Karl Marx said, is like a vengeful god that demands human sacrifices before it deigns to bless its worshippers.

And now, when their god has taken us to the edge of global catastrophe, the system's faithful acolytes insist that only minor repairs are needed, that everything will be all right if we just rejig the tax code, or let corporations trade pollution credits, or have fewer babies.

In contrast, the essays and manifestos in this book argue that the climate crisis involves profound issues of political, economic and social justice, issues that cannot be resolved without equally profound changes in the political, economic and social systems that are causing the crisis. They expose the profound injustice that makes the world's poorest and most vulnerable people suffer for the crimes of the richest nations and the biggest corporations. They insist that we must view global warming as an issue of oppression, exploitation and injustice, and that we must focus our fight on winning climate justice — for the global south, for indigenous peoples, for workers and farmers around the world.

Marx famously wrote that philosophers have only interpreted the world in various ways but the task is to change it. That statement is often misunderstood. It wasn't just a call to move from discussion to action — Marx was also saying that we can't properly understand the world *unless* we work to change it.

For that reason, it's important to point out that the authors of this book aren't ivory tower theorists: every one of them is actively involved in building movements to stop climate change, to change the world. So the articles in this book aren't abstract meditations: they are products of the authors' concrete experiences in building movements against global warming and environmental destruction. The authors aren't passive observers: they are partisans who don't hesitate to declare their outrage at ecological vandalism and their determination to stop the vandals.

Our task is to change the world. This book is a contribution to that task.

Acknowledgements

As editor of *Climate and Capitalism*, I have met (in person or electronically) many comrades from all around the world, of many political persuasions, who have shared their experiences and the lessons they have drawn from those experiences. Many of them contributed articles to this book, and all of them have helped me to think through my own views on ecosocialism. Their suggestions, criticisms and contributions have been invaluable.

I owe particular debts of gratitude to the many people, organizations and publications who made this book possible, including these:

▸ All of the authors who are listed below in "About the authors."

▸ The publications that granted permission to reprint articles: *Climate and Capitalism, Green Left Weekly, International Socialist Review, International Viewpoint, Links International Journal of Socialist Renewal, New Scientist, Socialist Resistance, Socialist Voice*, and *Socialist Worker* (U.S.A.)

▸ Zed Books, for permission to include an excerpt from Joel's Kovel's pathbreaking book *The Enemy of Nature: The End of Capitalism or the End of the World*.

▸ Oxfam International, for permission to include the Executive Summary of *Climate Wrongs and Human Rights*.

▸ Robb Johnson, who enthusiastically granted permission to include the lyrics of *Red and Green*. Roy Bailey's singing introduced me to this song

— it's on his CD *Coda*, which I highly recommend.
▸ Richard Fidler, who translated Hugo Blanco's article on very short notice.
▸ Duncan Chapel, who suggested this project in the first place, and who supported it through to publication.
▸ Jane Kelly and Sheila Malone,whose book *Ecosocialism or Barbarism* paved the way for this one.

About the authors

Hugo Blanco has been a leader of the indigenous peasant movement in Peru since the Land or Death uprising in the 1960s. He publishes the newspaper *La Lucha Indígena*.

Patrick Bond is director of the Centre for Civil Society at the University of KwaZulu-Natal, South Africa. His books include *Climate Change, Carbon Trading and Civil Society*.

Simon Butler writes for *Green Left Weekly* and maintains Climate Change Social Change, an ecosocialist blog.

Fidel Castro led the Cuban revolution and was the Cuba's head of state from 1960 until he retired in 2007.

Nicole Colson writes for *Socialist Worker*, the newspaper of the US-based International Socialist Organization.

Kamala Emanuel is a climate activist and a member of the Socialist Alliance in Perth, Australia.

John Bellamy Foster is editor of *Monthly Review* and the author of many books, including *Marx's Ecology* (2000) and *The Ecological Revolution* (2009).

Robb Johnson is a UK-based singer-songwriter.

Tony Kearns is Senior Deputy General Secretary of the Communication Workers Union in the U.K.

Joel Kovel is the author of The *Enemy of Nature: The End of Capitalism or the End of the World?* and a founding member of the Ecosocialist International Network.

Juan Esteban Lazo Hernandez is Vice-President of Cuba's Council of State and a member of the Central Committee of the Communist Party of Cuba.

Larry Lohmann is the author of *Carbon Trading: A Critical Conversation on Climate Change, Privatization and Power*.

Michael Löwy, who co-wrote the first *Ecosocialist Manifesto* in 2001, is a supporter of the Fourth International in France.

José Ramón Machado Ventura, who fought with Fidel Castro in the guerrilla war in the 1950s, is first vice president of Cuba's Councils of

State and Ministers .

Liam Mac Uaid is an editor of *Socialist Resistance* magazine.

Evo Morales, the president of Bolivia, is the first indigenous head of state in Latin America.

Anne Petermann and **Orin Langelle** are Executive Director and Co-Director/Strategist of Global Justice Ecology Project.

Andrew Simms is the author of *Ecological Debt: Global Warming and the Wealth of Nations*, and policy director of the UK-based New Economics Foundation.

Kevin Smith is the author of *The Carbon Neutral Myth: Offset Indulgences for your Climate Sins.*

Sean Thompson is a supporter of Green Left, the anti-capitalist current in the Green Party of England and Wales.

Terry Townsend is a member of Socialist Alliance and Managing Editor of *Links: International Journal of Socialist Renewal.*

David Travis works with sustainable agriculture, community economics and alternative land tenure systems. He is currently developing a perennial agriculture project in North Carolina, USA.

Daniel Tanuro, a certified agriculturalist and ecosocialist environmentalist, is a supporter of the Fourth International in Belgium.

Chris Williams is a physics and chemistry teacher in New York City. He writes for *International Socialist Review.*

Texts and translations

Articles that were originally published in English have been lightly edited for style to ensure consistency, and obvious typographical errors have been corrected. A few articles are abridged: in those cases I have indicated where the full text can be found.

Previously published translations from other languages have been re-checked for accuracy and consistency, and changes have been made where appropriate.

The articles by Hugo Blanco and Daniel Tanuro were translated specifically for this book.

1: CLIMATE EMERGENCY

*"We are on the precipice of climate system tipping points,
beyond which there is no redemption."*
—climate scientist James Hansen—

In the decades following World War II, it seemed that civilization might be destroyed in nuclear war. That danger still exists, but we now face an even greater threat: global devastation caused not by someone deciding to enter launch codes, but simply by continuing business as usual.

In Part One:

‣ **Tomorrow Will Be Too Late.** *Fidel Castro's compelling statement to the 1992 Rio Earth Summit, in which described the crisis, explained its causes, and posed solutions. No other world leader was as clear or decisive.*

‣ **Some Impacts of Global Warming** *and* **Not a Distant Prospect**. *Two articles that summarize in point form the probable effects of uncontrolled global warming, and recent evidence that climate change is already changing the world.*

‣ **Climate Wrongs and Human Rights.** *A 2008 Oxfam report showing that climate change will undermine human rights on a massive scale.*

‣ **If Socialism Fails: The Spectre of 21st Century Barbarism.** *An essay on the horrifying consequences that face the world if the existing social order isn't replaced.*

Tomorrow Will Be Too Late

Fidel Castro

Earth Summit, Rio De Janeiro, Brazil, June 12, 1992

Mr. President of Brazil Fernando Collor de Melo;

Mr. UN Secretary General Brutru Butrus-Ghali; Your Excellencies;

An important biological species is in danger of disappearing due to the fast and progressive destruction of its natural living conditions: humanity. We have become aware of this problem when it is almost too late to stop it.

It is necessary to point out that consumer societies are fundamentally responsible for the brutal destruction of the environment. They arose from the old colonial powers and from imperialist policies which in turn engendered the backwardness and poverty which today afflicts the vast majority of mankind.

With only 20 percent of the world's population, these societies consume two-thirds of the metals and three-fourths of the energy produced in the world. They have poisoned the seas and rivers, polluted the air, weakened and punctured the ozone layer, saturated the atmosphere with gases that are changing weather conditions with a catastrophic effect we are already beginning to experience.

The forests are disappearing. The deserts are expanding. Every year billons of tons of fertile soil end up in the sea. Numerous species are becoming extinct. Population pressures and poverty trigger frenzied efforts to survive even when it is at the expense of the environment. It is not possible to blame the Third World countries for this. Yesterday, they were colonies; today, they are nations exploited and pillaged by an unjust international economic order.

The solution cannot be to prevent the development of those who need it most. The reality is that anything that nowadays contributes to underdevelopment and poverty constitutes a flagrant violation of ecology. Tens of millions of men, women, and children die every year in the Third World as a result of this, more than in each of the two world wars. Unequal terms of trade, protectionism, and the foreign debt assault the ecology and promote the destruction of the environment.

If we want to save mankind from this self-destruction, we have to better distribute the wealth and technologies available in the world. Less luxury and less waste by a few countries is needed so there is less poverty and less hunger on a large part of the Earth. We do not need any more transferring to the Third World of lifestyles and consumption habits that ruin the environment. Let human life become more rational. Let us implement a just international economic order. Let us use all the science necessary for pollution-free, sustained development. Let us pay the ecological debt, and not the foreign debt. Let hunger disappear, and not mankind.

Now that the alleged threat of communism has disappeared and there are no longer any more excuses for cold wars, arms races, and military spending, what is blocking the immediate use of these resources to promote the development of the Third World and fight the threat of the ecological destruction of the planet?

Let selfishness end. Let hegemonies end. Let insensitivity, irresponsibility, and deceit end. Tomorrow it will be too late to do what we should have done a long time ago. Thank you.

Some Impacts of Global Warming

Climate and Capitalism, November 19, 2007
From the *Synthesis Report* of the Intergovernmental Panel on Climate Change, November 17, 2007....

Africa
▸ By 2020, between 75 and 250 million people are projected to be exposed to increased water stress due to climate change.
▸ By 2020, in some countries, yields from rain-fed agriculture could be reduced by up to 50%. Agricultural production, including access to food, in many African countries is projected to be severely compromised. This would further adversely affect food security and exacerbate malnutrition.
▸ Towards the end of the 21st century, the projected sea-level rise will affect low-lying coastal areas with large populations. The cost of adaptation could amount to at least 5-10% of Gross Domestic Product (GDP).
▸ By 2080, an increase of 5-8% of arid and semi-arid land in Africa is projected under a range of climate scenarios.

Asia
▸ By the 2050s, freshwater availability in Central, South, East and South-East Asia, particularly in large river basins, is projected to decrease.
▸ Coastal areas, especially heavily-populated megadelta regions in South, East and South-East Asia, will be at greatest risk due to increased flooding from the sea and, in some megadeltas, flooding from the rivers.
▸ Climate change is projected to compound the pressures on natural resources and the environment, associated with rapid urbanization, indus-

trialization and economic development.

▸ Endemic morbidity and mortality due to diarrhoeal disease primarily associated with floods and droughts are expected to rise in East, South and South-East Asia due to projected changes in the hydrological cycle.

Australia and New Zealand

▸ By 2020, significant loss of biodiversity is projected to occur in some ecologically rich sites including the Great Barrier Reef and Queensland Wet Tropics.

▸ By 2030, water security problems are projected to intensify in southern and eastern Australia and, in New Zealand, in North Island and some eastern regions.

▸ By 2030, production from agriculture and forestry is projected to decline over much of southern and eastern Australia, and over parts of eastern New Zealand, due to increased drought and fire. However, in New Zealand, initial benefits are projected in some other regions.

▸ By 2050, ongoing coastal development and population growth in some areas of Australia and New Zealand are projected to exacerbate risks from sea level rise and increases in the severity and frequency of storms and coastal flooding.

Europe

▸ Climate change is expected to magnify regional differences in Europe's natural resources and assets. Negative impacts will include increased risk of inland flash floods, and more frequent coastal flooding and increased erosion (due to storminess and sea-level rise).

▸ Mountainous areas will face glacier retreat, reduced snow cover and winter tourism, and extensive species losses (in some areas up to 60% under high emissions scenarios by 2080).

▸ In Southern Europe, climate change is projected to worsen conditions (high temperatures and drought) in a region already vulnerable to climate variability, and to reduce water availability, hydropower potential, summer tourism and, in general, crop productivity.

▸ Climate change is also projected to increase the health risks due to heat-waves, and the frequency of wildfires.

Latin America

▸ By mid century, increases in temperature and associated decreases in soil water are projected to lead to gradual replacement of tropical forest by savanna in eastern Amazonia. Semi-arid vegetation will tend to be replaced by arid-land vegetation.

▸ There is a risk of significant biodiversity loss through species extinction

in many areas of tropical Latin America.
▸ Productivity of some important crops is projected to decrease and live-stock productivity to decline, with adverse consequences for food security. In temperate zones soybean yields are projected to increase. Overall, the number of people at risk of hunger is projected to increase.
▸ Changes in precipitation patterns and the disappearance of glaciers are projected to significantly affect water availability for human consumption, agriculture and energy generation.

North America
▸ Warming in western mountains is projected to cause decreased snow-pack, more winter flooding, and reduced summer flows, exacerbating competition for over-allocated water resources.
▸ In the early decades of the century, moderate climate change is projected to increase aggregate yields of rain-fed agriculture by 5-20%, but with important variability among regions. Major challenges are projected for crops that are near the warm end of their suitable range or which depend on highly utilized water resources.
▸ During the course of this century, cities that currently experience heat-waves are expected to be further challenged by an increased number, intensity and duration of heatwaves during the course of the century, with potential for adverse health impacts.
▸ Coastal communities and habitats will be increasingly stressed by climate change impacts interacting with development and pollution.

Polar Regions
▸ The main projected biophysical effects are reductions in the thickness and extent of glaciers and ice sheets and sea ice, and changes in natural ecosystems with detrimental effects on many organisms including migratory birds, mammals and higher predators.
▸ For human communities in the Arctic, impacts, particularly those resulting from changing snow and ice conditions are projected to be mixed.
▸ Detrimental impacts would include those on infrastructure and traditional indigenous ways of life.
▸ In both polar regions, specific ecosystems and habitats are projected to be vulnerable, as climatic barriers to species invasions are lowered.

Small Islands
▸ Sea-level rise is expected to exacerbate inundation, storm surge, erosion and other coastal hazards, thus threatening vital infrastructure, settlements and facilities that support the livelihood of island communities.
▸ Deterioration in coastal conditions, for example through erosion of

beaches and coral bleaching is expected to affect local resources.

▸ By mid-century, climate change is expected to reduce water resources in many small islands, e.g., in the Caribbean and Pacific, to the point where they become insufficient to meet demand during low-rainfall periods.

▸ With higher temperatures, increased invasion by non-native species is expected to occur, particularly on mid- and high-latitude islands.

Not a Distant Prospect

Ian Angus

Climate and Capitalism, March 10, 2009

Global warming is not a distant prospect that might affect our grandchildren at the end of the century.

Anyone who opens a newspaper has read about the devastating heat wave and fires in Australia. And you've probably seen news of several studies that conclude that global warming and CO2 emissions have already exceeded the worst case scenarios in the IPCC's 2007 reports.

But those big stories are just the tip of the (rapidly melting) iceberg. The following items from various news sources are just a sampling of many I gathered in January and February, 2009. Most are based on peer-reviewed reports by climate scientists.

It's here, and it's very real.

▸ Canada's forests, stressed by global warming, insect infestations and persistent fires, are now pumping out more carbon dioxide than they absorb. *Chicago Tribune, Jan. 2*

▸ Ten million people are facing hunger in Kenya after harvests failed because of drought. The government has declared a national emergency. *Associated Press, Jan. 9*

▸ Some regions of Antarctica, particularly the peninsula that stretches toward South America, have warmed rapidly in recent years, contributing to the disintegration of ice shelves and accelerating the sliding of glaciers. *New York Times, Jan. 22*

▸ There has been a "sudden and dramatic collapse" in the amount of CO2 absorbed by the Sea of Japan. Absorption from 1999 to 2007 was half the level of 1992 to 1999. *Guardian (UK) Jan. 12*

▸ A study of past heat waves of the past predicts severe food shortages and rising malnutrition, especially in places where people are already poor and hungry. Crop yields may fall 20, 30, or 40 percent in some cases. *Discover.com, Jan. 21*

▸ The U.S. Geological Survey says the death rates of trees in western U.S. forests have doubled over the past two to three decades, driven in large part by warmer temperatures and water scarcity linked to climate change. *Washington Post, Jan. 22*

▸ If CO2 concentrations reach 450 to 600 parts per million, up from about 385 ppm today, problems like inexorable sea level rise and massive droughts will last for at least a thousand years. *New York Times, Jan. 27*

▸ The world's marine ecosystems risk being severely damaged by ocean acidification. PH levels are changing 100 times faster than natural variability. *BBCNews.com, Feb. 1*

▸ The Earth's seasons have shifted back in the calendar year, with the hottest and coldest days of the years now occurring almost two days earlier. *LiveScience, Feb. 3*

▸ 33 countries, including Malawi, Guinea, Senegal, Uganda, Bangladesh, Cambodia, Vietnam, Peru and Colombia are highly vulnerable to the effects of climate change because of their heavy reliance on fisheries and limited alternative sources of protein. *Agence France-Presse, Feb. 5*

▸ U.S. energy secretary Steven Chu says water shortages could eliminate all agriculture in California by the end of the century. *Los Angeles Times, Feb. 4*

▸ The ice caps are melting so fast that the world's oceans are rising more than twice as fast as they were in the 1970s. *Times (UK), Feb. 8*

▸ Since October, drought has killed 1.5 million cattle in Argentina. *Washington Post, Feb. 9*

▸ The Audubon Society says more than half of 305 bird species in North America are spending the winter about 35 miles farther north than they did 40 years ago. *Associated Press, Feb. 10*

▸ One of the largest penguin colonies in the world is under threat because the birds are being forced to swim 25 miles further from their nesting sites than they did only a decade ago, to find food. The colony has already declined by a fifth in the past 22 years. *Independent (UK). Feb. 9*

▸ Researchers in Norway report that atmospheric levels of carbon dioxide rose to 392 parts per million in December, up 2-3 ppm from the same time a year earlier. *Reuters, Feb. 12*

▸ Warmer temperatures are at least partly to blame for a surge in malaria cases in the highlands of East Africa and the increasing development of drug-resistant strains of the disease. *Daily Climate, Feb. 16*

▸ Indonesia's outermost islands face the risk of disappearing altogether because of human-induced climate change. *Jakarta Post, Feb. 17*

▸ The U.N. Environment Program says that up to a quarter of global food production could be lost by 2050 due to the combined impact of climate change, land degradation and loss, water scarcity and species infestation.

Cereal yields have already stagnated worldwide and fish catches are declining. *Reuters, Feb. 17*

▸ Global climate change threatens the complete disappearance of the Andes' tropical glaciers within the next 20 years, putting water, energy and food sources at risk, the World Bank says. Glacial retreat has already reduced by 12 percent the water supply to Peru's dry coastline, where 60 percent of the country's population lives. *Associated Press, Feb. 18*

▸ Russia will likely see more forest fires, droughts and floods in the coming century due to global warming, and policy makers need to prepare for large-scale change. Over the past 100 years, air temperatures in Russia warmed by around 1.29 degrees C., compared with 0.74 degrees C. globally. *Associated Press, Feb. 18*

▸ Nearly one quarter of Papua New Guinea's rainforests were damaged or destroyed between 1972 and 2002. *Mongobay, Feb. 23*

▸ Glaciers in the Pyrenees, which covered 3300 hectares a century ago, now cover 390 hectares. Worldwide, in 1996-2005, glaciers melted twice as fast as in the previous 10 years. *Guardian, Feb. 23*

▸ As a result of drought in Northern China, about 4.7 million people and 2.5 million head of livestock now lack adequate drinking water. *New York Times, Feb. 26*

▸ California's Governor Arnold Schwarzenegger has declared a state of emergency because of a severe drought. *BBCNews.com, Feb. 28*

And by the way: poor countries have received less than 10% of the money promised by rich countries to help them adapt to global warming. The world's richest countries have together pledged nearly $18bn (£12.5bn) in the last seven years, but less than $0.9bn has been delivered. (*Guardian*, Feb. 20)

Climate Wrongs and Human Rights

Oxfam

> Within an international community based upon the rule of law and universal values of equality, human rights and dignity, it is surely wrong for small, vulnerable communities to suffer because of the actions of other more powerful resource-rich countries, actions over which they have no control, and little or no protection. – *President Gayoom, Republic of the Maldives*

> Human rights law is relevant because climate change causes human rights violations. But a human rights lens can also be helpful in approaching and managing climate change. – *Mary Robinson, President, Realising Rights*

Climate change is set to undermine human rights on a massive scale. International human-rights law states that, '*In no case may a people be deprived of its own means of subsistence.*' But – as the Inter-governmental Panel on Climate Change (IPCC) has documented in detail – rich countries' continued excessive greenhouse-gas emissions are depriving millions of people of the very water, soil and land on which they subsist.

Oxfam International believes that realising human rights is essential to lift people out of poverty and injustice. Our staff and local partners work with communities in over 100 countries and are increasingly witnessing the devastating effects of more frequent and severe climatic events on poor people's prospects for development. According to the IPCC, climate change could halve yields from rain-fed crops in parts of Africa as early as 2020, and put 50 million more people worldwide at risk of hunger. Almost half a million people today live on islands that are threatened with extinction by sea-level rise, and up to one billion people could face water shortages in Asia by the 2050s due to melted glaciers. These kinds of impacts, in turn, are likely to lead to mass migration across borders and increasing conflict over scarce resources.

Rich countries' emissions are effectively violating the rights of millions of the world's poorest people. Twenty-three rich countries – including the USA, western Europe, Canada, Australia, and Japan – are home to just 14 per cent of the world's population but have produced 60 per cent of the world's carbon emissions since 1850, and they still produce 40 per cent of

---

Executive Summary from Climate Wrongs and Human Rights *pp. 2-4, Oxfam International 9 September 2008, reproduced with the permission of Oxfam GB, Oxfam House, John Smith Drive, Cowley, Oxford OX4 2JY, UK www.oxfam.org.uk. Oxfam GB does not necessarily endorse any text or activities that accompany the materials.*

annual carbon emissions today. In 1992, these countries committed to return their annual emissions to 1990 levels by 2000. Instead, by 2005 they had allowed their collective emissions to rise more than ten per cent above 1990 levels – with increases exceeding 15 per cent in Canada, Greece, Ireland, New Zealand, Portugal, Spain, and the USA. Their collective failure to act has raised the scientific risk – and the political risk – of global warming exceeding the critical threshold of 2°C.

Economics – which influences many current climate-policy debates – approaches decision-making by weighing up competing costs and benefits. But in a global context, how can the financial costs of cutting emissions in the richest countries be compared with the human costs of climate change for the world's poorest people? The implications of such a trade-off are appalling. Human-rights principles provide an alternative to the assumption that everything – from carbon to malnutrition – can be priced, compared, and traded. Human rights are a fundamental moral claim each person has to life's essentials – such as food, water, shelter and security – no matter how much or how little money or power they have.

When the Universal Declaration of Human Rights was drawn up in 1948, its authors could not have imagined the complex global interconnectedness that climate change would create. Human-rights laws and institutions now need to evolve fast to rise to this unprecedented challenge, if they are to provide a means of stopping human rights worldwide from being further undermined by rich countries' excessive greenhouse-gas emissions.

Sixty years on from the Universal Declaration, this paper sets out a new vision for a rights-centred approach to climate-change policies. It uses the norms and principles of human rights to guide national and international climate policy making now.

Based on these principles, Oxfam calls for urgent action on the following human-rights hotspots:

▸ *Rich countries must lead now in cutting global emissions to keep global warming well below 2°C.* Global emissions must fall at least 80 per cent below 1990 levels by 2050, with rich countries delivering domestic cuts of at least 25–40 per cent by 2020.

▸ *Rich countries must provide the finance needed for international adaptation.* They have so far delivered only $92m to the fund set up for the least-developed countries – less than what people in the USA spend on sun-tan lotion in one month. Innovative financing is urgently needed to raise at least $50bn per year.

▸ *Rich countries must provide the finance needed for low-carbon technologies in developing countries.* Over 20 years, their contributions to multilateral climate funds for technology transfer have been on average $437m annually: western Europeans spent ten times that much buying vacuum cleaners last year. Commitment to a new scale of financing must be delivered in the post-2012 regime.

▸ *Rich countries must halt their biofuel policies* which are undermining poor people's right to food and leading to land and labour rights violations. Developing-country governments must likewise protect poor people's rights through domestic regulation of biofuel production.

▸ *Developing countries must focus their adaptation strategies on the most vulnerable people* by putting poor communities at the heart of planning, addressing women's needs and interests, and providing social-protection schemes.

▸ *Developing countries must have ownership in managing international adaptation funds* and, in turn, must be accountable to vulnerable communities for how the finance is spent.

▸ *Companies must call on governments to act with far greater urgency in cutting global emissions* and must not lobby to block effective regulation.

▸ *Companies must take significant steps to cut their global emissions* in line with keeping global warming well below 2°C.

▸ *Companies must ensure that their mitigation or adaptation projects do not undermine people's rights*, either due to the technologies used, or due to implementing them without consulting affected communities.

▸ *Companies that source and sell globally can go much further in building communities' climate resilience* through their own supply-chain operations.

The ongoing climate negotiations – from Bali in 2007 to Copenhagen at the end of 2009 – are the best available chance for achieving the international co-operation needed to prevent dangerous climate change and to enable communities to adapt. That is why human rights must be placed at the heart of their deliberations. Indeed the impacts of climate change on the rights of the world's most vulnerable people will be the critical test of whether these negotiations succeed.

If Socialism Fails:
The Spectre of 21st Century Barbarism

Ian Angus

Socialist Voice, July 27, 2008.

From the first day it appeared online, *Climate and Capitalism*'s masthead has carried the slogan "Ecosocialism or Barbarism: there is no third way." We've been quite clear that ecosocialism is not a new theory or brand of socialism – it is socialism with Marx's important insights on ecology restored, socialism committed to the fight against ecological destruction. But why do we say that the alternative to ecosocialism is barbarism?

Marxists have used the word "barbarism" in various ways, but most often to describe actions or social conditions that are grossly inhumane, brutal, and violent. It is not a word we use lightly, because it implies not just bad behaviour but violations of the most important norms of human solidarity and civilized life.[1]

The slogan "Socialism or Barbarism" originated with the great German revolutionary socialist leader Rosa Luxemburg, who repeatedly raised it during World War I. It was a profound concept, one that has become ever more relevant as the years have passed.

Rosa Luxemburg spent her entire adult life organizing and educating the working class to fight for socialism. She was convinced that if socialism didn't triumph, capitalism would become ever more barbaric, wiping out centuries of gains in civilization. In a major 1915 antiwar polemic, she referred to Friedrich Engels' view that society must advance to socialism or revert to barbarism and then asked, "What does a 'reversion to barbarism' mean at the present stage of European civilization?"

She gave two related answers.

In the long run, she said, a continuation of capitalism would lead to the literal collapse of civilized society and the coming of a new Dark Age, similar to Europe after the fall of the Roman Empire: "The collapse of all civilization as in ancient Rome, depopulation, desolation, degeneration – a great cemetery." (*The Junius Pamphlet*)[2]

By saying this, Rosa Luxemburg was reminding the revolutionary left that socialism is not inevitable, that if the socialist movement failed, capitalism might destroy modern civilization, leaving behind a much poorer and much harsher world. That wasn't a new concept – it has been part of Marxist thought from its very beginning. In 1848, in The Communist Manifesto, Karl Marx and Friedrich Engels wrote: "The history of all hitherto existing society is the history of class struggles. ... that each time ended, either in the revolutionary reconstitution of society at large, *or in the common ruin of the contending classes.*" (emphasis added)

In Luxemburg's words: "Humanity is facing the alternative: Dissolution and downfall in capitalist anarchy, or regeneration through the social revolution." (*A Call to the Workers of the World*)

Capitalism's two faces

But Luxemburg, again following the example of Marx and Engels, also used the term "barbarism" another way, to contrast capitalism's loudly proclaimed noble ideals with its actual practice of torture, starvation, murder and war.

Marx many times described the two-sided nature of capitalist "progress." In 1853, writing about the British colonial regime in India, he described the "profound hypocrisy and inherent barbarism of bourgeois civilization [that] lies unveiled before our eyes, turning from its home, where it assumes respectable forms, to the colonies, where it goes naked." Capitalist progress, he said, resembled a "hideous, pagan idol, who would not drink the nectar but from the skulls of the slain." (*The Future Results of British Rule in India*)

Similarly, in a speech to radical workers in London in 1856, he said:

> On the one hand, there have started into life industrial and scientific forces, which no epoch of the former human history had ever suspected. On the other hand, there exist symptoms of decay, far surpassing the horrors recorded of the latter times of the Roman Empire. (*Speech at the Anniversary of the People's Paper*)

Immense improvements to the human condition have been made under capitalism – in health, culture, philosophy, literature, music and more. But capitalism has also led to starvation, destitution, mass violence, torture and even genocide – all on an unprecedented scale. As capitalism has expanded and aged, the barbarous side of its nature has come ever more to the fore.

Bourgeois society, which came to power promising equality, democracy, and human rights, has never had any compunction about throwing those ideals overboard to expand and protect its wealth and profits. That's the view of barbarism that Rosa Luxemburg was primarily concerned about during World War I. She wrote:

> Shamed, dishonoured, wading in blood and dripping in filth, this capitalist society stands. Not as we usually see it, playing the roles of peace and righteousness, of order, of philosophy, of ethics – as a roaring beast, as an orgy of anarchy, as pestilential breath, devastating culture and humanity – so it appears in all its hideous nakedness ...
>
> A look around us at this moment shows what the regression of bourgeois society into barbarism means. This world war is a regression into barbarism. (*The Junius Pamphlet*)

For Luxemburg, barbarism wasn't a future possibility. It was the *present reality* of imperialism, a reality that was destined to get much worse if socialism failed to stop it. Tragically, she was proven correct. The defeat of the German revolutions of 1919 to 1923, coupled with the isolation and degeneration of the Russian Revolution, opened the way to a century of genocide and constant war.

In 1933, Leon Trotsky described the rise of fascism as "capitalist society ... puking up undigested barbarism." (*What is National Socialism?*)

Later he wrote: "The delay of the socialist revolution engenders the indubitable phenomena of barbarism – chronic unemployment, pauperization of the petty bourgeoisie, fascism, finally wars of extermination which do not open up any new road." (*In Defense of Marxism*)

More than 250 million people, most of them civilians, were killed in the wars of extermination and mass atrocities of the 20th Century. The 21st century continues that record: in less than eight years over three million people have died in wars in Iraq, Afghanistan and elsewhere in the Third World, and at least 700,000 have died in "natural" disasters.

As Luxemburg and Trotsky warned, barbarism is already upon us. Only mass action can stop barbarism from advancing, and only socialism can definitively defeat it. Their call to action is even more important today, when capitalism has added massive ecological destruction, primarily affecting the poor, to the wars and other horrors of the 20th Century.

That view has been expressed repeatedly and forcefully by Venezuelan president Hugo Chavez. Speaking in Vienna in May 2006, he referred explicitly to Luxemburg's words:

> The choice before humanity is socialism or barbarism. ... When Rosa Luxemburg made this statement, she was speaking of a relatively distant future. But now the situation of the world is so bad that the threat to the human race is not in the future, but now.[3]

A few months earlier, in Caracas, he argued that capitalism's destruction of the environment gives particular urgency to the fight against barbarism today:

> I was remembering Karl Marx and Rosa Luxemburg and the phrase that each one of them, in their particular time and context put forward; the dilemma "socialism or barbarism." ...
>
> I believe it is time that we take up with courage and clarity a political, social, collective and ideological offensive across the world – a real offensive that permits us to move progressively, over the next years, the next decades, leaving behind the perverse, destructive, destroyer, capitalist model and go forward in constructing the socialist model to avoid barbarism and beyond that the annihilation of life on this planet.

I believe this idea has a strong connection with reality. I don't think we have much time. Fidel Castro said in one of his speeches I read not so long ago, "tomorrow could be too late, let's do now what we need to do." I don't believe that this is an exaggeration. The environment is suffering damage that could be irreversible – global warming, the greenhouse effect, the melting of the polar ice caps, the rising sea level, hurricanes – with terrible social consequences that will shake life on this planet.[4]

Chavez and the revolutionary Bolivarian movement in Venezuela have proudly raised the banner of 21st Century Socialism to describe their goals. As these comments show, they are also raising a warning flag, that the alternative to socialism is 21st Century Barbarism – the barbarism of the previous century amplified and intensified by ecological crisis.

Climate change and 'barbarization'

The Intergovernmental Panel on Climate Change (IPCC) has been studying and reporting on climate change for two decades. Recently the Vice-Chair of the IPCC, Professor Mohan Munasinghe, gave a lecture at Cambridge University that described "a dystopic possible future world in which social problems are made much worse by the environmental consequences of rising greenhouse gas emissions."

He said: "Climate change is, or could be, the additional factor which will exacerbate the existing problems of poverty, environmental degradation, social polarisation and terrorism and it could lead to a very chaotic situation."

"Barbarization," Munasinghe said, is already underway. We face "a situation where the rich live in enclaves, protected, and the poor live outside in unsustainable conditions."[5]

A common criticism of the IPCC is that its reports are too conservative, that they understate how fast climate change is occurring and how disastrous the effects may be. So when the Vice-Chair of the IPCC says that "barbarization" is already happening, no one should suggest that it's an exaggeration.

The present reality of barbarism

The idea of 21st Century Barbarism may seem farfetched. Even with food and fuel inflation, growing unemployment and housing crises, many working people in the advanced capitalist countries still enjoy a considerable degree of comfort and security.

But outside the protected enclaves of the global north, the reality of "barbarization" is all too evident.

- ▸ 2.5 billion people, nearly half of the world's population, survive on less than two dollars a day.
- ▸ Over 850 million people are chronically undernourished and three times that many frequently go hungry.

▶ Every hour of every day, 180 children die of hunger and 1200 die of preventable diseases.

▶ Over half a million women die every year from complications of pregnancy and childbirth. 99% of them are in the global south.

▶ Over a billion people live in vast urban slums, without sanitation, sufficient living space, or durable housing.

▶ 1.3 billion people have no safe water. 3 million die of water-related diseases every year.

The *United Nations Human Development Report 2007-2008* warns that unmitigated climate change will lock the world's poorest countries and their poorest citizens in a downward spiral, leaving hundreds of millions facing malnutrition, water scarcity, ecological threats, and a loss of livelihoods.[6]

In UNDP Administrator Kemal Dervi's words: "Ultimately, climate change is a threat to humanity as a whole. But it is the poor, a constituency with no responsibility for the ecological debt we are running up, who face the immediate and most severe human costs."[7]

Among the 21st Century threats identified by the *Human Development Report*:

▶ The breakdown of agricultural systems as a result of increased exposure to drought, rising temperatures, and more erratic rainfall, leaving up to 600 million more people facing malnutrition.

▶ An additional 1.8 billion people facing water stress by 2080, with large areas of South Asia and northern China facing a grave ecological crisis as a result of glacial retreat and changed rainfall patterns.

▶ Displacement through flooding and tropical storm activity of up to 332 million people in coastal and low-lying areas. Over 70 million Bangladeshis, 22 million Vietnamese, and six million Egyptians could be affected by global warming-related flooding.

▶ Expanding health risks, including up to 400 million more people facing the risk of malaria.

To these we can add the certainty that at least 100 million people will be added to the ranks of the permanently hungry this year as a result of food price inflation.

In the UN report, former South African Archbishop Desmond Tutu echoes Munasinghe's prediction of protected enclaves for the rich within a world of ecological destruction:

> While the citizens of the rich world are protected from harm, the poor, the vulnerable and the hungry are exposed to the harsh reality of climate change in their everyday lives.... We are drifting into a world of "adaptation apartheid."

As capitalism continues with business as usual, climate change is fast expanding the gap between rich and poor between and within nations, and imposing unparalleled suffering on those least able to protect themselves. That is the reality of 21st Century Barbarism.

No society that *permits* that to happen can be called civilized. No social order that *causes* it to happen deserves to survive.

Notes

1 In "Empire of Barbarism" (*Monthly Review*, December 2004), John Bellamy Foster and Brett Clark provide an excellent account of the evolution of the word "barbarism" and its present-day implications.

The best discussion of Rosa Luxemburg's use of the word is in Norman Geras, *The Legacy of Rosa Luxemburg* (NLB 1976), which unfortunately is out of print.

2 The works of Marx, Engels, Luxemburg and Trotsky that are quoted in this article can be found online in the Marxists Internet Archive, www.marxists.org/

3 Hands Off Venezuela, May 13, 2006

4 *Green Left Weekly*, August 31, 2005

5 "Expert warns climate change will lead to 'barbarisation'" *Guardian*, May 15, 2008

6 United Nations Development Program, *Human Development Report 2007/2008*

7 "Climate change threatens unprecedented human development reversals." UNDP News Release, Nov. 27, 2007

2: STARVING THE POOR

*"Nowhere in the world, in no act of genocide,
in no war, are so many people killed per minute,
per hour and per day as those who are killed
by hunger and poverty on our planet."*
—Fidel Castro—

The most devastating effects of climate change will be felt by the poor, by those who already live on the edge of starvation. The climate crisis and the food crisis are inseparably linked.

In Part Two:

▸ **World Hunger, Agribusiness, and the Food Sovereignty Alternative**. *An analysis of today's food crisis, and its relationship to the neoliberal restructuring of agriculture and the domination of food production and distribution by a handful of huge agribusiness.*

▸ **A New International Order is Needed** *and* **The Food Crisis is Systemic and Structural** *by two Cuban leaders: Esteban Lazo Hernandez at a meeting of 14 Latin American countries in Nicaragua in May 2008; and José Ramón Machado at the United Nations in June 2008.*

▸ **Peasants and Small Farmers Can Feed the World** *and* **Our Heritage as Food Producers is Critical to the Future of Humanity.** *Peasant farming activists explain why "food sovereignty" is the only possible basis for a sustainable global food system.*

▸ **The Rich Do Not Know Hunger.** *Fidel Castro's vehement condemnation of the 1996 World Food Summit's decision to abandon its long-standing goal of ending world hunger.*

World Hunger, Agribusiness, and the Food Sovereignty Alternative

Ian Angus

Socialist Voice, April 28 and May 12, 2008

> If the government cannot lower the cost of living it simply has to leave. If the police and UN troops want to shoot at us, that's OK, because in the end, if we are not killed by bullets, we'll die of hunger. – *A demonstrator in Port-au-Prince, Haiti*

In Haiti, where most people get 22% fewer calories than the minimum needed for good health, some are staving off their hunger pangs by eating "mud biscuits" made by mixing clay and water with a bit of vegetable oil and salt.[1]

Meanwhile, in Canada, the federal government is currently paying $225 for each pig killed in a mass cull of breeding swine, as part of a plan to reduce hog production. Hog farmers, squeezed by low hog prices and high feed costs, have responded so enthusiastically that the kill will likely use up all the allocated funds before the program ends in September.

Some of the slaughtered hogs may be given to local Food Banks, but most will be destroyed or made into pet food.

None will go to Haiti.

This is the brutal world of capitalist agriculture – a world where some people destroy food because prices are too low, and others literally eat dirt because food prices are too high.

Record prices for staple foods

We are in the midst of an unprecedented worldwide food price inflation that has driven prices to their highest levels in decades. The increases affect most kinds of food, but in particular the most important staples – wheat, corn, and rice.

The UN Food and Agriculture Organization says that between March 2007 and March 2008 prices of cereals increased 88%, oils and fats 106%, and dairy 48%. The FAO food price index as a whole rose 57% in one year – and most of the increase occurred in the past few months.

Another source, the World Bank, says that that in the 36 months ending February 2008, global wheat prices rose 181% and overall global food prices increased by 83%. The Bank expects most food prices to remain well above 2004 levels until at least 2015.

The most popular grade of Thailand rice sold for $198 a tonne five years ago and $323 a tonne a year ago. On April 24, the price hit $1,000.

Increases are even greater on local markets – in Haiti, the market price for a 50 kilo bag of rice doubled in one week at the end of March.

These increases are catastrophic for the 2.6 billion people around the world who live on less than US$2 a day and spend 60% to 80% of their incomes on food. Hundreds of millions cannot afford to eat.

This month, the hungry fought back.

Taking to the streets

In Haiti, on April 3, demonstrators in the southern city of Les Cayes built barricades, stopped trucks carrying rice and distributed the food, and tried to burn a United Nations compound. The protests quickly spread to the capital, Port-au-Prince, where thousands marched on the presidential palace, chanting "We are hungry!" Many called for the withdrawal of UN troops and the return of Jean-Bertrand Aristide, the exiled president whose government was overthrown by foreign powers in 2004.

President René Préval, who initially said nothing could be done, has announced a 16% cut in the wholesale price of rice. This is at best a stop-gap measure, since the reduction is for one month only, and retailers are not obligated to cut their prices.

The actions in Haiti paralleled similar protests by hungry people in more than twenty other countries.

▸ In Burkino Faso, a two-day general strike by unions and shopkeepers demanded "significant and effective" reductions in the price of rice and other staple foods.

▸ In Bangladesh, over 20,000 workers from textile factories in Fatullah went on strike to demand lower prices and higher wages. They hurled bricks and stones at police, who fired tear gas into the crowd.

▸ The Egyptian government sent thousands of troops into the Mahalla textile complex in the Nile Delta, to prevent a general strike demanding higher wages, an independent union, and lower prices. Two people were killed and over 600 have been jailed.

▸ In Abidjan, Côte d'Ivoire, police used tear gas against women who had set up barricades, burned tires and closed major roads. Thousands marched to the President's home, chanting "We are hungry," and "Life is too expensive, you are killing us."

▸ In Pakistan and Thailand, armed soldiers have been deployed to prevent the poor from seizing food from fields and warehouses.

Similar protests have taken place in Cameroon, Ethiopia, Honduras, Indonesia, Madagascar, Mauritania, Niger, Peru, Philippines, Senegal, Thailand, Uzbekistan, and Zambia. On April 2, the president of the World Bank told a meeting in Washington that there are 33 countries where price hikes could cause social unrest.

A Senior Editor of *Time* magazine warned:

The idea of the starving masses driven by their desperation to take to the streets and overthrow the *ancien regime* has seemed impossibly quaint since capitalism triumphed so decisively in the Cold War.... And yet, the headlines of the past month suggest that skyrocketing food prices are threatening the stability of a growing number of governments around the world. .... when circumstances render it impossible to feed their hungry children, normally passive citizens can very quickly become militants with nothing to lose.[2]

What's Driving Food Inflation?

Since the 1970s, food production has become increasingly globalized and concentrated. A handful of countries dominate the global trade in staple foods. 80% of wheat exports come from six exporters, as does 85% of rice. Three countries produce 70% of exported corn. This leaves the world's poorest countries, the ones that must import food to survive, at the mercy of economic trends and policies in those few exporting countries. When the global food trade system stops delivering, it's the poor who pay the price.

For several years, the global trade in staple foods has been heading towards a crisis. Four related trends have slowed production growth and pushed prices up.

The End of the Green Revolution: In the 1960s and 1970s, in an effort to counter peasant discontent in south and southeast Asia, the U.S. poured money and technical support into agricultural development in India and other countries. The "green revolution" – new seeds, fertilizers, pesticides, agricultural techniques and infrastructure – led to spectacular increases in food production, particularly rice. Yield per hectare continued expanding until the 1990s.

Today, it's not fashionable for governments to help poor people grow food for other poor people, because "the market" is supposed to take care of all problems. The *Economist* reports that "spending on farming as a share of total public spending in developing countries fell by half between 1980 and 2004."[3] Subsidies and R&D money have dried up, and production growth has stalled.

As a result, in seven of the past eight years the world consumed more grain than it produced, which means that rice was being removed from the inventories that governments and dealers normally hold as insurance against bad harvests. World grain stocks are now at their lowest point ever, leaving very little cushion for bad times.

Climate Change: Scientists say that climate change could cut food production in parts of the world by 50% in the next 12 years. But that isn't just a matter for the future:

▶ Australia is normally the world's second-largest exporter of grain, but a savage multi-year drought has reduced the wheat crop by 60% and rice production has been completely wiped out.

▶ In Bangladesh in November, one of the strongest cyclones in decades wiped out a million tonnes of rice and severely damaged the wheat crop, making the huge country even more dependent on imported food.

Other examples abound. It's clear that the global climate crisis is already here, and it is affecting food.

Agrofuels: It is now official policy in the U.S., Canada and Europe to convert food into fuel. U.S. vehicles burn enough corn to cover the entire import needs of the poorest 82 countries.[4]

Ethanol and biodiesel are very heavily subsidized, which means, inevitably, that crops like corn (maize) are being diverted out of the food chain and into gas tanks, and that new agricultural investment worldwide is being directed towards palm, soy, canola and other oil-producing plants. The demand for agrofuels increases the prices of those crops directly, and indirectly boosts the price of other grains by encouraging growers to switch to agrofuel. As Canadian hog producers have found, it also drives up the cost of producing meat, because corn is the main ingredient in North American animal feed.

Oil Prices: The price of food is linked to the price of oil because food can be made into a substitute for oil. But rising oil prices also affect the cost of producing food. Fertilizer and pesticides are made from petroleum and natural gas. Gas and diesel fuel are used in planting, harvesting and shipping.[5]

It's been estimated that 80% of the cost of growing corn is fossil fuel related – so it is no accident that food prices rise when oil prices rise.

* * *

By the end of 2007, reduced investment in third world agriculture, rising oil prices, and climate change meant that production growth was slowing and prices were rising. Good harvests and strong export growth might have staved off a crisis – but that isn't what happened. The trigger was rice, the staple food of three billion people.

Early this year, India announced that it was suspending most rice exports in order to rebuild its reserves. A few weeks later, Vietnam, whose rice crop was hit by a major insect infestation during the harvest, announced a four-month suspension of exports to ensure that enough would be available for its domestic market.

India and Vietnam together normally account for 30% of all rice exports, so their announcements were enough to push the already tight global rice market over the edge. Rice buyers immediately started buying up available stocks, hoarding whatever rice they could get in the expectation of future price increases, and bidding up the price for future crops. Prices soared. By mid-April, news reports described "panic buying" of rice futures on the Chicago Board of Trade, and there were rice shortages even on supermarket shelves in Canada and the U.S.A.

Why the rebellion?

There have been food price spikes before. Indeed, if we take inflation into account, global prices for staple foods were higher in the 1970s than they are today. So why has this inflationary explosion provoked mass protests around the world?

The answer is that since the 1970s the richest countries in the world, aided by the international agencies they control, have systematically undermined the poorest countries' ability to feed their populations and protect themselves in a crisis like this.

Haiti is a powerful and appalling example.

Rice has been grown in Haiti for centuries, and until twenty years ago Haitian farmers produced about 170,000 tonnes of rice a year, enough to cover 95% of domestic consumption. Rice farmers received no government subsidies, but, as in every other rice-producing country at the time, their access to local markets was protected by import tariffs.

In 1995, as a condition of providing a desperately needed loan, the International Monetary Fund required Haiti to cut its tariff on imported rice from 35% to 3%, the lowest in the Caribbean. The result was a massive influx of U.S. rice that sold for half the price of Haitian-grown rice. Thousands of rice farmers lost their lands and livelihoods, and today three-quarters of the rice eaten in Haiti comes from the U.S.[6]

U.S. rice didn't take over the Haitian market because it tastes better, or because U.S. rice growers are more efficient. It won out because rice exports are heavily subsidized by the U.S. government. In 2003, U.S. rice growers received $1.7 billion in government subsidies, an average of $232 per hectare of rice grown.[7] That money, most of which went to a handful of very large landowners and agribusiness corporations, allowed U.S. exporters to sell rice at 30% to 50% below their real production costs.

In short, Haiti was forced to abandon government protection of domestic agriculture – and the U.S. then used its government protection schemes to take over the market.

There have been many variations on this theme, with rich countries of the north imposing "liberalization" policies on poor and debt-ridden southern countries and then taking advantage of that liberalization to capture the market. Government subsidies account for 30% of farm revenue in the world's 30 richest countries, a total of US$280 billion a year,[8] an unbeatable advantage in a "free" market where the rich write the rules.

The global food trade game is rigged, and the poor have been left with reduced crops and no protections.

In addition, for several decades the World Bank and International Monetary Fund have refused to advance loans to poor countries unless they agree to "Structural Adjustment Programs" that require the loan recipients to devalue their currencies, cut taxes, privatize utilities, and reduce or eliminate support programs for farmers.

All this was done with the promise that the market would produce economic growth and prosperity – instead, poverty increased and support for agriculture was eliminated.

> The investment in improved agricultural input packages and extension support tapered and eventually disappeared in most rural areas of Africa under SAP. Concern for boosting smallholders' productivity was abandoned. Not only were governments rolled back, foreign aid to agriculture dwindled. World Bank funding for agriculture itself declined markedly from 32% of total lending in 1976-8 to 11.7% in 1997-9.[9]

During previous waves of food price inflation, the poor often had at least some access to food they grew themselves, or to food that was grown locally and available at locally set prices. Today, in many countries in Africa, Asia and Latin America, that's just not possible. Global markets now determine local prices – and often the only food available must be imported from far away.

* * *

Food is not just another commodity – it is absolutely essential for human survival. The very least that humanity should expect from any government or social system is that it try to prevent starvation – and above all that it not promote policies that deny food to hungry people.

That's why Venezuelan president Hugo Chavez was absolutely correct on April 24, when he described the food crisis as "the greatest demonstration of the historical failure of the capitalist model."

The people of Haiti are "suffering from the attacks of the empire's global capitalism," he said. "This calls for genuine and profound solidarity from all of us. It is the least we can do for Haiti."

When food riots broke out in Haiti, the first country to respond was Venezuela. Within days, planes were on their way from Caracas, carrying 364 tons of badly needed food.

Venezuela's action is in the finest tradition of human solidarity. When people are hungry, we should do our best to feed them. Venezuela's example should be applauded and emulated. But aid, however necessary, is only a stopgap. To truly address the problem of world hunger, we must understand and then change the system that causes it.

No shortage of food

The starting point for our analysis must be this: there is no shortage of food in the world today.

Contrary to the 18th century warnings of Thomas Malthus and his modern followers, study after study shows that global food production has consistently outstripped population growth, and that there is more than enough food to feed everyone. According to the United Nations Food and Agriculture Organization, enough food is produced in the world to provide over 2800 calories a day to everyone – substantially more than the minimum required for good health, and about 18% more calories per person than in the 1960s, despite a significant increase in total population.[10]

As the Food First Institute points out, "abundance, not scarcity, best describes the supply of food in the world today."[11]

Despite that, the most commonly proposed solution to world hunger is new technology to increase food production. The Alliance for a Green Revolution in Africa, funded by the Bill and Melinda Gates Foundation and the Rockefeller Foundation, aims to develop "more productive and resilient varieties of Africa's major food crops ... to enable Africa's small-scale farmers to produce larger, more diverse and reliable harvests."[12]

Similarly, the Manila-based International Rice Research Institute has initiated a public-private partnership "to increase rice production across Asia via the accelerated development and introduction of hybrid rice technologies."[13]

And the president of the World Bank promises to help developing countries gain "access to technology and science to boost yields."[14]

Scientific research is vitally important to the development of agriculture, but initiatives that assume in advance that new seeds and chemicals are needed are neither credible nor truly scientific. The fact that there is already enough food to feed the world shows that the food crisis is not a technical problem – it is a social and political problem.

Rather than asking how to increase production, our first question should be why, when so much food is available, are over 850 million people hungry and malnourished? Why do 18,000 children die of hunger every day? Why can't the global food industry feed the hungry?

The profit system

The answer can be stated in one sentence. The global food industry is not organized to feed the hungry; it is organized to generate profits for corporate agribusiness.

The agribusiness giants are achieving that objective very well indeed. This year, agribusiness profits are soaring above last year's levels, while hungry people from Haiti to Egypt to Senegal were taking to the streets to protest rising food prices.[15] These figures are for the first quarter of 2008:

▸ Grain Trading

Archer Daniels Midland (ADM). Gross profit: $1.15 billion, up 55% from last year

Cargill: Net earnings: $1.03 billion, up 86%

Bunge. Consolidated gross profit: $867 million, up 189%.

▸ Seeds & herbicides

Monsanto. Gross profit: $2.23 billion, up 54%.

Dupont Agriculture and Nutrition. Pre-tax operating income: $786 million, up 21%

▸ Fertilizer

Potash Corporation. Net income: $66 million, up 185.9%

Mosaic. Net earnings: $520.8 million, up more than 1,200%

The companies listed, plus a few more, are the monopoly or near-monopoly buyers and sellers of agricultural products around the world. Six companies control 85% of the world trade in grain; three control 83% of cocoa; three control 80% of the banana trade.[16] ADM, Cargill and Bunge effectively control the world's corn, which means that they alone decide how much of each year's crop goes to make ethanol, sweeteners, animal feed or human food.

As the editors of *Hungry for Profit* write, "The enormous power exerted by the largest agribusiness/food corporations allows them essentially to control the cost of their raw materials purchased from farmers while at the same time keeping prices of food to the general public at high enough levels to ensure large profits."[17]

Over the past three decades, transnational agribusiness companies have engineered a massive restructuring of global agriculture. Directly through their own market power and indirectly through governments and the World Bank, IMF and World Trade Organization, they have changed the way food is grown and distributed around the world. The changes have had wonderful effects on their profits, while simultaneously making global hunger worse and food crises inevitable.

The assault on traditional farming

Today's food crisis doesn't stand alone: it is a manifestation of a farm crisis that has been building for decades.

As we have seen, over the past three decades the rich countries of the north have forced poor countries to open their markets, then flooded those markets with subsidized food, with devastating results for Third World farming.

But the restructuring of global agriculture to the advantage of agribusiness giants didn't stop there. In the same period, southern countries were convinced, cajoled and bullied into adopting agricultural policies that promote export crops rather than food for domestic consumption, and favour large-scale industrial agriculture that requires single-crop (monoculture) production, heavy use of water, and massive quantities of fertilizer and pesticides. Increasingly, traditional farming, organized by and for communities

---

The global food industry is not organized to feed the hungry; it is organized to generate profits for corporate agribusiness.

---

and families, has been pushed aside by industrial farming organized by and for agribusinesses.

That transformation is the principal obstacle to a rational agriculture that could eliminate hunger.

The focus on export agriculture has produced the absurd and tragic result that millions of people are starving in countries that export food. In India, for example, over one-fifth of the population is chronically hungry and 48% of children under five years old are malnourished. Nevertheless, India exported US$1.5 billion worth of milled rice and $322 million worth of wheat in 2004.[18]

In other countries, farmland that used to grow food for domestic consumption now grows luxuries for the north. Colombia, where 13% of the population is malnourished, produces and exports 62% of all cut flowers sold in the United States.

In many cases the result of switching to export crops has produced results that would be laughable if they weren't so damaging. Kenya was self-sufficient in food until about 25 years ago. Today it imports 80% of its food – and 80% of its exports are other agricultural products.[19]

The shift to industrial agriculture has driven millions of people off the land and into unemployment and poverty in the immense slums that now surround many of the world's cities.

The people who best know the land are being separated from it; their farms enclosed into gigantic outdoor factories that produce only for export. Hundreds of millions of people now must depend on food that's grown thousands of miles away because their homeland agriculture has been transformed to meet the needs of agribusiness corporations.

As recent months have shown, the entire system is fragile: India's decision to rebuild its rice stocks made food unaffordable for millions half a world away.

If the purpose of agriculture is to feed people, the changes to global agriculture in the past 30 years make no sense. Industrial farming in the Third

World has produced increasing amounts of food, but at the cost of driving millions off the land and into lives of chronic hunger – and at the cost of poisoning air and water, and steadily decreasing the ability of the soil to deliver the food we need.

Contrary to the claims of agribusiness, the latest agricultural research, including more than a decade of concrete experience in Cuba, proves that small and mid-sized farms using sustainable agroecological methods are much more productive and vastly less damaging to the environment than huge industrial farms.[20]

Industrial farming continues not because it is more productive, but because it has been able, until now, to deliver uniform products in predictable quantities, bred specifically to resist damage during shipment to distant markets. That's where the profit is, and profit is what counts, no matter what the effect may be on earth, air, and water – or even on hungry people.

Fighting for food sovereignty

The changes imposed by transnational agribusiness and its agencies have not gone unchallenged. One of the most important developments in the past 15 years has been the emergence of La Vía Campesina (Peasant Way), an umbrella body that encompasses more than 120 small farmers' and peasants' organizations in 56 countries, ranging from the Landless Rural Workers Movement (MST) in Brazil to the National Farmers Union in Canada.

La Vía Campesina initially advanced its program as a challenge to the "World Food Summit," a 1996 UN-organized conference on global hunger that was attended by official representatives of 185 countries. The participants in that meeting promised (and subsequently did nothing to achieve) to reduce hunger and malnutrition by guaranteeing "sustainable food security for all people."[21]

As is typical of such events, the working people who are actually affected were excluded from the discussions. Outside the doors, La Vía Campesina proposed food sovereignty as an alternative to food security. Simple access to food is not enough, they argued: what's needed is access to land, water, and resources, and the people affected must have the right to know and to decide about food policies. Food is too important to be left to the global market and the manipulations of agribusiness: world hunger can only be ended by re-establishing small and mid-sized family farms as the key elements of food production.[22]

The central demand of the food sovereignty movement is that food should be treated primarily as a source of nutrition for the communities and countries where it is grown. In opposition to free-trade, agroexport policies, it urges a focus on domestic consumption and food self-sufficiency.

Contrary to the assertions of some critics, food sovereignty is not a call for economic isolationism or a return to an idealized rural past. Rather, it is a program for the defense and extension of human rights, for land reform, and for protection of the earth against capitalist ecocide. In addition to calling for food self-sufficiency and strengthening family farms, La Vía Campesina's original call for food sovereignty included these points:

▸ Guarantee everyone access to safe, nutritious and culturally appropriate food in sufficient quantity and quality to sustain a healthy life with full human dignity.

▸ Give landless and farming people – especially women – ownership and control of the land they work and return territories to indigenous peoples.

▸ Ensure the care and use of natural resources, especially land, water and seeds. End dependence on chemical inputs, on cash-crop monocultures and intensive, industrialized production.

▸ Oppose WTO, World Bank and IMF policies that facilitate the control of multinational corporations over agriculture. Regulate and tax speculative capital and enforce a strict Code of Conduct on transnational corporations.

▸ End the use of food as a weapon. Stop the displacement, forced urbanization and repression of peasants.

▸ Guarantee peasants and small farmers, and rural women input into formulating agricultural policies at all levels.[23]

La Vía Campesina's demand for food sovereignty constitutes a powerful agrarian program for the 21st century. Labour and left movements worldwide should give full support to it and to the campaigns of working farmers and peasants for land reform and against the industrialization and globalization of food and farming.

Stop the war on Third World farmers

Within that framework, we in the global north can and must demand that our governments stop all activities that weaken or damage Third World farming.

Stop using food for fuel. La Vía Campesina has said it simply and clearly: "Industrial agrofuels are an economic, social and environmental nonsense. Their development should be halted and agricultural production should focus on food as a priority."[24]

Cancel Third World debts. On April 30, Canada announced a special contribution of C$10 million for food relief to Haiti.[25] That's positive – but during 2008 Haiti will pay five times that much in interest on its $1.5 billion foreign debt, much of which was incurred during the imperialist-supported Duvalier dictatorships.

Haiti's situation is not unique and it is not an extreme case. The total external debt of Third World countries in 2005 was $2.7 trillion, and their debt payments that year totalled $513 billion.[26] Ending that cash drain, immediately and unconditionally, would provide essential resources to feed the hungry now and rebuild domestic farming over time.

Get the WTO out of agriculture. The regressive food policies that have been imposed on poor countries by the World Bank and IMF are codified and enforced by the World Trade Organization's Agreement on Agriculture. The AoA, as Afsar Jafri of *Focus on the Global South* writes, is "biased in favour of capital-intensive, corporate agribusiness-driven and export-oriented agriculture."[27] That's not surprising, since the U.S. official who drafted and then negotiated it was a former vice-president of agribusiness giant Cargill.

AoA should be abolished, and Third World countries should have the right to unilaterally cancel liberalization policies imposed through the World Bank, IMF, and WTO, as well as through bilateral free trade agreements such as NAFTA and CAFTA.

Self-Determination for the Global South. The current attempts by the U.S. to destabilize and overthrow the anti-imperialist governments of the ALBA group – Venezuela, Bolivia, Cuba, Nicaragua and Grenada – continue a long history of actions by northern countries to prevent Third World countries from asserting control over their own destinies. Organizing against such interventions "in the belly of the monster" is thus a key component of the fight to win food sovereignty around the world.

More than a century ago, Karl Marx wrote that despite its support for technical improvements, "the capitalist system works against a rational agriculture ... a rational agriculture is incompatible with the capitalist system."[28]

Today's food and farm crises completely confirm that judgment. A system that puts profit ahead of human needs has driven millions of producers off the land, undermined the earth's productivity while poisoning its air and water, and condemned nearly a billion people to chronic hunger and malnutrition.

The food crisis and the farm crisis are rooted in an irrational, anti-human system. To feed the world, urban and rural working people must join hands to sweep that system away.

Notes

1 Kevin Pina. "Mud Cookie Economics in Haiti." Haiti Action Network, Feb. 10, 2008. http://www.haitiaction.net/News/HIP/2_10_8/2_10_8.html

2 Tony Karon. "How Hunger Could Topple Regimes." *Time*, April 11, 2008. http://www.time.com/time/world/article/0,8599,1730107,00.html

3 "The New Face of Hunger." *Economist*, April 19, 2008.

4 Mark Lynas. "How the Rich Starved the World." *New Statesman*, April 17, 2008. http://www.newstatesman.com/200804170025

5 Dale Allen Pfeiffer. *Eating Fossil Fuels*. New Society Publishers, Gabriola Island BC, 2006. p. 1

6 "Kicking Down the Door." Oxfam International Briefing Paper, April 2005. http://www.oxfam.org/en/files/bp72_rice.pdf

7 Ibid.

8 "Agricultural Policy and Trade Reform." OECD Background Note. http://www.oecd.org/dataoecd/52/23/36896656.pdf

9 Kjell Havnevik, Deborah Bryceson, Lars-Erik Birgegård, Prosper Matondi & Atakilte Beyene. "African Agriculture and the World Bank: Development or Impoverishment?" *Links International Journal of Socialist Renewal*, http://www.links.org.au/node/328

10 Frederic Mousseau, *Food Aid or Food Sovereignty? Ending World Hunger in Our Time*. Oakland Institute, 2005. http://www.oaklandinstitute.org/pdfs/fasr.pdf. International Assessment of Agricultural Knowledge, Science and Technology for Development. *Global Summary for Decision Makers*. http://www.agassessment.org/docs/Global_SDM_210408_FINAL.pdf

11 Francis Moore Lappe, Joseph Collins, Peter Rosset. *World Hunger: Twelve Myths*. (Grove Press, New York, 1998) p. 8

12 "About the Alliance for a Green Revolution in Africa." http://www.agra-alliance.org/about/about_more.html

13 IRRI Press Release, April 4, 2008. http://www.irri.org/media/press/press.asp?id=171

14 "World Bank President Calls for Plan to Fight Hunger in Pre-Spring Meetings Address." News Release, April 2, 2008

15 These figures are taken from the companies' most recent quarterly reports, found on their websites. Because they report the numbers in different ways, they can't be compared to each other, only to their own previous reports.

16 Shawn Hattingh. "Liberalizing Food Trade to Death." *MRzine*, May 6, 2008. http://mrzine.monthlyreview.org/hattingh060508.html

17 Fred Magdoff, John Bellamy Foster and Frederick H. Buttel. *Hungry for Profit: The Agribusiness Threat to Farmers, Food, and the Environment*. Monthly Review Press, New York, 2000. p. 11

18 UN Food and Agriculture Organization. *Key Statistics Of Food And Agriculture External Trade*. http://www.fao.org/es/ess/toptrade/trade.asp?lang=EN&dir=exp&country=100

19 J. Madeley. *Hungry for Trade: How the poor pay for free trade*. Cited in Ibid

20 Jahi Campbell, "Shattering Myths: Can sustainable agriculture feed the world?" and "Editorial. Lessons from the Green Revolution." Food First Institute. www.foodfirst.org

21 World Food Summit. http://www.fao.org/wfs/index_en.htm

22 La Vía Campesina. "Food Sovereignty: A Future Without Hunger." (1996) http://www.voiceoftheturtle.org/library/1996%20Declaration%20of%20Food%20Sovereignty.pdf

23 Paraphrased and abridged from Ibid

24 La Vía Campesina. "A response to the Global Food Prices Crisis: Sustainable family farming can feed the world." http://www.viacampesina.org/main_en/index.php?option=com_content&task=view&id=483&Itemid=38

25 By way of comparison, this year Canada will spend $1 billion on the illegal occupation of and war in Afghanistan

26 Jubilee Debt Campaign. "The Basics About Debt." http://www.jubileedebtcampaign.org.uk/?lid=98

27 Afsar H. Jafri. "WTO: Agriculture at the Mercy of Rich Nations." *Focus on the Global South*, November 7, 2005. http://www.focusweb.org/india/content/view/733/30/

28 *Capital*, Volume III. Karl Marx & Frederick Engels, *Collected Works*, Volume 37, p. 123

A New International Order is Needed

Esteban Lazo Hernandez

Managua, May 2008
The facts speak clearly for themselves. In 2005, we used to pay 250 dollars for every ton of rice we imported; now we pay 1,050 dollars, four times as much. For a ton of wheat, we used to pay 132 dollars; now we pay 330 dollars, two and a half times as much. For a ton of corn, we used to pay 82 dollars; now we pay 230 dollars, nearly three times as much. For a ton of powdered milk, we used to pay 2,200 dollars; now it's 4,800 dollars. This is a perverse and unsustainable trend.

This phenomenon undermines the internal markets of most countries in our region and around the world, affecting the population directly, particularly the poorest sectors, bringing poverty to millions of people. A few decades ago, there were countries that grew their own rice and corn. But, following the neo-liberal recipes of the IMF, they liberalized the market and began to import subsidized US and European cereals, eradicating domestic production. With the rise in prices at the pace we've mentioned, a growing number of people can no longer afford to eat these basic food products. It comes as no surprise, thus, that they should resort to protests, that they should take to the streets to find whatever means they can to feed their children.

As Fidel underscored in 1996 during the World Food Summit, "hunger, the inseparable companion of the poor, is born of the unequal distribution of riches and of the world's injustices. The rich do not know hunger ... Millions of people around the world have perished in struggle against hunger and injustice."

The food crisis we face today is exacerbated by high oil prices and by the impact that the military adventure in Iraq has upon these; by the effect these prices have on the production and transportation of food; by climate change; by the fact that significant volumes of US and EU-grown grains and cereals are destined, more and more, to the production of biofuels and by the speculative practices surrounding transnational big capital, which gambles with food inventories at the cost of hunger for the poor.

But the essence of the crisis is not to be found in these recent phenomena; it lies, rather, in the unequal and unfair distribution of riches at the global level and in the unsustainable neo-liberal economic model that has been imposed upon us in an irresponsible and fanatical fashion over the course of the last twenty years.

Poor countries, dependent on food imports, are in no condition to take the blow. Their populations have no protection whatsoever and the market, needless to say, has neither the capacity nor the sense of responsibility to offer such protection. This is not a strictly economic problem. It is a humanitarian drama of incalculable consequences which even places our countries' very national security at risk.

To attribute the crisis to increased consumption by important sectors in certain developing countries that report accelerated economic growth, such as China and India, is not only an unfounded argument, it also conveys a racist and discriminatory message, which portrays as a problem the fact that millions of human beings should have access, for the first time, to decent and healthy food.

The problem, as it manifests itself in our region, is, in essence, linked to the precarious situation of small farmers and rural populations living in underdeveloped countries, and to the oligopolistic nature of the large transnational companies that control the agricultural food industry.

These companies control prices, technologies, standards, certifications, distribution channels and sources of funding for world food production. They also control transportation, scientific research, genetic pools and the fertilizer and pesticide industries. Their governments, in Europe, North America and other parts of the world, set down the international rules that govern trade in food, technologies and the supplies needed to produce these.

Agricultural subsidies in the United States and the European Union not only make the food these countries sell more expensive, they also constitute a fundamental obstacle for developing countries seeking to access their markets with their products, something which has a direct impact on the situation of agriculture and producers in the South.

This is a structural problem generated by today's international economic order, not a passing crisis that can be alleviated with palliative or emergency measures. The World Bank's recent promises to allocate 500 million devalued dollars as an emergency measure to alleviate the crisis are ridiculous and an insult to our intelligence.

To strike at the very heart and at the causes of the dilemma, we must examine and change the written and unwritten rules, both agreed to and imposed upon us, that today govern the international economic order and the creation and distribution of wealth, particularly in the food production and distribution sector.

Today, the truly decisive move is to undertake a profound, structural change of the current international economic and political order, an order which is anti-democratic, unjust, exclusive and unsustainable. An order which is predatory, as a result of which, as Fidel said twelve years ago, "waters are contaminated, the atmosphere is poisoned and nature is destroyed. It is not only the fact that investments, education and technologies are lacking or the population is growing at an accelerated pace; the environment is deteriorating and the future that is growing more hazardous with every passing day."

Having said this, we agree that international cooperation, as a means of confronting this time of crisis, can no longer be postponed. We need emergency measures to quickly alleviate the situation of those countries which already face social turmoil. In the middle term, we must also give impetus to cooperation and exchange plans that entail joint investments and accelerate agricultural production and food distribution in our region, through the firm commitment and resolute participation of the State. Cuba is willing to contribute its modest efforts to this.

The program brought to us today by comrade Daniel [Ortega], a call to join forces and wills and to combine the resources of ALBA members and countries in Central America and the Caribbean, is worthy of our support. It presupposes the clear understanding that the current food crises the world faces is not an opportunity, as some believe, but a very dangerous crisis. It involves express recognition that our efforts must be aimed at defending everyone's right to food and at securing a decent life for the millions of peasant families that have been plundered to this day, not at availing ourselves of the occasion to pursue corporate interests or petty commercial opportunities.

We have debated on the matter extensively. Now, it is time to act with unity, audacity, solidarity and a practical spirit. If this is our common goal, you can rely on Cuba.

Allow me to conclude with the farsighted words Fidel pronounced in 1996, which reverberate today with undiminished pertinence and profundity: "The bells that toll today for those who starve to death each day shall toll tomorrow for the whole of humanity if it refuses, or is unable, or is not wise enough to save itself."

The Food Crisis is Systemic and Structural

José Ramón Machado

Juventud Rebelde, June 4, 2000. Translated by Ian Angus

Two years ago, in this very hall, the international community agreed to eradicate world hunger. It adopted a goal of halving the number of malnourished people by 2015. Today that modest and inadequate goal seems like a pipedream.

The world food crisis is not a passing phenomenon. Its recent appearance in such serious form, in a world that produces enough food for all its inhabitants, clearly reveals that the crisis is systemic and structural.

Hunger and malnourishment are the result of an international economic order that maintains and deepens poverty, inequality and injustice.

It is undeniable that the countries of the North bear responsibility for the hunger and malnourishment of 854 million people. They imposed trade liberalization and financial rules that demanded structural adjustment, on a world composed of clearly unequal actors. They brought ruin to many small producers in the South and turned self-sufficient and even exporting nations into net importers of food products.

The governments of developed countries refuse to eliminate their outrageous agricultural subsidies while imposing their rules of international trade on the rest of the world. Their voracious transnational corporations set prices, monopolize technologies, impose unfair certification processes on trade, and manipulate distribution channels, sources of financing, trade and supplies for the production of food worldwide. They also control transportation, scientific research, gene banks and the production of fertilizers and pesticides.

The worst of it all is that, if things continue as they are, the crisis will become even more serious. The production and consumption patterns of developed countries are accelerating global climate change, threatening humanity's very existence. These patterns must be changed. The irrational attempt to perpetuate these disastrous forms of consumerism is behind the sinister strategy of transforming grains and cereals into fuels.

The Non-Aligned Countries Summit in Havana called for the establishment of a peaceful and prosperous world and a just and equitable international order. This is the only way to an end to the food crisis.

The right to food is an inalienable human right. Since 1997, this has been confirmed on Cuba's initiative by successive resolutions adopted by the former Commission on Human Rights and later by the Council and the UN General Assembly. Our country, representing the Non-Aligned Movement, and with the support of more than two thirds of UN member states, also proposed the calling of a seventh special session of the Human Rights Council, which has just called for concrete actions to address the world food crisis.

Hunger and malnourishment cannot be eradicated through palliatives, nor with symbolic donations which – let us be honest – will not satisfy peoples' needs and will not be sustainable.

At the very least, agricultural production in South countries must first be rebuilt and developed. The developed countries have more than enough resources to do this. What's required is the political will of their governments.

▸ If NATO's military budget were reduced by a mere 10% a year, nearly 100 billion dollars would be freed up.

▸ If the foreign debt of developing countries, a debt they have paid several times over, were cancelled, the countries of the South would have at their disposal the 345 billion dollars now used for annual debt service payments.

▸ If the developed countries honoured their commitment to devote 0.7 % of the Gross Domestic Product to Official Development Aid, the countries of the South would have at least an additional 130 billion dollars a year.

▸ If only one fourth of the money squandered each year on commercial advertising were devoted to food production, nearly 250 billion dollars could be dedicated to fighting hunger and malnutrition.

▸ If the money devoted to agricultural subsidies in the North were directed to agricultural development in the South, our countries would have around a billion dollars a day to invest in food production.

Mr. Chairman, I bring this message from Cuba, a country ferociously blockaded but standing proudly by its principles and the unity of its people: yes, we can successfully confront this food crisis, but only if we go to the root of the problem, address its real causes and reject demagogy, hypocrisy and false promises.

Allow me to conclude by recalling the words of Fidel Castro, when he addressed the UN General Assembly in New York in October 1979:

> The din of weapons, of threatening language, and of arrogance on the international scene must cease. Abandon the illusion that the problems of the world can be solved by nuclear weapons. Bombs may kill the hungry, the sick and the uneducated, but bombs cannot kill hunger, disease and illiteracy.

'Peasants and Small Farmers Can Feed The World'

La Via Campesina

Open letter to the FAO, the G8, and the Group of 77, May 1, 2008
Our movement, La Via Campesina, consists of millions of small farmers and landless workers in more than 60 countries around the world. Although we are the ones producing food for our families and communities, many of us are hungry or living in poverty. Over the last months, the situation has worsened due to the sudden rise in food prices.

We are also severely hit by the crisis because many of us do not have enough land to feed our families, and because most producers do not benefit from those high prices. Large traders, speculators, supermarkets and industrial farms are cashing in on and benefiting from this crisis.

This current food crisis is the result of many years of deregulation of agricultural markets, the privatization of state regulatory bodies and the dumping of agricultural products on the markets of developing countries. According to the FAO, liberalized markets have attracted huge cash flows that seek to speculate on agricultural products on the "futures" markets and other financial instruments.

The corporate expansion of agrofuels and the initially enthusiastic support for agrofuels in countries such as the US, EU and Brazil have added to the expectation that land for food will become more and more scarce.

On top of this in many southern countries hundreds of thousands of hectares are converted from agricultural uses in an uncontrolled way for so-called economic development zones, urbanization and infrastructure. The ongoing land grabbing by transnational companies and other speculators will expel millions more peasants who will end up in the mega cities where they will be added to the ranks of the hungry and poor in the slums.

Besides this, we may expect, especially in Africa and South Asia, more severe droughts and floods caused by global climate change. These are severe threats for the rural as well as for the urban areas.

These are highly worrying developments that need active and urgent action! We need a fundamental change in the approach to food production and agricultural markets!

Time to rebuild national food economies!
Rebuilding national food economies will require immediate and long-term political commitments from governments. An absolute priority has to be given to domestic food production in order to decrease dependency on the international market.

Peasants and small farmers should be encouraged through better prices for their farm products and stable markets to produce food for themselves and their communities.

Landless families from rural and urban areas have to get access to land, seeds and water to produce their own food. This means increased investment in peasant and farmer-based food production for domestic markets.

Governments have to provide financial support for the poorest consumers to allow them to eat. Speculation and extremely high prices forced upon consumers by traders and retailers have to be controlled. Peasants and small farmers need better access to their domestic markets so that they can sell food at fair prices for themselves and for consumers.

Countries need to set up intervention mechanisms aimed at stabilizing market prices. In order to achieve this, import controls with taxes and quotas are needed to avoid low-priced imports which undermine domestic production. National buffer stocks managed by the state have to be built up to stabilize domestic markets: in times of surplus, cereals can be taken from the market to build up the reserve stocks and in case of shortages, cereals can be released.

Regulating international markets and supporting countries to strengthen their food production

At the international level, stabilization measures also have to be undertaken. International buffer stocks have to be built up and an intervention mechanism put in place to stabilize prices on international markets at a reasonable level. Exporting countries have to accept international rules to control the quantities they can bring to the market, in order to stop dumping. The right to implement import controls, set up programs to support the poorest consumers, implement agrarian reform and invest in domestic, farmer peasant-based food production has to be fully respected and supported at the international level.

We ask the FAO, based on its mandate, to take the initiative and create the political environment for a fundamental change in food policies. In the International Conference on Agrarian Reform and Rural Development a broad majority of governments recognized and agreed on the importance of rural development and agrarian reform to combat poverty and hunger in the rural areas.

The International Assessment of Agricultural Knowledge, Science and Technology for Development (IAASTD), an assessment of the agricultural sector that involved Civil Society organizations, the private sector, and governments as well as the FAO and the World Bank came to the conclusion that corporate-led agriculture and the increasing dependence of peasants and small farmers is at the heart of the problem.

They also concluded that peasant, and farmer-based sustainable agriculture has to be supported and strengthened. The International Fund on Agricultural Development also recognizes the key role of peasants and small farmers in the production of food.

We request that G8 governments allow these initiatives to be taken. They should stop the promotion of agrofuels as these are no solution for the climate crisis and add to the destruction of forests. Especially in the southern countries, agrofuels occupy millions of hectares that should remain available for food production.

We also demand that the G8 analyze critically their own agricultural policies, take initiatives to stop the ongoing volatility of the international markets and shift their financial support away from industrial agriculture towards sustainable family farmer-based food production.

We also demand that the G8 stop and cancel any free trade agreements that will only contribute to the destruction of food production in developing countries and block any possibility of autonomous industrial development.

The influence of transnational corporations and financial speculative interests has to be controlled as much as possible and kept away from the international food market. Food is too important to be left to business alone.

A possible WTO agreement in the Doha Round will mean another blow for peasant-based food production. We demand that the governments of the G77 assess again the WTO negotiations on agriculture in the Doha round and reject any agreement that has negative implications for domestic food production and does not allow the taking of all necessary measures to strengthen food production and increase national self sufficiency.

Peasants and small farmers are the main food producers

La Via Campesina is convinced that peasants and small farmers can feed the world. They have to be the key part of the solution. With sufficient political will and the implementation of adequate policies, more peasants and small farmers, men and women, will easily produce sufficient food to feed the growing population. The current situation shows that changes are needed!

The time for Food Sovereignty has come!

'Our Heritage as Food Producers is Critical to the Future of Humanty'

Nyéléni Forum for Food Sovereignty

Mali, February 2007

We, more than 500 representatives from more than 80 countries, of organizations of peasants/family farmers, artisanal fisher folk, indigenous peoples, landless peoples, rural workers, migrants, pastoralists, forest communities, women, youth, consumers and environmental and urban movements have gathered together in the village of Nyéléni in Sélingué, Mali to strengthen a global movement for food sovereignty. We are doing this, brick by brick, as we live here in huts constructed by hand in the local tradition, and eat food that is produced and prepared by the Sélingué community. We give our collective endeavour the name "Nyéléni" as a tribute to and inspiration from a legendary Malian peasant woman who farmed and fed her peoples well.

Most of us are food producers and are ready, able and willing to feed all the world's peoples. Our heritage as food producers is critical to the future of humanity. This is specially so in the case of women and indigenous peoples who are the historical creators of knowledge about food and agriculture and are devalued. But this heritage and our capacities to produce healthy, good and abundant food are being threatened and undermined by neo-liberalism and global capitalism. Food sovereignty gives us the hope and power to preserve, recover and build on our food producing knowledge and capacity.

Food sovereignty is the right of peoples to healthy and culturally appropriate food produced through ecologically sound and sustainable methods, and their right to define their own food and agriculture systems. It puts the aspirations and needs of those who produce, distribute and consume food at the heart of food systems and policies rather than the demands of markets and corporations. It defends the interests and inclusion of the next generation. It offers a strategy to resist and dismantle the current corporate trade and food regime, and directions for food, farming, pastoral and fisheries systems determined by local producers and users.

Food sovereignty prioritizes local and national economies and markets and empowers peasant and family farmer-driven agriculture, artisanal — fishing, pastoralist-led grazing, and food production, distribution and consumption based on environmental, social and economic sustainability.

Food sovereignty promotes transparent trade that guarantees just incomes to all peoples as well as the rights of consumers to control their food and nutrition. It ensures that the rights to use and manage lands, territories, waters, seeds, livestock and biodiversity are in the hands of those of us who produce food. Food sovereignty implies new social relations free of oppression and inequality between men and women, peoples, racial groups, social and economic classes and generations.

In Nyéléni, through numerous debates and interactions, we are deepening our collective understanding of food sovereignty and learning about the realities of the struggles of our respective movements to retain autonomy and regain our powers. We now understand better the tools we need to build our movement and advance our collective vision.

What are we fighting for?

A world where...

All peoples, nations and states are able to determine their own food producing systems and policies that provide every one of us with good quality, adequate, affordable, healthy and culturally appropriate food.

There is recognition and respect of women's roles and rights in food production, and representation of women in all decision making bodies.

All peoples in each of our countries are able to live with dignity, earn a living wage for their labour and have the opportunity to remain in their homes, if they so choose.

Food sovereignty is considered a basic human right, recognised and implemented by communities, peoples, states and international bodies.

We are able to conserve and rehabilitate rural environments, fish populations, landscapes and food traditions based on ecologically sustainable management of land, soils, water, seas, seeds, livestock and all other biodiversity.

We value, recognize and respect our diversity of traditional knowledge, food, language and culture, and the way we organize and express ourselves.

There is genuine and integral agrarian reform that guarantees peasants full rights to land, defends and recovers the territories of indigenous peoples, ensures fishing communities' access and control over their fishing areas and eco-systems, honours access and control by pastoral communities over pastoral lands and migratory routes, assures decent jobs with fair remuneration and labour rights for all, and a future for young people in the countryside.

Agrarian reform revitalizes inter-dependence between producers and consumers, ensures community survival, social and economic justice, ecological sustainability, and respect for local autonomy and governance with equal rights for women and men.

Agrarian reform guarantees rights to territory and self-determination for our peoples.

We share our lands and territories peacefully and fairly among our peoples, be we peasants, indigenous peoples, artisanal fishers, pastoralists, or others.

In the case of natural and human-created disasters and conflict-recovery situations, food sovereignty acts as a form of "insurance" that strengthens local recovery efforts and mitigates negative impacts.

We remember that communities affected by disasters are not helpless, and that strong local organization for self-help is the key to recovery.

Peoples' power to make decisions about their material, natural and spiritual heritage are defended.

All peoples have the right to defend their territories from the actions of transnational corporations.

What are we fighting against?

Imperialism, neo-liberalism, neo-colonialism and patriarchy, and all systems that impoverish life, resources and ecosystems, and the agents that promote the above such as international financial institutions, the World Trade Organization, free trade agreements, transnational corporations, and governments that are antagonistic to their peoples.

The dumping of food at prices below the cost of production in the global economy.

The domination of our food and food producing systems by corporations that place profits before people, health and the environment.

Technologies and practices that undercut our future food producing capacities, damage the environment and put our health at risk. These include transgenic crops and animals, terminator technology, industrial aquaculture and destructive fishing practices, the so-called White Revolution of industrial dairy practices, the so-called "old" and "new" Green Revolutions, and the "Green Deserts" of industrial bio-fuel monocultures and other plantations.

The privatization and commodification of food, basic and public services, knowledge, land, water, seeds, livestock and our natural heritage.

Development projects/models and extractive industries that displace people and destroy our environments and natural heritage;

Wars, conflicts, occupations, economic blockades, famines, forced displacement of peoples and confiscation of their lands, and all forces and governments that cause and support these.

Post-disaster and conflict reconstruction programmes that destroy our environments and capacities.

The criminalization of all those who struggle to protect and defend our rights.

Food aid that disguises dumping, introduces GMOs [genetically nodified organisms] into local environments and food systems and creates new colonialism patterns.

The internationalization and globalization of paternalistic and patriarchal values, that marginalize women, and diverse agricultural, indigenous, pastoral and fisher communities around the world.

What can and will we do about it?

Just as we are working with the local community in Sélingué to create a meeting space at Nyéléni, we are committed to building our collective movement for food sovereignty by forging alliances, supporting each others' struggles and extending our solidarity, strengths, and creativity to peoples all over the world who are committed to food sovereignty. Every struggle, in any part of the world for food sovereignty, is our struggle.

We have arrived at a number of collective actions to share our vision of food sovereignty with all peoples of this world, which are elaborated in our synthesis document. We will implement these actions in our respective local areas and regions, in our own movements and jointly in solidarity with other movements. We will share our vision and action agenda for food sovereignty with others who are not able to be with us here in Nyéléni so that the spirit of Nyéléni permeates across the world and becomes a powerful force to make food sovereignty a reality for peoples all over the world.

Finally, we give our unconditional and unwavering support to the peasant movements of Mali and ROPPA [Network of Farmers' and Agricultural Producers' Organizations of West Africa] in their demands that food sovereignty become a reality in Mali and by extension in all of Africa.

Now is the time for food sovereignty!

_____

The Rich Do Not Know Hunger

Fidel Castro

World Food Summit, 1996

Hunger, the inseparable companion of the poor, is born of the unequal distribution of the wealth and of the world's injustices. The rich do not know hunger.

Colonialism was not alien to the poverty and underdevelopment afflicting today a large segment of mankind. Neither is the offensive opulence and the squandering by the consumer societies of the former metropolises which have subjected to exploitation a large number of countries on Earth. Millions of people around the world have perished in struggle against hunger and injustice.

What kind of cosmetic solutions are we going to provide so that in 20 years from now there would be 400 million instead of 800 million starving people? The very modesty of these goals is shameful. If 35,000 people – half of them children – are starving to death every day, why is it that in the developed countries olive groves are being torn down, cattle herds are being sacrificed and large amounts of money are being paid so that the land is kept unproductive?

If the world is rightly moved by accidents and natural or social catastrophes that bring death to hundreds or thousands of people, why is it not equally moved by the genocide that is taking place every day in front of our eyes?

Intervention forces are organised to prevent the death of hundreds of thousands of people in eastern Zaire. What are we going to do to prevent the starvation of one million people every month in the rest of the world?

It is capitalism, neoliberalism, the laws of a wild market, external debt, underdevelopment and unequal terms of trade that are killing so many people in the world.

Why is $700 billion invested every year in the military instead of investing a portion of those resources in fighting hunger, preventing the deterioration of the soils, the desertification and deforestation of millions of hectares every year, the warming up of the atmosphere and the greenhouse effect that increase the number of hurricanes, the scarcity or excess of rain, the destruction of the ozone layer and other natural phenomena which negatively affect food production and humanity's life on Earth?

Waters are polluted, the atmosphere is poisoned, and nature is destroyed. It is not only lack of investment, education and technologies or the accelerated pace of the population growth; the environment is deteriorating and the future that is growing more hazardous with every passing day.

Why are increasingly sophisticated weapons still being produced after the Cold War is over? What are those weapons for if not to dominate the world? Why is there ferocious competition to sell underdeveloped countries weapons that will not make them more able to defend their independence while they would rather be killing hunger?

Why are criminal policies and absurd blockades that include food and medicines being added to all this with the purpose of annihilating whole populations out of hunger and diseases? Where is the ethic, the justification, the respect for the most basic human rights and the common sense of such policies?

Let the truth prevail and not hypocrisy and deceit. Let us build an awareness on the fact that hegemonism, arrogance and selfishness must cease in this world.

The bells that are now tolling for those starving to death every day will tomorrow toll for all humanity if it refuses, or is unable, or is not wise enough to save itself.

3: FALSE EXPLANATIONS, FALSE SOLUTIONS

"Despite the fact that economists have long insisted that there is no such thing as a free lunch, we are now being told on every side – even by Gore – that where global warming is concerned there is a free lunch after all."
—John Bellamy Foster—

Two of the most widely-held explanations of the ecological and climate crises attribute both to overpopulation or to human nature. Those explanations are just as spurious as capitalist promises that biofuels will reduce energy use, or that burying carbon dioxide will slash greenhouse gas emissions.

In Part Three:

▸ **Too Many People?** *Simon Butler critiques the neo-Malthusian view that the world's poor have too many children, and that population control is the solution to global warming.*

▸ **The Myth of the 'Tragedy of the Commons.'** *An analysis of the most important and frequently-quoted "human nature" argument — the theory invented by Garrett Hardin, a far-right advocate of population control and eugenics.*

▸ **Magic Bullets: The Ethanol Scam *and* Carbon Capture and Storage**. *Evaluations of two much-hyped technologies: replacing gasoline with fuel derived from corn, sugar and other plants; and keeping emissions out of the atmosphere by burying them underground.*

▸ **A New War on the Planet?** *John Bellamy Foster says that the magic bullet solutions proposed for global warming actually involve launching new and more destructive assaults on the Earth.*

Too Many People?

Simon Butler

Green Left Weekly, November 8 and November 14, 2008
Many environmentalists believe that environmental destruction is a product of "overpopulation," and that the world is already "full up." So are population reduction strategies essential to solving the climate crisis?

At best, population control schemes focus on treating a symptom of an irrational, polluting social and economic system rather than the causes. In China, for instance, such measures haven't solved that country's environmental problems. At worst, populationist theories shift the blame for climate change onto the poorest and most vulnerable people in the Third World.

They do not address the reasons why environmental damage, or even instances of overpopulation, happens in the first place and they divert attention away from the main challenge facing the climate movement – the urgent need to construct a new economy based on environmentally sustainable technologies and the raising of living standards globally.

For at least 200 years, "overpopulation" has been used to explain a host of social problems such as poverty, famine, unemployment and – more recently – environmental destruction.

Between 1798 and 1826, the conservative English economist and clergyman Thomas Malthus published six editions of his influential *Essay on the Principle of Population*, which argued that population growth inevitably outstrips food production.

Malthus' argument was that the English working class was poor because they were too numerous, not because they were exploited. He opposed welfare or higher wages because, he said, that would allow the poor to survive and breed, compounding "overpopulation" and leading to more poverty.

Malthus was wrong about food production. In the last two centuries, food production has grown faster than population – but his theories nevertheless gained wide acceptance among the English elite of the day because they provided a convenient excuse to blame the poor for their own predicament.

In the 1960s, Malthus' anti-human ideas were resuscitated by a new generation of conservative theorists who argued that the people of the global South remained hungry because there were too many to feed. US environmentalist Paul Erlich, in his 1968 bestseller *The Population Bomb*, argued for population control measures in the Third World to, he said, avert an ecological crisis.

Populationists like Erlich usually don't question the unequal allocation of resources on a global scale. Nor do they admit that high birth rates in the Third

World are largely a response to dire poverty. Instead, they look at the world's resources as though they were dividing up a pie: reduce the world's population and those remaining will each get a bigger slice. They fail to address the question of power and, therefore, unequal access to global resources.

Most environmentalists who believe that population control is necessary would still reject the most extreme forms of the populationist argument.

But the fact remains that the real driver of climate change is not population growth but a market economy locked into burning fossil fuels for energy. The corporations that profit most from taking the lion's share of global resources are the same polluting industries that, today, are resisting the necessary shift away from carbon-based economies.

Populationists tend to downplay the question of power. As renowned US ecologist Barry Commoner commented, populationist solutions to environmental destruction are "equivalent to attempting to save a leaking ship by lightening the load by forcing passengers overboard."

He went on to ask the question that populationists tend to ignore: "One is constrained to ask if there is not something wrong with the ship."

The world is not experiencing runaway population growth. Global population is growing, but the rate of growth is slowing. It peaked in the 1960s and has been in decline ever since. Global population grew by 140% between 1950 and 2000. Experts predict a further rise of 50% between 2000 and 2050, and just 11% in the 50 years after that.

The simplistic view that population control is the main way to reverse runaway climate change can obscure debate over other measures. These include: the rapid replacement of fossil fuel-generated energy with renewables; improvements in energy efficiency; and the introduction of sustainable agricultural methods.

In rich countries such as Australia, we need to campaign for environmental outcomes that sharply reduce Third World poverty, including cancelling debt owed to First World nations.

It is well documented – including in the wealthy countries – that birth rates fall as living standards rise. Furthermore, the greater economic independence women have, and the more control women have over their own bodies, the fewer children they have. Development, along with women's emancipation, is the best contraception.

It is undeniable that parts of the world are overcrowded, and that land degradation through over-logging, erosion, over-hunting, over-fishing and poor waste disposal are massive problems in the countries of the global South. These social, economic and environment problems are interlinked, and point to the real causes of overpopulation and environmental destruction of the Third World – extreme poverty. Liberty and justice and rights for the poor, especially women, have to be our concern.

Diverting attention from real change

Population-based arguments wrongly treat population levels as the cause, rather than an effect, of an unsustainable economic system. This means they tend to divert attention away from pushing for the real changes urgently needed.

Campaigning for such measures as the rapid introduction of renewable energy and the phasing-out of fossil fuels, along with a shift to sustainable agricultural methods, should instead be the highest priority of the environmental movement.

Strategies to reduce human population also end up blaming some of the world's poorest people for the looming climate crisis, when they are the people least responsible. Instead, it is the powerful, vested interests that profit most from the fossil-fuel economy who pose the real threat to the planet. They must be confronted.

A section of those who accept the idea of population reduction on environmental grounds would protest that their own ideas aren't designed to substitute for the introduction of renewable energy, but to complement it.

Others would be indignant at the suggestion that their views have anything in common with the overt racism expressed by the likes of prominent US population theorist Garrett Hardin.

Hardin argued against providing food and medical aid to countries in the Third World facing famine. Such humanitarian aid only encourage more babies to survive, driving up "overpopulation" and resulting, he said, in further environmental destruction.[1]

Population theories still retain their appeal to people who are genuinely worried about the threat of global warming, are concerned with enduring poverty in the global South and who would reject Hardin's callous conclusions.

The rapid world population increase over the past two centuries appears to offer a plausible explanation of how the world got itself into ecological distress – reducing world population seems like a plausible solution.

Sustainable Population Australia (SPA) is an example of an environmental group that couches its population reduction arguments in the framework of a professed humanitarian response to the perils of climate change.[2]

A "key document" published in 2007 by SPA and available on its website predicts a depressingly dire future for humanity. According to SPA: "Without a planned humane contraction, this century will see social chaos and human suffering on an unprecedented scale."[3] If population reduction schemes are not implemented, they warn, then population reduction will be inflicted on us anyway – in the form of famine, war and disease.

SPA supports the introduction of renewable energy, believes foreign aid should be increased, opposes immigration selection on racial grounds and argues that wasteful and excessive consumption in the big polluting countries in the First World must be reduced.

But SPA contends that the environmental benefits of these measures will not be enough. Any gains, SPA asserts, will be wiped out by increased human consumption unless a planned world population reduction occurs as well.[5]

SPA concludes the "most important single action ... governments should take is to begin at once to implement humane strategies to reduce population."[6] But SPA's "humane" position still fails to provide either an effective, or a truly humane, strategy to avert the consequences of climate change for a number of reasons.

There is no factual basis to the SPA's claim that a shift to renewable energy could be simply negated by population increases. Clearly, in a zero-emissions or low-emissions economy, population levels will impact on the

---

Population control theories all relegate the billions of people in the global South to being just a part of the problem.

---

environment in a very different, more sustainable way. SPA simply does not take this into account.

Furthermore, the argument still serves to divert attention away from the genuine, urgent need for widespread renewable energy by insisting population reduction schemes should take number one priority. This is dangerous because it dovetails with the message coming from the advocates of "business as usual" policies who imply, against the evidence, that renewable technology is not advanced enough to replace fossil fuels today.

SPA recommends a global average of one child per family as part of its strategy for a sustainable world. Yet they fail to examine the case of China, which has enforced a one-child policy on its population for three decades.

There are many problems with this far-from-humane policy. But if assessed solely on sustainable climate outcomes then China's population reduction scheme can only be considered to be a spectacular failure.

To sustain their emphasis on population control, SPA has to downplay the inconvenient truth that the world's rate of population growth is actually declining, not blowing out of control. The growth rate of greenhouse gas emissions, however, is expanding dangerously today.

While there is no direct link between population increase and greenhouse gas emissions there is a clear and obvious link between expanding fossil fuel use and greenhouse gas increases.

In common with other populationist arguments, SPA fails to tackle the question of political power in society. That's why SPA's "humane" argument is couched largely in terms of containing, or mitigating, the apparently inevitable effects of environmental destruction.

There's little in SPA's position that gives hope that the climate justice movement can actually win the political battle for social justice and a safe climate in time. Population control measures assume the absolute worst case scenario from the outset – a future world so harsh and so polluted they hold it will become more "humane" to stop people in the global South from being born at all!

There is a kernel of truth in this apocalyptic scenario. Left unchecked, human-induced climate change is a serious threat to life on the planet. But the challenge this poses, however, is to fight for an alternative model of development based on meeting the needs of people and the planet, before it is too late.

Part of the problem is that groups such as SPA tend to see the people of the global South as passive victims of climate change – not as potential agents of sustainable change.

Environmental movements in the Third World are active, growing and involving far greater numbers than the movements in the First World. Millions are fighting for a sustainable world today, so their children and grandchildren can have hope for a decent life in the future.

As Walden Bello, executive director of Focus on the Global South, has pointed out:

> "The challenge facing activists in the global North and global South is to discover or bring about those circumstances that will trigger the formation of a global mass movement that will decisively confront the most crucial challenge of our times."[7]

Population control theories all relegate the billions of people in the global South to being just a part of the problem. But this outlook is radically false. They are, in fact, what Bello calls "the pivotal agent in the fight against global warming."

The populations of the global South are not responsible for climate change. Rather, they are an essential component of a safe climate solution. Our strategy should be to join up with them in this fight for the future – not draw up plans to reduce their numbers.

Notes

1 Richard Lynn's "Tribute to Garrett Hardin" unabashedly praises these racist, anti-human, misanthropic ideas. A good indication of how far away Hardin's populationism is from the ideology of the left. http://www.garretthardinsociety.org/tributes/tr_lynn_2001.html.

2 http://www.population.org.au

3 Global Population Reduction: A 21st century strategy to avoid human suffering and environmental devastation. p.3. Available at http://www.population.org.au/GPR_SPA_2007.pdf.

4 "So the world faces a stark choice: either act now to reduce population or do nothing and allow this population reduction to be inflicted upon us either directly through famine or indirectly through disease or civil and regional wars motivated by resource scarcity." Ibid. p 1.

5 " Savings made by implementing renewable technologies (lowering T) and reducing unnecessary affluence (lowering A) would soon be offset by consumption growth due to the rate at which the population (P) continues to expand. The most enduring way to lower total human environmental impact (I) is therefore to lower the value of the population size (P)." ibid, p5.

6 Ibid, p10.

7 Walden Bello. "The Environmental Movement in the Global South: The Pivotal Agent in the Fight against Global Warming." http://climateandcapitalism.com/?p=239

The Myth of the 'Tragedy of the Commons'

Ian Angus

Socialist Voice, August 24, 2008

Will shared resources always be misused and overused? Is community ownership of land, forests, and fisheries a guaranteed road to ecological disaster? Is privatization the only way to protect the environment and end Third World poverty? Most economists and development planners will answer "yes" – and for proof they will point to the most influential article ever written on those important questions.

Since its publication in *Science* in December 1968, "The Tragedy of the Commons" has been anthologized in at least 111 books, making it one of the most-reprinted articles ever to appear in any scientific journal. It is also one of the most-quoted: a recent Google search found "about 302,000" results for the phrase "tragedy of the commons."

For 40 years it has been, in the words of a World Bank discussion paper, "the dominant paradigm within which social scientists assess natural resource issues." (Bromley and Cernea 1989: 6) It has been used time and again to justify stealing indigenous peoples' lands, privatizing health care and other social services, giving corporations "tradable permits" to pollute the air and water, and much more.

Noted anthropologist Dr. G.N. Appell (1995) writes that the article "has been embraced as a sacred text by scholars and professionals in the practice of designing futures for others and imposing their own economic and environmental rationality on other social systems of which they have incomplete understanding and knowledge."

Like most sacred texts, "The Tragedy of the Commons" is more often cited than read. As we will see, although its title sounds authoritative and scientific, it fell far short of science.

Hardin hatches a myth

The author of "The Tragedy of the Commons" was Garrett Hardin, a University of California professor who until then was best known as the author of a biology textbook that argued for "control of breeding" of "genetically defective" people. (Hardin 1966: 707) In his 1968 essay he argued that communities that share resources inevitably pave the way for their own destruction; instead of wealth for all, there is wealth for none.

He based his argument on a story about the commons in rural England.

(The term "commons" was used in England to refer to the shared pastures, fields, forests, irrigation systems, and other resources that were found in many rural areas until well into the 1800s. Similar communal farming arrangements existed in most of Europe, and they still exist today in various forms around the world, particularly in indigenous communities.)

"Picture a pasture open to all," Hardin wrote. A herdsmen who wants to expand his personal herd will calculate that the cost of additional grazing (reduced food for all animals, rapid soil depletion) will be divided among all, but he alone will get the benefit of having more cattle to sell.

Inevitably, "the rational herdsman concludes that the only sensible course for him to pursue is to add another animal to his herd." But every "rational herdsman" will do the same thing, so the commons is soon overstocked and overgrazed to the point where it supports no animals at all.

Hardin used the word "tragedy" as Aristotle did, to refer to a dramatic outcome that is the inevitable but unplanned result of a character's actions. He called the destruction of the commons through overuse a tragedy not because it is sad, but because it is the inevitable result of shared use of the pasture. "Freedom in a commons brings ruin to all."

Where's the evidence?

Given the subsequent influence of Hardin's essay, it's shocking to realize that he provided no evidence at all to support his sweeping conclusions. He claimed that the "tragedy" was inevitable – but he didn't show that it had happened even once.

Hardin simply ignored what actually happens in a real commons: self-regulation by the communities involved. One such process was described years earlier in Friedrich Engels' account of the "mark," the form taken by commons-based communities in parts of pre-capitalist Germany:

> The use of arable and meadowlands was under the supervision and direction of the community ... Just as the share of each member in so much of the

mark as was distributed was of equal size, so was his share also in the use of the 'common mark.' The nature of this use was determined by the members of the community as a whole. ...

At fixed times and, if necessary, more frequently, they met in the open air to discuss the affairs of the mark and to sit in judgment upon breaches of regulations and disputes concerning the mark. (Engels 1892)

Historians and other scholars have broadly confirmed Engels' description of communal management of shared resources. A summary of recent research concludes:

What existed in fact was not a 'tragedy of the commons' but rather a triumph: that for hundreds of years – and perhaps thousands, although written records do not exist to prove the longer era – land was managed successfully by communities. (Cox 1985: 60)

Part of that self-regulation process was known in England as "stinting" – establishing limits for the number of cows, pigs, sheep and other livestock that each commoner could graze on the common pasture. Such "stints" pro-

---

In the real world, small farmers, fishers and others have created their own institutions and rules for preserving resources and ensuring that the commons community survived through good years and bad.

---

tected the land from overuse (a concept that experienced farmers understood long before Hardin arrived) and allowed the community to allocate resources according to its own concepts of fairness.

The only significant cases of overstocking found by the leading modern expert on the English commons involved wealthy landowners who deliberately put too many animals onto the pasture in order to weaken their much poorer neighbours' position in disputes over the enclosure (privatization) of common lands (Neeson 1993: 156).

Hardin assumed that peasant farmers are unable to change their behaviour in the face of certain disaster. But in the real world, small farmers, fishers and others have created their own institutions and rules for preserving resources and ensuring that the commons community survived through good years and bad.

Why does the herder want more?

Hardin's argument started with the unproven assertion that herdsmen always want to expand their herds: "It is to be expected that each herdsman will try to keep as many cattle as possible on the commons. ... As a rational being, each herdsman seeks to maximize his gain."

In short, Hardin's conclusion was predetermined by his assumptions. "It is to be expected" that each herdsman will try to maximize the size of his herd – and each one does exactly that. It's a circular argument that proves nothing.

Hardin assumed that human nature is selfish and unchanging, and that society is just an assemblage of self-interested individuals who don't care about the impact of their actions on the community. The same idea, explicitly or implicitly, is a fundamental component of mainstream (i.e., pro-capitalist) economic theory. All the evidence (not to mention common sense) shows that this is absurd: people are social beings, and society is much more than the arithmetic sum of its members. Even capitalist society, which rewards the most anti-social behaviour, has not crushed human cooperation and solidarity. The very fact that for centuries "rational herdsmen" did not overgraze the commons disproves Hardin's most fundamental assumptions – but that hasn't stopped him or his disciples from erecting policy castles on foundations of sand.

Even if the herdsman wanted to behave as Hardin described, he couldn't do so unless certain conditions existed.

There would have to be a market for the cattle, and he would have to be focused on producing for that market, not for local consumption. He would have to have enough capital to buy the additional cattle and the fodder they would need in winter. He would have to be able to hire workers to care for the larger herd, build bigger barns, etc. And his desire for profit would have to outweigh his interest in the long-term survival of his community.

In short, Hardin didn't describe the behaviour of herdsmen in pre-capitalist farming communities – he described the behaviour of capitalists operating in a capitalist economy. The universal human nature that he claimed would always destroy common resources is actually the profit-driven "grow or die" behaviour of corporations.

Will private ownership do better?

That leads us to another fatal flaw in Hardin's argument: in addition to providing no evidence that maintaining the commons will inevitably destroy the environment, he offered no justification for his opinion that privatization would save it. Once again he simply presented his own prejudices as fact:

> We must admit that our legal system of private property plus inheritance is unjust – but we put up with it because we are not convinced, at the moment, that anyone has invented a better system. The alternative of the commons is too horrifying to contemplate. Injustice is preferable to total ruin.

The implication is that private owners will do a better job of caring for the environment because they want to preserve the value of their assets. In reality, scholars and activists have documented scores of cases in which the division and privatization of communally managed lands had disastrous results. Privatizing the commons has repeatedly led to deforestation, soil erosion and depletion, overuse of fertilizers and pesticides, and the ruin of ecosystems.

As Karl Marx wrote, nature requires long cycles of birth, development and regeneration, but capitalism requires short-term returns.

> The entire spirit of capitalist production, which is oriented towards the most immediate monetary profits, stands in contradiction to agriculture, which has to concern itself with the whole gamut of permanent conditions of life required by the chain of human generations. A striking illustration of this is furnished by the forests, which are only rarely managed in a way more or less corresponding to the interests of society as a whole... (Marx 1998: 611n)

Contrary to Hardin's claims, a community that shares fields and forests has a strong incentive to protect them to the best of its ability, even if that means not maximizing current production, because those resources will be essential to the community's survival for centuries to come. Capitalist owners have the opposite incentive, because they will not survive in business if they don't maximize short-term profit. If ethanol promises bigger and faster profits than centuries-old rain forests, the trees will fall.

This focus on short-term gain has reached a point of appalling absurdity in recent best-selling books by Bjorn Lomborg, William Nordhaus and others, who argue that it is irrational to spend money to stop greenhouse gas emissions today, because the payoff is too far in the future. Other investments, they say, will produce much better returns, more quickly.

Community management isn't an infallible way of protecting shared resources: some communities have mismanaged common resources, and some commons may have been overused to extinction. But no commons-based community has capitalism's built-in drive to put current profits ahead of the well-being of future generations.

A politically useful myth

The truly appalling thing about "The Tragedy of the Commons" is not its lack of evidence or logic – badly researched and argued articles are not unknown in academic journals. What's shocking is the fact that this piece of reactionary nonsense has been hailed as a brilliant analysis of the causes of human suffering and environmental destruction, and adopted as a basis for social policy by supposed experts ranging from economists and environmentalists to governments and United Nations agencies.

Despite being refuted again and again, it is still used today to support private ownership and uncontrolled markets as sure-fire roads to economic growth.

The success of Hardin's argument reflects its usefulness as a pseudo-scientific explanation of global poverty and inequality, an explanation that doesn't question the dominant social and political order. It confirms the prejudices of those in power: logical and factual errors are nothing com-

---

Community management isn't an infallible way of protecting shared resources, but no commons-based community has capitalism's built-in drive to put current profits ahead of the well-being of future generations.

---

pared to the very attractive (to the rich) claim that the poor are responsible for their own poverty. The fact that Hardin's argument also blames the poor for ecological destruction is a bonus.

Hardin's essay has been widely used as an ideological response to anti-imperialist movements in the Third World and discontent among indigenous and other oppressed peoples everywhere in the world.

> Hardin's fable was taken up by the gathering forces of neo-liberal reaction in the 1970s, and his essay became the 'scientific' foundation of World Bank and IMF policies, viz. enclosure of commons and privatization of public property. ... The message is clear: we must never treat the earth as a 'common treasury.' We must be ruthless and greedy or else we will perish. (Boal 2007)

In Canada, conservative lobbyists use arguments derived from Hardin's political tract to explain away poverty on First Nations' reserves, and to argue for further dismantling of indigenous communities. A study published by the influential Fraser Institute urges privatization of reserve land:

> These large amounts of land, with their attendant natural resources, will never yield their maximum benefit to Canada's native people as long as they are held as collective property subject to political management. ... collective property is the path of poverty, and private property is the path of prosperity. (Fraser 2002: 16-17)

This isn't just right-wing posturing. Canada's federal government, which has refused to sign the United Nations Declaration on the Rights of Indigenous Peoples, announced in 2007 that it will "develop approaches to support the development of individual property ownership on reserves," and created a $300 million fund to do just that.

In Hardin's world, poverty has nothing to do with centuries of racism, colonialism, and exploitation: poverty is inevitable and natural in all times and places, the product of immutable human nature. The poor bring it on themselves by having too many babies and clinging to self-destructive collectivism.

The tragedy of the commons is a useful political myth – a scientific-sounding way of saying that there is no alternative to the dominant world order. Stripped of excess verbiage, Hardin's essay asserted, without proof, that human beings are helpless prisoners of biology and the market. Unless restrained, we will inevitably destroy our communities and environment for a few extra pennies of profit. There is nothing we can do to make the world better or more just.

In 1844 Friedrich Engels described a similar argument as a "repulsive blasphemy against man and nature." Those words apply with full force to the myth of the tragedy of the commons.

* * *

ONCE AGAIN: "THE MYTH OF THE TRAGEDY OF THE COMMONS"
Climate and Capitalism, November 3, 2008

The response to my recent article, "The Myth of the Tragedy of the Commons," has been very encouraging. It prompted a small flood of emails to my inbox, was reposted on many websites and blogs around the world, and has been discussed in a variety of online forums.

The majority of the comments were positive, but many readers challenged my critique of Garrett Hardin's very influential 1968 essay, "The Tragedy of the Commons." A gratifying number wrote serious and thoughtful criticisms. While they differed in specifics, these responses consistently made one or more of these three points:

▸ How can you say that the tragedy of the commons is a myth? Look at the ecological destruction around us. Isn't that tragic?

▸ It doesn't matter if Hardin's account of the historical commons was wrong. He wasn't writing history: he just used the commons as a model, or a metaphor.

▸ Hardin wasn't rejecting all commons, just "unmanaged commons." A "managed commons" would not be subject to the tragedy.

This article responds to those points. Except under the first heading, I've tried to avoid repeating arguments I made in the first article.

How can you say that?

Some respondents described ecological horrors and catastrophes – vanished fisheries, poisoned rivers, greenhouse gases, and more – and then said, in various ways, "The destruction of the world we all share is a terrible tragedy. How can you call it a myth?"

This question reflects an understandable problem with terminology. When Hardin wrote "The Tragedy of the Commons," he wasn't using the word "tragedy" in its normal everyday sense of a sad or unfortunate event. I tried to explain this in my article:

> Hardin used the word 'tragedy' as Aristotle did, to refer to a dramatic outcome that is the inevitable but unplanned result of a character's actions. He called the destruction of the commons through overuse a tragedy not because it is sad, but because it is the inevitable result of shared use of the pasture.

So the point is not whether ecological destruction is real. Of course it is. The point is, did Hardin's essay correctly explain why that destruction is taking place? Is there something about human nature that is inimical to shared resources? Hardin said yes, and I say that's a myth.

But it was only a model!

During the 1970s and 1980s, Hardin's description of the historical commons was so thoroughly debunked by historians and anthropologists that he resorted to denying that he ever meant to be historically accurate. In 1991, he claimed that his account was actually a "hypothetical model" and "whether any particular case is a materialization of that model is a historical question – and of only secondary importance." (Hardin 1991)

Similarly, an academic who called Hardin "one of the most important thinkers of the 20th century" wrote that his description of the traditional commons was a "thought experiment," so criticism of his historical errors is irrelevant. (Elliot 2003)

But Hardin offered no such qualification in his 1968 essay, or in the many books and articles he wrote on related subjects in the next 20 years. Quite the opposite, in fact.

In a 1977 essay, for example, Hardin referred explicitly to "the way the common pasture lands of England were converted to private property," by Parliamentary Enclosure Acts in the 1700s and 1800s. These Acts, he wrote, "put an end to the tragedy of the commons in this aspect of agriculture." That's a very explicit statement about historical facts – there's nothing "hypothetical" about it (Hardin 1977: p. 46).

So Hardin's later claim that historical facts don't matter was an attempt to rewrite his own history. He only claimed the story was "just a model" after it had been thoroughly disproved.

But it was only a metaphor!

In his 1968 essay and many subsequent articles, Hardin lumped together very different social situations and problems, labelled them all "commons" and claimed that the "tragedy of the commons" explained them all. He argued that the destruction of the historical commons explained the collapse of fisheries, overcrowding in US national parks, air and water pollution, "distracting and unpleasant advertising signs," overpopulation, and even "mindless music" in shopping malls.

While his account is often labelled a metaphor, Hardin didn't say that those situations were similar to commons. He said they *were* commons, and he repeatedly referred to their problems not as similar to but as *aspects of* the tragedy of the commons.

If all of those things were commons, then the fact that he was wrong about the historical "tragedy" completely undermines his core argument.

In reality, however, none of the examples he mentions are "commons" in any meaningful sense. Shopping malls and billboard locations are private property, with access controlled by the owners. National Parks are managed or mismanaged by government bureaucrats. Unmanaged shared resources like air and water are being polluted by giant corporations, not by "rational herdsmen." And Hardin's claim that population growth results from a "commons in breeding" is just plain bizarre.

There's no evidence that Hardin meant the "tragedy" to be seen as "only a metaphor" – but if he did, it was a very poor metaphor indeed.

He really meant the "unmanaged commons"

Several people suggested that Hardin was really criticizing "unmanaged commons," and thus presumably favoured a "managed commons." The problem with that idea is that Hardin clearly thought that "managed commons" was a contradiction in terms.

In his original 1968 essay Hardin wrote that a commons "if justifiable at all, is only justifiable under conditions of low-population density." As population grew, "the commons has had to be abandoned in one aspect after another." The "tragedy of the commons" could only be avoided by abandoning the commons: either by converting it to private property, or by imposing external controls that effectively eliminate the sharing of resources.

He repeated that argument many times in later articles and books. In 1985, for example:

> A commons is a resource to which a population has free and unmanaged access: it contrasts with private property (access only to the owner) and with socialized property (access to which is controlled by managers appointed by some political unit). (Hardin 1985: p. 90)

In short, Hardin *defined* the commons as unmanaged – so the claim that he was arguing for "managed commons" doesn't make sense. When he argued for management, he was arguing for *enclosing* the commons.

He was more explicit in an article written to mark the 30th anniversary of his original essay: "A 'managed commons' describes either socialism or the privatism of free enterprise" (Hardin, 1998). Since he equated socialism with bureaucratic state control, it is clear that for him the "managed commons" was not a commons at all.

Several readers said they understood that Hardin later changed his mind, that he said the tragedy only occurred in "unmanaged commons." One pointed to this sentence, in a speech Hardin gave in 1980:

> As a result of discussions carried out during the past decade I now suggest a better wording of the central idea: Under conditions of overpopulation, freedom in an unmanaged commons brings ruin to all. (Hardin 1980)

Note, however, that Hardin only says that this is "better wording." There is nothing in this restatement of his "central idea" that doesn't appear in the original essay. Far from recanting, he was trying to be more explicit.

In any event, as we've seen, five years later Hardin still defined the commons as unmanaged, so it's evident that he only added the word "unmanaged" in 1980 to clarify his argument, not to change it.

(Nor did the addition of "under conditions of overpopulation" add anything to what he wrote in 1968. Since Hardin believed that overpopulation was the biggest problem in the third world countries where most commons-based communities exist today, that qualification just reinforced his general anti-commons argument.)

What does "unmanaged" mean?

While Hardin's later articles did not revise his original argument fundamentally, they did expand it in a way that provides an important insight into the way he thought about commons-based communities. In the 1980 speech quoted above, he accepted that an unmanaged commons can work if (a) "the informal power of shame" is used to keep people in line, and (b) "the community does not exceed about 150 people."

As evidence for these apparently arbitrary requirements, he cited the example of Hutterite religious communes. Between forty and fifty thousand people live in such communities in western Canada and the United States: they hold all property in common, and communities normally divide in two when the population reaches 150 or so. The issue of size is a red herring: many shared resource communities are much larger than the limit the Hutterites have chosen.

But what's truly remarkable here is that Hardin classified Hutterite colonies as *unmanaged*, with the "informal power of shame" as its only means of staving off the tragedy of the commons. Compare that to this account of Hutterite governance in Canada:

> Each colony elects an executive council from the managers of various en-
> terprises, and together with the colony minister, the executive deals with
> important matters that will be brought before the assembly (all baptized
> male members – in effect, men 20 years of age and older). Although women
> have an official subordinate status, their informal influence on colony life
> is significant. They hold managerial positions in the kitchen, kindergarten,
> the purchase of dry goods, and vegetable production. (Ryan 1999: p. 1125)

Obviously, the word "unmanaged" simply doesn't apply to Hutterite
communities. The fact that Hardin thought it did shows how limited his con-
ceptions were. Anything that wasn't either privately owned or controlled by
the state was, by definition, "unmanaged."

As Derek Wall points out, such blindness to non-capitalist social structures is widespread in mainstream social science:

> The commons is important because it provides a way of regulating activity
> without the state or the market.... Throughout history, the commons has
> been the dominant form of regulation providing an alternative almost uni-
> versally ignored by economists who are reluctant to admit that substitutes
> to the market and the state even exist. (Wall 2005: p. 184)

Hutterite colonies don't just share resources – they democratically organize and govern their communities to manage those resources. That was also
true of the historical commons in Europe, and it's true of indigenous societies
in many parts of the world today. As historian Peter Linebaugh writes:

> To speak of the commons as if it were a natural resource is misleading at
> best and dangerous at worst – the commons is an activity and, if anything,
> it expresses relationships in society that are inseparable from relations to
> nature. (Linebaugh 2008: p. 279)

Hardin, like the economists Wall describes, looked at the world with
capitalist blinders on. As a result, he couldn't recognize a community-man-
aged non-tragic commons when it was right before his eyes.

Works cited in this article

Appell, G.N. 1993. "Hardin's Myth of the Commons: The Tragedy of Conceptual Confu-
sions." http://tinyurl.com/5knwou

Boal, Iain. 2007. "Interview: Spectres of Malthus: Scarcity, Poverty, Apocalypse." *Coun-
terpunch*, September 11, 2007. http://tinyurl.com/5vepm5

Bromley, Daniel W. and Cernea, Michael M. 1989. "The Management of Common Property Natural Resources: Some Conceptual and Operational Fallacies." World Bank Discussion Paper. http://tinyurl.com/5853qn

Cox, Susan Jane Buck. 1985, "No Tragedy on the Commons." *Environmental Ethics 7*.
http://tinyurl.com/5bys8h

Elliot, Herschel. 2003. "The Revolutionary Import of Garrett Hardin's Work." http://tinyurl.com/5tokrk

Engels, Friedrich. 1844. *Outlines of a Critique of Political Economy*. http://tinyurl.com/5p24t5

Engels, Friedrich. 1892. "The Mark." http://tinyurl.com/6e58e7

Fraser Institute. 2002. *Individual Property Rights on Canadian Indian Reserves*. http://tinyurl.com/5pjfjj

Hardin, Garrett. 1966. *Biology: Its Principles and Implications*. Second edition. San Francisco. W.H. Freeman & Co.

Hardin, Garrett. 1968. "The Tragedy of the Commons." http://tinyurl.com/0827

Hardin, Garrett. 1977. "Denial and Disguise." in Garrett Hardin and John Baden, editors, *Managing the Commons*. San Francisco: W.H. Freeman and Co. pp. 45-52

Hardin, Garrett. 1980. "An ecolate view of the human predicament." http://tinyurl.com/t98c

Hardin, Garrett. 1985. *Filters Against Folly: How to Survive Despite Economists, Ecologists and the Merely Eloquent*. New York: Viking Press.

Hardin, Garrett. 1991. "The Tragedy of the Unmanaged Commons: Population and the Disguises of Providence." in Robert V. Andelson, editor, *Commons Without Tragedy: Protecting the Environment from Over-Population - A New Approach*. Savage MD: Barnes & Noble

Hardin, Garrett. 1998. "Extension of the Tragedy of the Commons." http://tinyurl.com/bow6h

Linebaugh, Peter. 2008. *The Magna Carta Manifesto: Liberties and Commons for All*. Los Angeles: University of California Press

Marx, Karl. [1867] 1998. *Marx Engels Collected Works* Vol. 37 (*Capital*, Vol. 3). New York: International Publishers.

Neeson, J.M. 1993. *Commoners: Common Right, Enclosure and Social Change in England, 1700-1820*. Cambridge University Press.

Ryan, John. 1999. "Hutterites." in James Marsh, editor, *The Canadian Encyclopedia*, Year 2000 Edition. Toronto: McClelland and Stewart, pp. 1124-5.

Wall, Derek. 2005. *Babylon and Beyond: The Economics of Anti-Capitalist, Anti-Globalist and Radical Green Movements*. London: Pluto Books.

Magic Bullet #1: The Ethanol Scam

Nicole Colson

Socialist Worker, July 10, 2008
Unless you're delusional or in the pay of the energy industry, you know that the burning of fossil fuels is the primary cause of global warming and destructive climate change that is already wreaking havoc around the globe. Not to mention that fossil fuels are a limited resource, costly to extract and refine, and increasingly sought-after by competing nations.

So if a more environmentally friendly fuel could be derived from renewable plant-based sources, wouldn't it be logical to make the switch?

This is the justification for the recent boom in biofuel production in the U.S. and around the globe. Since biofuels (which can be made from corn, sugar cane, soybeans or other organic sources) are produced from "renewable resources," goes the argument, they can go a long way to helping break America from its 21-million-barrels-a-day oil habit and provide a more environmentally friendly alternative to fossil fuels.

Biofuels – especially, in the U.S., corn-derived ethanol – are being promoted as the saviour of both the planet and humankind.

Think that's an exaggeration? Check out the National Corn Growers Association's online comic book adventures of "Captain Cornelius," who uses his corn superpowers to "protect the environment." Or the association's online promotional video, a Star Wars parody in which "ethanol" is depicted as a wise Yoda-like figure, and "gasoline" is Darth Vader.

Rolling Stone quoted Senator Chuck Grassley of Iowa – "the king of ethanol hype," the magazine pointed out – as saying "Everything about ethanol is good, good, good." But if you scratch a bit beneath the surface, ethanol stops looking quite so "good, good, good."

For one thing, although biofuels are promoted as a cure-all for an ailing environment, many scientists say that they aren't necessarily any better than traditional fossil fuels. As *National Geographic* reported in October:

> Biofuels as currently rendered in the U.S. are doing great things for some farmers and for agricultural giants like Archer Daniels Midland and Cargill, but little for the environment.
>
> Corn requires large doses of herbicide and nitrogen fertilizer and can cause more soil erosion than any other crop. And producing corn ethanol consumes just about as much fossil fuel as the ethanol itself replaces. Biodiesel from soybeans fares only slightly better. Environmentalists also fear that rising prices for both crops will push farmers to plough up some 35 million acres ... of marginal farmland now set aside for soil and wildlife conservation, potentially releasing even more carbon bound in the fallow fields.

According to research reported last year by a team led by Nobel Prize-winning chemist Paul Crutzen, ethanol derived from corn may generate up to 50 percent more greenhouse gases than gasoline, because up to twice as much nitrous oxide may be released by the production process due to increased use of nitrogen fertilizers on corn (one of the most fertilizer-heavy crops).

In addition, in the U.S. and across the globe, forests, grasslands and other fragile ecosystems are being cleared to make way for production of corn, soybeans or other biofuel crops, causing further environmental harm.

According to one study published earlier this year in the journal *Science*, using a worldwide agricultural model to estimate emissions from land-use changes, researchers found that corn-based ethanol, "instead of producing a 20 percent savings in greenhouse gases, nearly doubles greenhouse emissions over 30 years and increases greenhouse gases for 167 years."

As Nature Conservancy researcher Joe Fargione told *Science Daily*, "If you're trying to mitigate global warming, it simply does not make sense to convert land for biofuels production. All the biofuels we use now cause habitat destruction, either directly or indirectly."

In the Midwest "Corn Belt," for example, increased corn production for ethanol has now pushed out nearly 20 million acres of soybean production. Until recently, soybeans were regularly rotated with corn crops, but many farmers are now abandoning them in order to chase the big government subsidies that now come with corn.

Brazilian farmers, driven to plant more of the world's soybeans as a result (not to mention sugar cane for Brazil's own biofuel production), have in turn increased the conversion of the Brazilian Amazon and Cerrado – some of the richest areas in the world in terms of biodiversity – into croplands and cattle pastures. Overall, the effect has been to push soybean prices higher, while encouraging intensive use of nitrogen and phosphorus fertilizers for corn crops.

This increase in fertilizer use is already causing environmental harm. Fertilizer runoff from Midwestern farms into the Gulf of Mexico has created an algae bloom that suffocates the ocean life underneath it.

In the 1970s, the bloom used to occur just once every two to three years. Intense factory farming has made the bloom a yearly phenomenon since the 1980s. And last year, when Midwestern farmers devoted a tract of land nearly the size of California to corn cultivation – a 15 percent increase over the previous year – the "dead zone" grew to the third-largest size ever observed. Reports suggest that the dead zone this year will expand to more than 10,000 square miles, the largest size on record and nearly 20 percent larger than the previous record.

It's also worth noting that ethanol production is often bad for the health of those who live in the communities surrounding the distilleries. Reports of fires, toxic spills and air pollution are common. The Environmental Protection Agency (EPA) concluded this year that "ozone levels generally increase with increased ethanol use."

A 2005 report by the *Des Moines Register* – when Iowa had a total of 17 ethanol plants – found that these facilities "emitted so much [cancer-causing] formaldehyde and toluene into the air that the U.S. Environmental Protection Agency forced several large companies to install new equipment," that several plants were built without construction permits, and that some released bad batches of ethanol and sewage into streams, threatening fish and wildlife.

Yet last year, the EPA relaxed regulations for the ethanol industry, allowing fuel-producing ethanol plants to raise their emissions of pollutants like carbon monoxide, nitrous oxide and sulphur dioxide from 100 tons per year to 250 tons per year.

In the years since the *Register* completed its investigation, the number of ethanol distilleries in the U.S. has skyrocketed – particularly since 2005, when the *Energy Policy Act* was passed, tripling the U.S. government mandate of biofuel production to 7.5 billion gallons of ethanol per year by 2012.

In early 2006, the U.S. had just 95 ethanol plants in operation. Today, according to the Renewable Fuels Association, there are a total of 161 ethanol distilleries in the U.S. – with another 42 plants under construction and seven undergoing expansion. Iowa alone now has 41 ethanol refineries.

And will this boom in ethanol production have an impact on U.S. oil dependence? Not likely. As the Energy Justice Network noted:

> Meeting the lifetime fuel requirements of just one year's worth of U.S. population growth with straight ethanol (assuming each baby lived 70 years), would cost 52,000 tons of insecticides, 735,000 tons of herbicides, 93 million tons of fertilizer, and the loss of 2 inches of soil from the 12.3 billion acres on which the corn was grown. The U.S. only has 2.263 billion acres of land, and soil depletion is already a critical issue. Soil is being lost from corn plantations about 12 times faster than it is being rebuilt.

As the U.S. General Accounting Office concluded in 1997, "ethanol's potential for substituting for petroleum is so small that it is unlikely to significantly affect overall energy security."

One of the biggest negative impacts of the ethanol boom has been the human cost for the world's poor.

As *Foreign Affairs* reported in May, "The current biofuels craze ... has disrupted food and commodities markets and inflicted heavy penalties on poor consumers. These developments have occurred despite record global grain harvests in 2007."

Rising demand over the past several years has helped lead to a global spike in the price of corn – one of the most important staple crops for the world's poor. Between May 2007 and today, the average price of corn increased by some 60 percent (soybeans, also used for biofuel, went up by more than 75 percent).

According to the USDA's annual *Food Security Assessment*, the soaring cost of food increased the number of hungry people in the world by 122 million in 2007 to some 982 million (and poverty groups say the real number is likely much higher). The number of new hungry people – roughly equal to the population of Japan – is the biggest increase since the USDA started producing the report 16 years ago.

As *Time* magazine reported:

> The grain it takes to fill an SUV tank with ethanol could feed a person for a year. Harvests are being plucked to fuel our cars instead of ourselves. The UN's World Food Program says it needs $500 million in additional funding and supplies, calling the rising costs for food nothing less than a global emergency. Soaring corn prices have sparked tortilla riots in Mexico City, and skyrocketing flour prices have destabilized Pakistan, which wasn't exactly tranquil when flour was affordable.

Though some portion of these price increases can be attributed to natural (and man-made) phenomenon like drought and floods, the skyrocketing costs of gasoline (which adds to the price of almost every stage of agriculture, from petroleum-based chemical fertilizers to harvesting and shipping costs) and market speculation due to a declining dollar, biofuels have also played a critical role.

As *Foreign Affairs* noted, "Although controversy remains over how much of the food price increase since 2006 can be attributed to biofuels, their effects cannot be overlooked. In 2008, 30 percent of the U.S. corn crop will be used for ethanol." That percentage is expected to rise through 2015, especially since Congress approved a law in December that mandates the use of at least 36 billion gallons of biofuels by 2020.

As ethanol distilleries suddenly multiplied in the Midwest, as much as 50 percent of some states' corn crop has been diverted to ethanol – taking up land and corn that was once used to feed livestock, which in turn pushes up prices on meat as well. By next year, the U.S. ethanol industry will need 4 billion bushels of corn – 1 billion bushels more than this year and nearly double 2007 levels – to meet anticipated production.

In the same period, however, U.S. corn production is projected to grow by only 11 percent. "The USDA has said that if the ethanol industry gets 1 billion more bushels of corn, it means that the domestic livestock industry will have to cut back 16 percent in feeding corn," said Purdue University Extension agricultural economist Chris Hurt, "And then our foreign buyers [i.e. countries that import U.S. corn] will have to cut back 18 percent."

Given that U.S. trade policies – particularly NAFTA – have decimated the ability of countries like Mexico to feed themselves (pushing farmers out of business by opening markets to imports of U.S. grain), the consequences of a further spike in corn prices will be felt not only on the tables of U.S. consumers, but even more keenly among the world's poor. According to *Le Monde Diplomatique*, since 1994, Mexico has been forced to triple its imports of all cereals, and now must import nearly 25 percent of its corn. But since a portion of Mexico's population is now dependent on U.S. corn, any further spike in corn prices will cause further misery for masses of poor Mexicans.

U.S. officials and business, meanwhile, deny any responsibility. Agriculture Secretary Edward Schafer, for example, recently claimed that biofuel production pushed up global food prices by only 2 or 3 percent. But even USDA chief economist Joseph Glauber admitted in testimony to Congress in June that biofuels account for at least ten percent of global food price rises.

A recent World Bank report leaked to Britain's Guardian newspaper suggested that biofuels may be responsible for as much as 75 percent of global food price increases. World Bank officials say the report isn't finalized, and the number seems inflated.

But other studies show the same direction. *The Gallagher Report*, a British study released last week, found that the "negative impacts from biofuels are real and significant." The study stated that, among other things, current biofuel policies could drive 10.7 million people in India into poverty and force grain prices up in the European Union by 15 percent.

Yet at the recent Group of Eight (G8) summit in Japan, leaders of the world's richest nations – who dined on an elaborate six-course lunch, followed by an eight-course dinner banquet – had little in the way of solutions for the current energy or food crises plunging millions into misery, except to encourage more of the same policies that created the problems in the first place.

As the global women's organization MADRE noted in a statement:

> The root cause of the food crisis is not scarcity, but the failed economic policies long championed by the G8, namely, trade liberalization and industrial agriculture... Yet in the search for solutions, the G8 is considering expanded support for the very measures that caused this web of problems. Calls for more tariff reductions, biofuel plantations, genetically modified crops and wider use of petroleum-based fertilizers and chemical pesticides are at the forefront of discussions in Japan.
>
> These measures cannot resolve the global food crisis. They may, however, further boost this year's record profits for agricultural corporations. There are viable solutions to the food crisis, but they will not emerge from a narrow pursuit of the financial interests of multinational corporations.

The agribusinesses cashing in on the twin bonanzas of spiking food prices and biofuels couldn't get away with it without a little help from their friends in Washington – and not only the Republican variety.

Barack Obama, for example, is a senator from Illinois, where Archer Daniels Midland, the leading producer of ethanol, is a major political force. ADM has spent years lobbying for ethanol, and it's paid off with politicians like Obama.

"Since entering the Senate in 2005," reported the *Washington Post,* "Obama has been a staunch supporter of ethanol – he justified his vote for the Bush administration's 2005 energy bill, which was favourable to the oil industry, on the grounds that it also contained subsidies for ethanol and other forms of alternative energy, and he has sought earmarks for research projects on ethanol and other biofuels in his home state of Illinois, the second-highest corn-producing state after Iowa."

More than anything, the ethanol scam shows that corporate, market-based "solutions" to global warming and oil dependence are no solution at all.

The sane and rational creation of biofuels – using, for example, non-food plants and wise land-use – could be one part of working toward solutions to the environmental crisis.

But that would only succeed if it were combined with other measures: real improvements in fuel efficiency in cars; massive government investment in public transit and alternative energy sources such as solar and wind power; restructuring of industrial manufacturing and agriculture away from oil dependence; and a reordering of urban areas so that people were not forced out of economic necessity to drive long distances from home to and from work, to name a few.

However, as Phil Gasper recently noted in the *International Socialist Review,* such measures "would require wresting control of large quantities of economic resources from corporate control and radically democratizing the entire political process. At the very least, this would require the emergence of social movements on a scale that has not been seen in the U.S. since the 1930s, capable of forcing capital to concede significant concessions. But to push the process through to completion would require breaking entirely with the logic of the profit system."

Magic Bullet #2: Carbon Capture and Storage

Ian Angus

Climate and Capitalism, March 15, 2008
This week, Canada's federal government revealed new details about its supposed plan for reducing greenhouse gas emissions.

Last year in *Canadian Dimension,* I described the plan as "a complete and total fraud" and "a recipe for inaction and delay." The latest announcement amply confirms that judgment.

Energy Minister John Baird has revealed new details, but the plan still aims to reduce "emissions-intensity," while allowing actual emissions to increase – tar sands operators will be able to triple their emissions with no penalty. It still includes loopholes and exemptions that are big enough to drive a tar sands loader through. It still allows big emitters to buy their way out of doing anything at all.

Betting on CCS, Sort Of

The one new thing in this announcement is a claim that the very worst polluters in Canada – power plants and tar sands operations – will be required to implement Carbon Capture and Storage (CCS). They'll have to install equipment that captures CO_2 and other greenhouse gases, and then they'll have to pump the gas underground, where it will remain forever.

Like the rest of the plan, this sounds good until you examine the details. Most notably:

▸ The CCS requirement only applies to plants and tar sands operations that begin operations in 2012 and later. Existing facilities, and those completed in the next three years, are exempt.

▸ The CCS requirement – actually "a cleaner fuel Standard based on carbon capture and storage technology" – won't actually apply until 2018.

Most companies are exempt, and there's a 10-year delay on regulations. That's what the Harper government means by "Getting Tough on Industry's Emissions."

The Harper-Baird cabal present CCS as a silver bullet, a new technology that will magically solve a problem that they'd really rather ignore.

But getting magic to work in the real world can be difficult. Just two months ago, a major report to the Minister from the pro-business and pro-CCS National Roundtable on the Environment and the Economy said: "Technologies such as CCS are largely untested on a massive scale ... While small-scale CCS has been proven, the scalability of these small initiatives is untested."

Let's be more explicit: only a handful of working Carbon Capture facilities exist, in the entire world. All are very small. Not one could handle the CO_2 from the smallest coal-fired power plant in Canada or anywhere else. No one knows when or if the technology will work on a large scale, or how much CO_2 a large-scale operation would actually capture.

And no one knows what it will cost. The Integrated CO_2 Network (ICO2N), a very pro-CCS coalition of big Canadian energy companies, says "capture costs are significant and present an economic challenge." That's a critical issue, because under capitalism CCS will not be deployed – it won't even be developed – unless there are substantial profits to be made.

Is It Safe?

But even if carbon capture works and is cost-effective, there are significant questions about the long-term reliability and safety of underground geologic storage. The Union of Concerned Scientists warns:

> While the potential environmental consequences and risks to public safety are generally acknowledged but frequently dismissed as minor, these environmental concerns are insufficiently studied through systematic research to date. These risks include:

> Direct risks to humans
> ▸ the potential for environmental risks to humans, such as catastrophic venting of CO_2, i.e., the rapid re-release of stored gas in toxic concentrations from underground storage sites;
> ▸ the potential for potable aquifer contamination; and
> ▸ the possible risk of induced seismicity (earthquakes) due to underground movement of displaced fluids.

> Environmental risks
> ▸ the yet-unknown permanence of underground carbon storage, i.e., the re-release of carbon dioxide, thus delaying, but ultimately not solving the emission problem; given the energy penalty associated with carbon separation, if stored carbon is re-released to the atmosphere over time scales of years or decades, atmospheric carbon dioxide concentrations will increase;
> ▸ continued (and possibly increased) reliance on fossil fuels with the associated adverse environmental consequences at fossil-fuel extraction sites, particularly in ecologically sensitive areas;
> ▸ adverse environmental impacts associated with extensive expansion of pipeline facilities necessary for the transfer of CO_2 to deposition sites if implemented on a large scale; and
> ▸ unknown impacts on the biological communities that live in deep saline formations and other storage sites.

In the words of the International Energy Agency, "Unless it can be proven that CO_2 can be permanently and safely stored over the long term, the option will be untenable, whatever its additional benefits."

They Don't Care

Harper, Baird and Co. know all this. They don't care.

In politics, a decade is several lifetimes. By putting off the CCS requirement to 2018, they are offloading the problem onto other politicians and other governments. They are ensuring that the corporations affected will have lots of time to lobby for changes and exemptions and further delays. (The president of the Canadian Association of Petroleum Producers has already said that his group will ask Ottawa for more time.)

When a politician promises to do something in ten years, he is putting it off forever. Where climate change is concerned, that's worse than irresponsible – it's downright criminal.

* * *

AN OPEN LETTER TO CANADA'S ENVIRONMENT MINISTER
Climate and Capitalism, April 4, 2008
Dear Mr. Baird:

You recently announced that your government will impose tough measures "cut our greenhouse gas emissions an absolute 20% by 2020." Central to that promise was a proposed regulation requiring that any electrical plants opened after 2012 be designed to use Carbon Capture and Storage, and that CCS be actually implemented in those plants by 2018.

CCS, as you know, involves "capturing" CO_2 emissions at their source, and then "storing" them at least a kilometre underground, where the pressure will keep the gas in liquid form, and where, you hope, they will stay indefinitely. That's the theory – there are no working commercial CCS operations anywhere in the world, only a handful of tiny test sites.

When you made the announcement, I wrote that this was just another attempt to delay action on emissions. Unfortunately, evidence confirming that judgment continues to flow in.

A recent issue of *New Scientist* magazine (March 27, 2008) features an article by Fred Pearce, who sums up the state of CCS science and technology, and asks the very pertinent question "Can clean coal live up to its promise?" You should read it. According to that article, the UK government is almost as enthusiastic about CCS as you are. The senior minister for industry has predicted that by 2030 up to a third of electricity in Britain could be generated by "clean coal" plants using CCS. Pearse comments:

> Unfortunately, few in the energy industry believe these deadlines are remotely achievable. A study by the Massachusetts Institute of Technology called *The Future of Coal*, published last year, suggests that the first commercial CCS plants won't be on stream until 2030 at the earliest.
>
> Thomas Kuhn of the Edison Electric Institute, which represents most US power generators, half of whose fuel is coal, takes a similar line. In September, he told a House Select Committee that commercial deployment of CCS for emissions from large coal-burning power stations will require 25 years of R&D and cost about $20 billion.
>
> The energy company Shell, though enthusiastic about the technology, doesn't foresee CCS being in widespread use until 2050.

Pearce also discusses the problem of safety and longevity – will the CO_2 actually stay in the ground? A scientist familiar with a CCS test site in Norway says that it hasn't leaked, but she admits it may not be typical.

> So far, tests have been small-scale, short-term and largely at sites that geologists judge will perform best. In the real world, Hovorka points out, geologists will be under pressure to find burial sites close to power plants, where the rock formations may be less than perfect. .... She also admits there is no method yet for deciding how much CO_2 a particular rock formation can absorb before leaking, and how to spot if things are going wrong.

Even if it works – CCS will not capture all the CO_2 generated by a power plant, and it will actually create emissions of its own.

> Yet even the best CCS systems will not capture all the CO_2, and existing methods typically capture only about 85 per cent. In reality the figures are even more unfavourable, as the CCS process itself consumes anything from 10 to 40 per cent of the energy produced by a fossil-fuel power station.
>
> Another factor to be taken into account is the energy used by diggers, trucks and trains to extract coal and transport it to the power station. In all, this may take up to a quarter of the energy the coal produces at the power plant ...

The most detailed assessment of this problem published to date concludes that CCS would reduce GHG emissions from coal-fired power stations by two-thirds – at best!

But of course you know all this. There are many very knowledgeable, very intelligent people in your department, and I'm sure they have told you the truth about CCS: it won't do the job, no one knows if it is safe, and it won't arrive in time. You have been told that, and yet you chose to tell the public that CCS is the silver bullet needed to stop Canada from continuing as one of the worst GHG emitters in the world.

Given that, Mr. Baird, why should we believe that you really want to cut greenhouse gas emissions and deal effectively with global warming? Why shouldn't we draw the obvious conclusion that your "Turning the Corner" plan is just more greenwash, that it simply continues the long-time Conservative and Liberal policy of avoiding action on climate change?

Yours truly,

Ian Angus, Editor

Climate and Capitalism

A New War on the Planet?

John Bellamy Foster

Indypendent, June 8, 2007

During the last year the global warming debate has reached a turning point. Due to the media hype surrounding Al Gore's film *An Inconvenient Truth*, followed by a new assessment by the U.N. Intergovernmental Panel on Climate Change (IPCC), the climate sceptics have suffered a major defeat. Suddenly the media and the public are awakening to what the scientific consensus has been saying for two decades on human-induced climate change and the dangers it poses to the future of life on earth.

Proposed solutions to global warming are popping up everywhere, from the current biofuels panacea to geoengineering solutions such as pumping sulphur particles into the stratosphere to shade the Earth from the sun to claims that a market in carbon dioxide emissions is the invisible hand that will save the world.

"Let's quit the debate about whether greenhouse gases are caused by mankind or by natural causes," President Bush said in a hastily organized retreat. "Let's just focus on technologies that deal with the issue."

It is characteristic of the magic-bullet solutions that now pervade the media that they promise to defend our current way of life while remaining virtually cost free. Despite the fact that economists have long insisted that there is no such thing as a free lunch, we are now being told on every side – even by Gore – that where global warming is concerned there is a free lunch after all. We can have our cars, our industrial waste, our endlessly expanding commodity economy, and climate stability too.

Even the IPCC, in its policy proposals, tells us that climate change can be stopped on the cheap – if only the magic of technology and markets is applied.

The goal is clearly to save the planet – but only if capitalism can be fully preserved at the same time.

Hence, the most prominent proposals are shaped by the fact that they are designed to fit within the capitalist box. There can be no disruption of existing class or power relations. All proposed solutions must be compatible with the treadmill of production.

Even progressive thinkers such as George Monbiot in his new book *Heat: How to Stop the Planet Burning* have gotten into the act. Monbiot pointedly tells us that the rich countries can solve the global warming problem without becoming "Third World" states or shaking up "middle-class" life – or indeed interfering with the distribution of riches at all. Politics is carefully excluded from his analysis, which instead focuses on such things as more buses, better insulated homes, virtual work, virtual shopping and improved cement. Corporations, we are led to believe, are part of the solution, not part of the problem.

Less progressive, more technocratic thinkers look for substitutes for hydrocarbons, such as biofuels or even nuclear power, or they talk of floating white plastic islands in the oceans (a geoengineering solution to replace the lost reflectivity due to melting ice).

The dominant answers to global warming thus amount to what might be thought of as a new declaration of war on nature. If nature has "struck back" at capitalism's degradation of the environment in the form of climate change, the answer is to unleash a more powerful array of technological and market innovations so that the system can continue to expand as before.

As Hannah Arendt, one of the leading political philosophers of the 20th century, explained: "Under modern [capitalist] conditions not destruction but conservation spells ruin." Hence, capitalism, faced by natural obstacles, sees no alternative to a new assault on nature, employing new, high-tech armaments.

The ecological irrationality of this response is evident in the tendency to dissociate global warming from the global environmental crisis as a whole, which includes such problems as species extinction, destruction of the oceans, tropical deforestation, desertification, toxic wastes, etc.

It is then possible, from this narrow perspective, to promote biofuels as a partial solution to global warming – without acknowledging that this will accelerate world hunger. Or it is thought pragmatic to dump iron filings in the ocean (the so-called Geritol solution to global warming) in order to grow phytoplankton and increase the carbon absorbing capacity of the ocean – without connecting this at all to the current oceanic catastrophe. The fact that the biosphere is one interconnected whole is downplayed in favour of mere economic expediency.

What all of this suggests is that a real solution to the planetary environmental crisis cannot be accomplished simply through new technologies or through turning nature into a market. It is necessary to go to the root of the problem by addressing the social relations of production.

We must recognize that today's ecological problems are related to a system of global inequality that demands ecological destruction as a necessary condition of its existence. New social and democratic solutions need to be developed, rooted in human community and sustainability, embodying principles of conservation that are essential to life. But this means stepping outside the capitalist box and making peace with the planet – and with other human beings.

4: THE FANTASY OF GREEN CAPITALISM

> *"You cannot, ladies and gentlemen, have green capitalism.*
> *It is a contradiction in terms."*
> *—George Monbiot—*

Most mainstream environmentalists base their hopes for change on the belief that capitalism can be "greened," through government policies or new technology. They ignore the reality of capitalism's built-in need to grow and pollute.

In Part Four:

▸ **The Failures of Green Economics.** *Joel Kovel on green economic theories that try to combine responsible environmental behaviour with capitalist markets.*

▸ **Sustainable Capitalism?** *David Travis explains why reform proposals from John Ikerd, Gus Speth and others fail in the face of capitalism's growth imperative.*

▸ **The Limits of Green Keynesianism.** *Sean Thompson reviews a proposal that is "more far sighted and radical" than any existing government plan, but which misses the point in crucial ways.*

▸ **Capitalism's Anti-ecology Treadmill.** *Terry Townsend identifies the factors that make capitalism the most destructive economic system of all time.*

The Failures of Green Economics

Joel Kovel

From The Enemy of Nature, second edition. (Zed Books 2007)
Given the collapse of twentieth-century socialism and the hegemony of neo-liberalism, it is not surprising that an influential and diverse body of opinion would arise claiming that a reformist economic path can be found out of the ecological crisis that does not require the overthrow and supersession of capital.

This "green," or ecological, economics echoes a number of the economic points made here – that our system suffers from a kind of gigantism, that its values, in particular the espousal of quantity over quality, are severely flawed, that it misallocates resources, promotes inequity, and generally has made a botch of the global ecology. But green economics goes on to insist that the system has recuperative powers.

It would not be entirely fair to say that the people who espouse it are part of the system, for they have at times suffered one sanction or another. But green economics is not really outside of the system, either. Its proponents want rather to stretch and reorganize the system to realize ecologically sound potentials, and they believe that the means are at hand for doing so.

Ecological economics represents the ecological wing of mainstream economics; it speaks with an authoritative and technical voice toward the entirety of economic relations with nature. Ecological economics comes packaged as a professional association with a refereed journal. As a recent quasi-official volume asks:

> Can we ... reorganize our society rapidly enough to avoid a catastrophic overshoot? Can we be humble enough to acknowledge the huge uncertainties involved and protect ourselves from their most dire consequences? Can we effectively develop policies to deal with the tricky issues of wealth distribution, population prudence, international trade, and energy supply in a world where the simple palliative of 'more growth' is no longer an option? Can we modify our systems of governance at international, national, and local levels to be better adapted to these and new and more difficult challenges? (R.J. Costanza et al., *An Introduction to Ecological Economics*. St. Lucie Press, p. 5)

Clearly, ecological economics is uninterested in social transformation, and accepts the potentials of the present system to absorb the crisis, that is, to "adapt." To this means, which has in effect become an end, ecological economists employ a great variety of instrumental measures, from "incentive-based" regulations (such as tradable emission credits) to various ecological tariffs and "natural capital" depletion taxes, as well as penalties against polluters. There is one very definite common denominator underlying all the various interventions of ecological economics, which ties this discourse firmly into the mainstream of capital, and that is the commodification of nature in all aspects, its quantification into a system of value.

The trading of pollution credits began in the United States in 1989 with the effort to control sulphur dioxide emissions, and was smoothly applied to the carbon trading regime in the Kyoto Protocols. The United States government under George W. Bush has refused to go along with this on the grounds that Kyoto would be bad for the economy, but not all American capitalists agree; and the main body lie in wait licking their chops for the huge market which will result if Kyoto is generalized. A trading credit is a license, granted by the state, to exploit some part of nature, like a mineral right over a certain territory.

There are actually two lines by which the Kyoto process is tied to accumulation. In the first, pollution credits are traded with a modest reduction in emissions and potentially a great deal of value being added to the transaction. In the second, named the Clean Development Mechanism, Northern firms are given license to create carbon sequestration projects in the South, for example, eucalyptus tree farms. This frees them to continue polluting in the chimerical hope that their carbon will be recycled in some future time. At the same time, more of the Southern commons is enclosed and more people are displaced from their traditional life and forced into the chaotic megalopolises.

That anyone would believe this scheme capable of containing global warming is testimony to the intense brainwashing that goes on these days. Of course the jargon of tradable permits uses all the latest buzzwords of the rationality that would allow business to have its cake and eat it as well. And it is a fine idea, except for two problems: that it cannot work, especially for global warming; and that if it did work, it only perpetuates the kind of world that gives us the ecological crisis in the first place.

As for the first, the notion presupposes a rational marketplace of nations in which rich developed ones pay poor developing ones for the right to emit greenhouse gases. But this kind of market requires an orderly world-society of cooperating nations – exactly what imperialism-as-globalization has made impossible, and what the sequestration projects, with their indeterminate outcome and neo-colonial impact, will make even more chaotic. Finally, to the extent that the project succeeds, so does it fail, for the new wealth which has been created remains like capital everywhere, constantly seeking investment outlets and placing yet more burdens on ecosystems. Under capital, with its ceaseless pressure to expand, wealth necessarily turns into ecological disintegration.

The idea of tradable credits owes a great deal to Stephen Breyer, who was rewarded by Clinton with a Supreme Court seat, as well as to major environmental NGOs, most notably, the Environmental Defense Fund, which see no contradiction in rationalizing pollution and turning it into a fresh source of profit. The story offers useful lessons in the co-optation of the mainstream environmental movement as this passes from citizen-based activism to ponderous bureaucratic scuffling for "a seat at the table."

Capital is more than happy to enlist mainstream enviros as partners in the management of nature. Big environmental groups offer capital a three-fold convenience: as legitimation, reminding the world that the system

---

With ecological economics defining nature in the terms of private property, the experts are given an extensive playing field on which they never have to contemplate the fact that unlimited accumulation and ecological integrity form an iron contradiction.

---

works; as control over popular dissent, a kind of sponge that sucks up and contains the ecological anxiety in the general population; and as rationalization, a useful governor to introduce some control and protect the system from its own worst tendencies, while ensuring the orderly flow of profits.

Ecological economics stands squarely midstream in this gigantic process of rationalizing capital, and provides a kind of *lingua franca* with which technocrats of all stripes – NGOs, foundations, environmental studies programs in academia – can gather around the table and discuss ways the ecological crisis can be kept from getting out of hand while preserving the integrity of accumulation. With ecological economics defining nature in the terms of private property, the experts are given an extensive playing field on which they never have to contemplate the fact that unlimited accumulation and ecological integrity form an iron contradiction.

Mainstream ecological economics is relatively unconcerned about the size of economic units. However, there are also those who cluster about a second strand of green economics and regard this question as primary. These may roughly be described as neo-Smithian, the Smith in question being the great Adam, father of modern political economy. Adam Smith's advocacy of free markets was in the interest of an end distinctly different from today's neoliberalism. Smith's vision – which in good measure also became Thomas Jefferson's – was of a capitalism of small producers, freely exchanging with each other. He feared and loathed monopolies, and felt that the competitive market of small buyers and sellers (where no single individual could by himself determine prices) would self-regulate to keep these at bay. Smith argued that state intervention, the *bête noire* of neoliberalism, leads to monopoly and economic gigantism. Neoliberalism, needless to say, has no difficulty at all with these latter ends.

The ambition of neo-Smithian thinking is to restore small, independent capitals to pre-eminence. For this purpose, as David Korten, one of the leading exponents of the view, puts it, Smith's assumption, "that capital would be rooted in a particular place," must be met. Korten's ecological society, the essence of which he describes as "democratic pluralism," is based upon "regulated markets," in which government and civil society combine to offset the tendencies of capitalist firms to expand and concentrate, even as these same capitalist firms, now reduced, continue to provide the mainspring of the economy. (D. Korten, "The Mythic Victory of Market Capitalism," in Mander and Goldsmith, eds., *The Case Against the Global Economy*, Sierra Club Books, 1996, pp. 183-191)

Korten has achieved prominence in presenting these views, a number of which parallel those argued here. However, he does so without any concentrated critique of capital itself, neither does he look into questions of class, gender, nor any other category of domination. This is because Korten sees the primary lesion in philosophical or religious terms, as a suddenly appearing colossal kind of mistake identifiable as the "Scientific Revolution," whose "materialism" stripped life of "meaning" and crushed the spirit of "generosity and caring." He regards this grandly:

> Failing to recognize and embrace their responsibility to the whole [human beings] turned their extraordinary abilities to ends ultimately destructive of the whole of life, destroying in a mere 100 years much of the living natural capital it had taken billions of years of evolution to create.

Note the reference to "natural capital," as though nature had toiled to put the gift of capital into human hands, who then abused this through, false science and materialism. Since capital – or class, or the capitalist state – is no big deal to Korten, and even, when nature produces it, a good thing, he has no difficulty in seeing it checked by "globalizing civil society," who will restrain and effectively domesticate the animal, leading to the neo-Smithian Promised Land.

This is essentially an upbeat fairytale standing in for history. If it were true, the world would be a much easier place to change; indeed, without capital and the capitalist state, we wouldn't have a problem in the first place.

Sustainable Capitalism?

David Travis

Links International Journal of Socialist Renewal, September 9, 2008
On the fringe of the green movement, one always hears the following phrases coming from the mainstream with great regularity: "green capitalism," "sustainable capitalism," "social entrepreneurs," "green entrepreneurs," etc. None of these terms tend to mean anything specific, and no one who uses them is in a great hurry to spell out, for example, how a green entrepreneur is different in any fundamental way from some other kind of entrepreneur, or how capitalism could be driven toward sustainability rather than profit. So you can imagine my pleasure at meeting John Ikerd, the author of a book called *Sustainable Capitalism: A Matter of Common Sense.*

I ran into Dr. Ikerd at an energy conference in 2006 where he was speaking, and had the pleasure of dining with him afterwards. He's a passionate speaker and is obviously concerned not only with ecological sustainability but with the social impact of contemporary forms of production, although the depth of his knowledge regarding the social and political dimension of the capitalist mode is more or less what one would expect from a professor of agricultural economics.

In his estimation, the problems caused by capitalism are accidental, in the sense that he does not see anything inherently wrong with the way capitalism operates. Its ill social and environmental effects are accidents caused by the way capitalism developed. He argues that the "scientific" view of neoclassical economists (as opposed to what he saw as the morally healthy humanism of Smith and Ricardo), paired with the institution of the multinational corporation, have created a business environment that facilitates the creation of profitable yet unethical decisions with impunity.[1]

Ikerd nevertheless regards capitalism as "the most efficient economic system," and in spite of the many "risks" that come with it, he – like many sustainability advocates and environmentalists – sees some permutation of its existence as essentially inevitable. The reasoning behind this "inevitability" of capitalism is usually unclear, with many of those who elect to speak about issues of sustainability unwilling to pursue (oddly enough) the question of whether or not our current economic system is inherently unsustainable, or the question of whether or not our present system of social and economic relations can in fact be changed. Nevertheless, one usually finds the following arguments in favour of the "inevitability thesis":

(a) Capitalism is "the most efficient" economic system or "the best" system so far, and therefore any economic change must take the form of an improvement or modification to its basic workings. Most people who make this argument never go very far in elaborating on what they mean by "efficient" or "productive" or any of the other adjectives they unreflectively apply to capitalism. To what end it is productive, or for whose benefit it is efficient, generally remains unknown and unasked.

(b) Alternatives to capitalism have all "failed." People who make this argument no doubt have the Soviet Union and communist China in mind. Ironically, proponents of these "historical" arguments often ignore all history in making them, and imagine instead a kind of "level playing field" in which nations experimenting with alternative economic systems somehow lost "fair and square" against the might of Western capitalism. This interpretation has no real basis in fact, what with embargoes, propaganda, espionage, terrorism, coups, political assassination, outright invasion and every other conceivable trick in the book routinely pulled against any state foolish enough to try playing for the wrong team. What the Soviet Union and other states demonstrate is never articulated with any clarity; the value of the US legacy is evaluated in a positive light that is similarly vague and unreflective, fuelled primarily by the safe assumption that US capitalism can be "the best" without being "good," and that this simple realization justifies it going unchanged, unchallenged and unquestioned.

Ikerd does not deviate from either of these articles of modern faith:

> Many people today question whether a capitalist economy can ever be sustainable. Admittedly, the ecological and social risks of capitalism are real. However, no other economic system has been found that can rival its efficiency and productivity in decisions and activities that are legitimately private, personal, or individual in nature. Societies that have tried communism, socialism, and religious theocracies have never been able to meet the physical and material needs of their people. They are ultimately rejected by their people because they are not economically sustainable. Most individual economic decisions do not deprive anyone of their basic social rights or violate any moral imperative. These decisions legitimately belong in the individual, private economy, where there is no logical alternative to capitalism. Capitalism, with all of its inherent risks, is still humanity's best hope for sustainability. Fortunately, sustainable capitalism does not require some radical, new-age value system; it only requires that we return to the foundational principles of classical capitalism and grass-roots democracy.[2]

By this Ikerd means finding some way of injecting moral sensibilities back into the US economy, as they were in the good old days of Adam Smith, when land was appropriated by war and genocide, and when labour was supplied by slaves and indentured servants.

The problem here is a failure to recognise the basic logic of capitalism.

The rational choice is not to attempt to reform capitalism with moralistic pleading, regulatory boondoggles, or vague hopes that an over-worked and under-educated public will miraculously coalesce and demand the enlightened and equitable oversight of policy and civil society. That seems idealistic and impractical. It would seem more productive to replace the entire system with one that is democratic, sustainable and non-exploitive at its very core, rather than as a jury-rigged afterthought. Call me a realist.

Fortunately, not all mainstreamers are quite as naive as the good Dr. Ikerd. James Gustave Speth's *The Bridge at the End of the World: Capitalism, the Environment, and Crossing from Crisis to Sustainability*, for example, clearly recognises the role of the modern capitalist economy in producing the climate crisis. All of this is carefully and compellingly laid out by John Bellamy Foster *et al.* in their article in the *Monthly Review*'s July-August 2008 issue.

Speth basically sees a kind of zero-growth capitalism as being necessary for an environmentally stable Earth. In the process, he supposedly challenges the mainstream optimism of technocrats, who believe that "dematerialisation" – a concept in industrial ecology that refers to the reduction of material impacts per unit of services or products – can preserve or even restore the environment while also providing the capacity for sustained economic growth.

So, for example, the United States might replace its vehicle fleet with cars and trucks that use only a half of the amount of fuel they do today. That's great. But to have economic growth, we need to be driving more and buying more cars – by building and marketing cars in China, for example. But having twice as much of a product that has half the environmental impact gets you nowhere. To begin moving toward sustainability, you would have to maintain the vehicle fleet at its current size and make it more efficient at the same time. That's all well and good for the environment, but it's not profitable.

Coming from Speth, this is quite challenging. He was a co-founder of the National Resources Defense Council, was the chair of the Council on Environmental Quality under US President Jimmy Carter, is the founder of the World Resources Institute, is a former administrator of the United Nations Development Program and he's currently the dean of the Yale School of Forestry and Environmental Studies. Which is to say this critique is coming from the heart of bourgeois liberal environmentalism.[3]

In case any of us were getting scared at this point:

> Speth is no Marxist, and he's not attacking capitalism in its ideal and theoretic form. But he's marshalled formidable evidence that American-style consumer capitalism of the early twenty-first century is incompatible with maintaining quality of life for all of us. It is generating unprecedented envi-

ronmental risks while failing to advance the happiness and social well-being of Americans, Speth argues. Our obsession with consumption and GDP growth has overshot its target and now causes more harm—to environment, social fabric, and world security—than good.[4]

God forbid we risk fire and brimstone by criticising capitalism in its "ideal or theoretic form." Instead:

▸ We must change the very nature of corporations so they become legally accountable to society at large, not just to themselves and their shareholders.

▸ We must challenge the current obsession with GDP growth and focus on growth in the areas that truly enhance human wellbeing: growth in good jobs, in the availability of health care, in education, in the deployment of green technologies, in the incomes of the poor, in security against illness and disability, in infrastructure, and more.

▸ We must challenge materialism and consumerism as the source of happiness and seek new values about quality of life, social solidarity, and connectedness to nature.

▸ We must transform the market through government action so that it works for the environment, rather than against it.

▸ We must transform democracy through deep political reforms that reassert popular control, encouraging locally strong, deliberative democracy and limiting corporate influence.

▸ We must forge a new environmental politics that recognises links among environmentalism, social liberalism, human and civil rights, the fight against poverty, and other issues.[5]

Granted, these are quick talking points aimed primarily at promoting a book and (presumably) providing basic information to the press. And there is (even for me) something enticing at least about the first proposal about making corporations legally accountable to society. I have no doubt that Mr. Speth has in mind something along the lines of mainstream environmental regulation, rather than – I don't know – prohibiting profit altogether and mandating democratic workplaces, although it's hard to say when someone actually advocates for a "zero growth" capitalism. The only other somewhat challenging phrase in this list is the call for "deep political reforms," by which he presumably means things like capping the power of lobbyists (the institution itself is something of a travesty) and making room for environmental voter initiatives. I don't know.

But the central theme is that we have to challenge the culture of consumerism. We need new values. We must transform the market. It is not all that different from the naive moralisms of Dr. Ikerd. This is a puzzling though not uncommon approach, and there are parts of this that make a great deal of sense. The perception of our social ills as being the result of a moral failure, or a failure to recognise value, seems immediate and commonsensical, particularly for members of a society easily fixated by personal responsibility as an explanatory device.

And part of the appeal of personal responsibility and moralising is precisely that it is individualistic: it enables the criticism of vast groups of people without specificity, it allows for the appearance of concern, outrage and various forms of progressive posturing, while at the same avoiding change and the tremendous ill will of interests aligned against it. Which is not to say that people don't mean well, of course; indeed "meaning well" and "doing good" is the other side of the personal responsibility escape hatch. Within the mainstream eco-yuppie paradigm, the most you can possibly be expected to do is "right thing" in your own life. You buy your indulgences in the form of a low-carbon lifestyle and an arsenal of "eco-friendly" products, and in return you are exempt from the uncomfortable task of looking your class, your politics and your job in the face.

Nature of capitalism

As for the puzzling part: such views, however well informed, ignore the nature of capitalism. The extraction of profit from labour and nature isn't some accidental part of what capitalism is. It's what makes the thing go. Similarly, growth and GDP aren't just bells and whistles that can be removed from some stripped-down, enviro-friendly version of the beast. Growth is why people invest. Without profit or growth, there would be no capitalists.

But the bourgeois apologists generally take the position that capitalism is value neutral and entirely mutable, freely reflecting the "values" of the consumer. For them capitalism is a form of economic tool and little more. The works of the apologists attest to an essentially technocratic understanding of capitalism, which itself has no tendency toward any particular society or way of living, at least not beyond the acceptance of certain unequivocal social goods such as private property rights, free association, equality under the law, etc. The idea that we would have to significantly alter or remove capitalism itself in order to rectify its ills appears nonsensical to the apologist, who regards capitalism as nothing more than the "most efficient" way of doing anything. Capitalism is even the "most efficient" way of "fixing" capitalism. Go figure.

Jurgen Habermas has a few things to say about ethics and technocracy:

> Technocratic consciousness reflects not the sundering of an ethical situation but the repression of "ethics" as a category of life. The common, positivist way of thinking renders inert the frame of reference of interaction in ordinary language, in which domination and ideology both arise under conditions of distorted communication and can be reflectively detected and broken down. The depoliticization of the mass of the population, which is

legitimated through technocratic consciousness, is at the same time men's self-objectification in categories equally of both purposive-rational action and adaptive behaviour. The reified models of the sciences migrate into the sociocultural life-world and gain objective power over the latter's self-understanding. The ideological nucleus of this consciousness is the elimination of the distinction between the practical and the technical.[6]

So what we're observing in Ikerd and Speth is a partial breakdown of this ideology. It is a breakdown in the sense that there is ultimately a recognition that the technocratic capitalism of the post-war era has failed in ways that are important enough to warrant "deep" changes in "our"social, political and economic behaviour.[7] But it has failed in terms of destroying the environment and investing in an energy, transportation and residential development infrastructure that is wildly unsustainable. The Cold War conviction that capitalism succeeds in delivering social goods with an adequate level of equal opportunity and fairness remains strong even in spite of its failures in regard to climate and energy.[8] That is one important sense in which the breakdown is partial, and it is fundamentally tied to the fact that environmentalism is a bourgeois movement.[9]

Values privatised

But the second and more important sense that this breakdown is only partial has to do with the fact that the cult of "corporate responsibility," of which people like Ikerd and Speth are the most advanced spokespeople, perceives "values" in a kind of vacuum. Values have no place to go. They are not social concepts connected to specific relations of class and power – values are privatized. To think that our collective social behaviour is the product of personal values is a mistake, one that obfuscates the basic structural and historical forces at work in society; indeed the very idea of society is a blanket to be thrown over the web of institutions, classes, movements, and power groups to which we actually relate and live.

In any case, you can't say you want an end to the GDP and economic growth as we know it without challenging these fundamental institutions. Similarly you can't say that profit is the problem yet be unwilling to challenge capitalism in its "ideal or theoretic form." Changing our "values" or our "culture" won't magically allow us to consume our way to sustainability. Like it or not, capitalism is about extraction and profit, and when it comes to change, the sustainability movement has to decide to either shit or get off the pot.

Notes

1 *Sustainable Capitalism: Our Best Hope for the Future.*

2 Ibid.

3 Wikipedia article on James Speth.

4 *Beyond Reform.*

5 *Bridge at the Edge of the World.*

6 Jurgen Habermas, "Technology and Science as Ideology."

7 Commentators on climate change often speak of it as being "our" fault, but these assertions of collective guilt are a little hard to understand given that a very small class of investors are the ones who ultimately drive the development, marketing and production decisions that determine the way we live. When isolated individuals who are overworked, lied to, swindled and presented with a limited number of bad options actually end up making bad environmental decisions, what exactly are we supposed to do? Blame them in the same way we blame highly informed and highly organised institutions looking for profit? No, I didn't think so either. Among those who like to deride those who shop at Wal-Mart, I wonder how many have mutual funds or pension plans that include Wal-Mart stock.

8 In this respect, there are some uncomfortable grains of truth to the common reactionary and otherwise idiotic claim that environmentalists care more about nature than their fellow human beings.

9 But not exclusively. Rising Tide, for example, has taken a good position against carbon offsets, the most popular technocratic answer to climate change.

The Limits of Green Keynesianism

Sean Thompson

Climate and Capitalism, October 2008

The authors of the New Economics Foundation (NEF) *Green New Deal* report deserve our thanks. At a time when most economists, politicians and bankers are rushing around like headless chickens, the *Green New Deal* Group has recognised what most others have signally failed to; that the current crisis is not just current and financial, it is the first of three overlapping and global crises that we face. This "triple crunch," as they call it, is a combination of the banking crisis we are now experiencing, the ongoing and ever growing threat of climate change and the explosion of energy prices caused by the imminent approach of peal oil. (see http://tinyurl.com/5jxcld.)

"These three overlapping events," they say, "threaten to develop into a perfect storm, the like of which we have not seen since the Great Depression."

The report proposes that we should deal with these three interlocked crises with twin strategies; first, "a structural transformation of the regulation of national and international financial systems, and major changes to taxation systems" and second, "a sustained programme to invest in and deploy energy conservation and renewable energies, coupled with effective demand management." These strategies are fleshed out by a number of specific(ish) policy proposals:

Infrastructure development

▸ A huge programme of investment in energy conservation (including a massive domestic insulation and micro CHP installation) and the development of renewable energy generation capacity.

▸ A vast environmental reconstruction programme, along with the recruitment and training/retraining of the hundreds of thousands of workers required.

▸ Significant increases in fossil fuel prices on order to force energy efficiency and to make alternative energy sources more attractive.

Fiscal measures

▸ The establishment of an Oil Legacy Fund, financed by a windfall tax on the profits of the oil and gas companies.

▸ The development of a package of other fund raising measures, such as government and local authority bonds, "Go Green" national savings bonds and investment from the pension funds.

▸ A significant reduction in the Bank Rate in order to help finance a new energy and transport infrastructure, along with much tighter controls on lending and on the generation of credit.

▸ The forced de-merger of large banking and finance groups, which should then be further split into smaller banks. At the same time, retail banking should be split from both corporate finance and from securities dealing.

▸ The reintroduction of capital controls by national governments.

▸ Strict regulation of derivatives and similar spivvy wheezes and, in the long term, downsizing of the financial sector in relation the rest of the economy.

▸ Minimising corporate tax evasion by clamping down on tax havens and ensuring transparent and honest corporate financial reporting

International negotiation

▸ The Government should negotiate international agreements that allow national autonomy over domestic monetary and fiscal policy, set an international target for atmospheric greenhouse gas concentrations, establish Kyoto 2, financing poor countries' investments in climate change adaptation and renewable energy generation and assisting the free transfer of new energy technologies to developing countries.

Farsighted, radical ... and too narrow

This is a more far sighted and radical package of proposals than any currently on the desk of any finance minister or central banker in the 1st World. However, I believe that the proposals come from a too narrow – if entirely understandable – focus on the immediate need for economic stability and big reductions in carbon emissions and fail to recognise the cyclical instability that is an inherent characteristic of the capitalist dynamic, or the unproductive speculative impulse that lies at the heart of capitalism.

The report hardly seems to notice the increase in the already wide inequality that neoliberalism has manufactured in our society, inequality which is getting worse as a result of the crisis we are currently facing, which will get much worse in the deep recession we are rushing towards, and which lie at the heart of the most intractable social problems we face, from fuel poverty, poor health and obesity to crime, drug addiction and family dislocation. As a result, the report in some crucial ways misses the point and consequently many of its proposals are too timid.

It is, of course, true that the current global financial crisis has been triggered by the collapse of the credit fuelled property bubble in the United States. It is also undeniable that the bubble was the inevitable outcome of the financial deregulation of the late seventies and eighties that led to an enormous expansion of financial markets, an explosion of credit and the development of ever more exotic and arcane speculative vehicles. For twenty five years or more there has been an ever flowing fountain of cash pouring into the financial markets. In the United States, total financial assets averaged around 440% of GDP from the early '50s to the late '70s. Then they started to climb steadily; to over 600% in 1990 and over 1000% by 2007.

With a few unpleasant interruptions (the stock market crash of the late '80s, the Asian and Mexican financial crises of the mid '90s, the dot-com bubble of the early 2000s) it seemed as if Wall Street and the City had entered an eternal bull market.

In reality, this ready access to credit – for speculative financial ventures (on the part of the rich) and for housing and unsustainably cheap consumer goods from China (for the rest of us) – helped disguise the ongoing relative decline of western (particularly US and UK) manufacturing industries and the hollowing out of their real economies. What this has led to is both an increase in personal indebtedness and a dramatic inflation in the value of assets (stocks and shares, houses etc.).

Commodity inflation was suppressed by falling labour costs, which were kept down by the introduction of the Anglo Saxon concept of "flexible labour markets," heavily reinforced labour discipline through the imposition of draconian labour laws and the export of manufacturing to China and the Far East. As the *Green New Deal* puts it, this asset inflation "explains why the rich have got richer within the liberalized financial system and the poor have become poorer and more indebted."

All this make it irresistibly tempting to call for the re-regulation of finance – and indeed, that is desperately needed. But this crisis hasn't happened just because Thatcher and Reagan's deregulation of finance introduced instability into the capitalist system, and that after each crisis since the late '70s the system, when it bounced back, was even more unequal, unbalanced and distorted than before. The underlying cause of the crisis is the inherent boom/bust instability that lies at the heart of the capitalist system, particularly the financial markets.

Why capitalism has to keep expanding and is inherently unstable

In pre-capitalist economies, where money played an enabling role, the circuit of commodities and money existed in a form in which particular commodities (or use-values) constituted the end of the economic cycle. A commodity embodying a particular use-value is sold for money which is used to purchase a different commodity, or C-M-C. So each circuit is closed by the consumption of a use-value.

However, in the case of a capitalist economy, the circuit of commodities and money begins and ends with money. Money is used to purchase commodities which are sold on for money, or M-C-M. Of course, since money is simply the abstract expression of a quantitative relationship, such an exchange would be meaningless if the same amount of money was exchanged at the end of the process as at the beginning.

So the actual formula in reality is M-C-M*, where M* is in fact M+m or profit, or capital, or, as we dried out bitter old Marxists say, surplus value. Of course, the big difference between this and simple commodity production is that there is no end to the process, since the object of the process is not final use but the accumulation of capital. So the M-C-M* produced in one year leads to the m being reinvested, leading to M-C-M** the next year, M-C-M*** the next, and so on ad infinitum. Just as a shark needs to continually keep on swimming in order to survive, so does capitalism need to continually go on expanding.

The mainspring of this drive to accumulate is competition. This competition forces every player in the market to grow through continual reinvestment in order to survive. In the case of banks, the commodity to be bought and sold is credit (or conversely, debt). Competition puts banks and brokerages continually under pressure to try to expand their markets by issuing loans to riskier and riskier customers and speculate on riskier and riskier derivatives.

As the Canadian economist Jim Stanford has said:

> Capitalism is nothing if not creative and the financial industry has lured some of humanity's smartest minds to focus on the utterly unproductive task of developing new pieces of financial paper, and new ways of buying and selling them. Despite the finger pointing at mortgage brokers and credit rate, therefore, the current meltdown is rooted squarely in the innovative but blinding greed that is the *raison d'être* of private finance.

So the financial system is both structurally unstable and impossibly un-predictable – although this crisis, triggered by the bursting of the US and UK housing bubbles, should have been predictable enough. This inherent instability, compounded by the deregulation of the markets demanded by financiers and the consequent global mobility of capital, has led us to shift, seamlessly and almost overnight, from a situation where credit was sloshing around our knees to one where credit has virtually dried up and bankers throughout the world are curled up and trembling in foetal positions with their eyes shut and their hands over their ears – apparently all as the result of the sleight of hand of a relatively tiny number of spivs and hucksters.

Credit creation is an essential social and economic function, but it has been largely handed over to private banks – with, it appears, bugger all regu-latory or social oversight – whose *raison d'être* is to maximise their own profit. When their cost-benefit or risk analyses diverge from those of soci-ety as a whole (and they do frequently), the economy finds itself with too much credit, too little, or in a really desperate crisis (like now) none at all. Of course, we need credit as an essential lubricant to ensure the liquidity of institutions and ordinary people in the real economy, but that credit supply needs to be stable and at the right level. We have the living proof before us that "the market" cannot ensure that: only governments can.

Beyond stabilisation to transformation

For that reason, we need to go beyond the proposals in the *Green New Deal*, which look more modest by the day. The report's key proposals for financial renewal include a big reduction in the Bank of England interest rate, tight controls on lending and on the generation of credit, the forced de-merger of large banking and finance groups, the divorce of retail banking from both corporate finance and securities dealing, the reintroduction of government controls on capital flows, strict regulation of derivatives and similar spivvy wheezes and the long term downsizing of the financial sector in relation the rest of the economy.

Now all these proposals are fine as far as they go but the report seems very shy about dealing with the central issue: the inevitable necessity to ex-ert direct state control over the domestic financial system in order to imple-ment any of the proposals in a meaningful way.

This certainly means making our central bank (the Bank of England) the main tool in the government's strategy of financial intervention by reversing its so-called independence and by changing its current narrow and negative neo-liberal remit of limiting price inflation to a much more positive one of actively promoting economic health and full employment.

Whether or not this will lead to the rapid nationalisation of the bank-ing system as a whole is currently uncertain. The Government has already nationalised Northern Rock and part of Bradford and Bingley and as I write, Alastair Darling is talking about the Government requiring equity holdings in return for the huge sums it is pumping into the banks to maintain at least some liquidity – and the banks are likely to become steadily more dependent on the Bank of England as their wholesale loans are not being rolled over as they become due for payment.

The BBC's Robert Peston (an essential source of information for us all at the moment) pointed out a few days ago that while in 2001 the gap between the money lent by the banks and what they took in from conventional deposits was zero, by the end of last year the gap had grown to £625b – a staggering dependence on the wholesale markets. Over the past few months the gap has been filled by loans from the Bank of England; effectively, says Peston, "It's a sort of nationalization by stealth."

Nationalization, through receiving equity in return for recapitalization, is a perfectly practical option – all the more so as yesterday shares in RBS dropped by 20% and the FTSE had its biggest ever one day drop, with shares losing £93bn off their values. HBOS has lost 76% of its value in the last year, Lloyds TSB has lost 52%, Barclays has lost 40% and RBS has lost 58%. So they have nowhere to go except the state.

To quote Jim Stanford again:

> At the end of the day, the risks associated with private finance will always be socialised (as they have been in the current crisis) simply because the costs of the major financial failures are too severe, and too widely distributed, to tolerate. So why don't we socialise the whole process, or at least part of it?

However, there is absolutely no point in the state taking all or part of the equity – and toxic debt – of the banks simply to ride this crisis out and then to return to business as usual. We have to find more equitable and publicly accountable ways to create a stable supply of credit without recourse to the anarchic and irrational monster that private finance has become. Rational lending in the real economy – to consumers, home buyers and productive undertakings – is a necessary public service we all depend on, but we can't trust the market to provide it reliably. So we need to develop alternative vehicles, including banks brought into public ownership, credit unions, building societies and other mutuals and not for profit institutions.

A few days ago one commentator said that the Government's apparent policy of allowing, or even encouraging, the development of ever larger financial institutions through amalgamations or take-overs in order to deal with the weakness of institutions like HBOS and B&B was in danger of creating a situation where instead of there being institutions the government couldn't afford to fail, there would soon be institutions the Government couldn't afford to save. The authors of the *Green New Deal* are quite right to suggest that we must reverse this policy, but I fail to see how the forced de-merger of behemoths like Lloyds TSB, Barclays, RBS etc. could be effected without complete state control – if not ownership – of their assets.

A new industrial revolution

The authors of the *Green New Deal* have taken their inspiration, as well as the title of their report, from the programme developed by Franklin D Roosevelt in response to the post 1929 Depression. Like him, and like Keynes, they propose an ambitious programme of public works and infrastructure development. Only it isn't ambitious enough.

While the proposals to spend £50-70b a year on a massive programme of energy conservation measures coupled with a similarly vast programme for the development of renewable energy sources are admirable, they are so tightly focussed on the trees that they don't notice that the wood is in danger of rotting away.

Manufacturing industry in the UK now only amounts for around 25% of the economy. At the beginning of October, the *Guardian* reported that the UK manufacturing sector is shrinking at the fastest rate since records began 17 years ago. It reported that levels of output, new orders and employment in the manufacturing sector had recorded unprecedented declines in the previous month. The British Chamber of Commerce has reported that all the main indices in its most recent quarterly survey – sales, orders, profitability and confidence – were down for manufacturing and services firms of all sizes, findings that are described as "exceptionally bad." The BCC is now predicting that unemployment will exceed two million next year. There can be no doubt that this situation can only get a great deal worse.

Our manufacturing base has been withering since Thatcher decided that a Post Industrial Britain didn't need to concern itself with making things; there was far more money (for some) in manipulating financial paper. In particular, our engineering and construction industries have been hollowed out and our previous army of skilled engineers and builders dispersed, with no one replacing them. So now, if we need more trains (and we do) we must buy them from Germany or France, because we have no locomotive building industry any more. If we want large wind powered generators we have to wait in the queue for them at German and Danish (the world leaders) manufacturers, because we currently have no large wind generator manufacturing capacity, despite having the best conditions for wind power on earth!

The *Green New Deal* report predicts that the development of the admirable low-carbon energy system and environmental reconstruction programme it proposes will "see hundreds of thousands of ... jobs created in the UK. It will be part of a wider shift from an economy focussed on financial services and shopping to one that is a an engine of environmental transformation." That is certainly a desirable goal, but it will not happen without the most massive and rapid programme of investment in the retooling of industry and reskilling of labour that we have seen since the Second World War.

If our aim is to build a whole new low-carbon energy system, along with other aims not mentioned by the report, such as a totally renewed public transport system, a sustainable water supply system and a massive programme of social housing to meet the needs of the five million families on waiting lists for a home, we are going to need nothing less than a new industrial revolution. We need to develop/redevelop the capacity to implement a to huge production programme encompassing mini and micro CHP equipment, wave and offshore wind generator production, a whole new grid infrastructure, energy efficient buses and rail/light rail vehicles, low impact buildings and building materials etc., etc. (which, incidentally, would almost certainly place us on a collision course with the EU Commission). As the report's authors put it, there is a "need for mobilization as though for war."

Although hundreds of thousands of jobs would be created by such a programme, the major changes in industrial strategy that are implied by the report – for example, contraction of the motor vehicle, armaments and aero-space industries and the run-down of much of the existing electricity generation capacity – would lead to a need to transfer and retrain workers moving from declining to rapidly expanding sectors. To gain public support, including crucially the support of the unions and the workers effected, such changes would have to be accompanied by an absolute guarantee of jobs and retraining with no loss of pay or security and a guarantee of rehousing rights where necessary.

Funding and the market

But of course, such a huge programme must be financed, and it is here that the report is either at its most optimistic or at its weakest, depending on the hue of your tinted glasses – and mine, I'm afraid, are not very pink at the moment. Having listed the three key planks of FDR's New Deal, authors of the report tell us that; "The *Green New Deal* will, however, differ from its 1930s predecessor in that there will be a much bigger role for investments from private savings, pensions, banks and insurance."

Every fund raising measure, in fact, apart from flag days and bring and buy sales. Strangely, even though the report points out that the programme will cost the equivalent of 3.5% of GDP – much the same as was committed to FDR's New Deal – it doesn't explain why, though FDR funded his programme largely with public spending, we should not do the same.

The report suggests that the government funding required could come in part from the increase in its income from rapidly rising carbon taxes and carbon trading. Leaving the issue of carbon trading aside at the moment (for a later day of vituperative diatribe), the report doesn't mention either the potential for the redistribution of existing government spending (on Trident, Iraq/Afghanistan, existing PFI contracts etc.) or increased taxation, both personal and corporate, so the prosperous, not to say the filthy rich, could pay their fair share.

However, it does mention government bonds. Now, there is nothing safer than a government bond. However, monetarist policy was to reduce government spending and debt and thus to reduce the supply of government bonds, encouraging institutions to go for riskier assets. Increasing the supply of government bonds not only produces a valuable stockpile of public debt, it can also serve as a stabiliser to the financial system.

So the idea of using government bonds as a funding vehicle for the project, along with local authority bonds and various novelty variations aimed at suitable sections of the public, particularly in the form of "green gilts" is a sound one. And the report is quite right to look to the pension funds as a long term source of funding.

However, as the report itself says, "Pension funds are not charities. They are governed by the obligations of fiduciary duty to pursue the best interests of their members [in other words, to maximise profits] rather than the ethical whims of their trustees." In reality, their policies have tended to be steered more by what is good for the fund managers' bonuses than anything else. The reports authors suggest that two factors might lead pension funds to change their investment strategies; a growing realization of the threat of climate change and the tightening of regulations on pension fund disclosure and valuation.

The first of these factors can, I think, fairly confidently discounted. It requires a long term view that is, for most fund managers, an unaffordable luxury, rather like expecting a football manager to plough most of his transfer funds into a training school for young players. However, the second factor is potentially significant. In practice it is about using the power of the state to determine the investment strategies of the fund managers. But why not simply cut through the Gordian Knot and require pension managers to put a minimum percentage of their funds into government bonds?

The report points out that the Norwegian state has used its oil income to establish a huge investment fund that underpins its state pension scheme. Thatcher, of course, used our oil revenue to fund tax cuts and mass unemployment. It suggests that we could follow Norway's lead (a couple of decades late) and set up an Oil Legacy Fund, paid for primarily by a windfall tax on oil and gas company profits. Part of these increased revenues, it is suggested, would be needed "to raise benefits for the poorest people in our society" who would otherwise suffer from the inevitable rises in the prices of fossil fuels that peak oil and carbon taxes would generate.

*Many of its proposals rely to a dangerous degree
on the goodwill, common sense or long term
thoughtfulness of the very groups who have got us into
this mess and who will pull the world down round their
ears rather than concede power.*

We already have five million households in Britain classified as suffering fuel poverty (that is, more than 10% of household income going on fuel). The recent huge increases in gas and electricity will literally be, literally, the death of hundreds, possibly thousands, more pensioners this winter. The report suggests that: "grants would be required to cover 100% of the cost of changes needed to the dwellings of the most disadvantaged, to increase energy efficiency and fit renewables."

Is that it? What about challenging poverty? What about equality?

Taming the market?

If we seriously want to gain popular support for the *Green New Deal* or similar strategies, we should be arguing that the policies we propose will constitute a war on poverty and unemployment right now, rather than a programme of grants and benefits to ameliorate the worst of effects of peak oil on the poorest. We must be clear, both to ourselves and to the mass of ordinary people who stand to gain from such a strategy and whose active support is necessary for its successful implementation, that it is going to be necessary to challenge both the domination of the market and its powerful defenders, whether they are financiers, EU Commissioners or the boards of multinational corporations. And here we come to the key limitation of Keynesianism, whether green or any other colour; essentially it has always been about trying to stabilise a fundamentally unstable system rather than transform it. It seeks to civilise the market rather than challenge its domination and tame it.

Not only can we not trust the market to find the funding for the sort of measures advocated in the *Green New Deal*, we can't trust the market – or its functionaries – to implement them. The report's failure to recognise this is a major weakness, as is its exclusive focus on energy conservation and renewable energy as the vehicles of economic restructuring.

In reality, there is little point in a new low-carbon energy system without a completely renewed public transport system, since transport accounts for 24% of our carbon footprint. And it is impossible to develop a sensible energy conservation programme for our homes, workplaces and public buildings, particularly the report's "every building a power station" policy, without dealing with the inextricably linked needs for a renewed and sustainable water supply system and a massive programme of social housing.

There is a consensus that we cannot trust the market to deliver or maintain a national railway service and that therefore the railways should be brought back into public ownership. I think that it is self evidently true that we cannot trust the power companies to develop a sustainable and equitable energy service, nor the water companies to deliver water and remove waste in a socially and environmentally just way. Therefore, I suggest that one of the preconditions of the sort of vast infrastructural reconstruction advocated in the report is the taking into public ownership not only the railways, but all public transport services and the power and water utilities.

While the idea of an Oil Legacy Fund is an excellent one, using it to continue to subsidise poverty rather than challenge it is hardly likely to excite the popular imagination. Far better that we use it, together with a hypothecated National Insurance Fund, to underpin a decent pensions scheme that does not leave the old, the disabled and the vulnerable in poverty. Fuel costs could be dealt with by a variation on Mayer Hillman's carbon rationing proposals; the allocation to all households a free energy allowance (weighted so that single person households were not disadvantaged) with all energy consumed above the free allowance charged at a progressively higher rate. Clearly, such a proposal would not be practicable in the context of privatised oil, gas and electricity suppliers.

Conclusion

The report is right to say that the current crisis, in which the US banks alone have lost something like $1.6 trillion so far, undermines the credibility of the whole neoliberal project. In the words of one of the *Green New Deal* Group, Ann Pettifor: "Flawed monetary policies are turning a crisis into a catastrophe." It is also right to point out the need for good old-fashioned direct government spending and job creation, putting new demand into the economy through investing in infrastructure and public services.

The report correctly argues that we should be shifting the focus of the economy away from the financial sector and back to the real economy, where real people produce real goods and services that actually contribute to our collective well being. It highlights the next crisis that is likely to sweep over us quite soon, that of peak oil, rightly emphases the scale and urgency of the threat of global warming, and points out that coping with those threats has to be an integral part of our infrastructural renewal.

However, the report does not sufficiently recognise that this crisis, like all those that have come before, is rooted in a deeper and more fundamental problem than the greed and recklessness unleashed by neoliberalism. The fundamental problem is that of a financial system orientated towards maximising private profit rather than assisting real progress for ordinary people.

As a result, many of its proposals rely to a dangerous degree on the goodwill, common sense or long term thoughtfulness of the very groups who have got us into this mess and who will pull the world down round their ears rather than concede power.

What is needed is a programme of infrastructural renewal even more ambitious than that envisioned by the report's authors. Such a programme will require determined government and popular action to end the domination of the market and to use society's resources, including the banks, building societies and other financial institutions and most importantly, the pension funds, for the common good.

Capitalism's Anti-ecology Treadmill

Terry Townsend

From a talk given in 2007 in Australia.
Full text at http://www.dsp.org.au/node/194

Al Gore's *An Inconvenient Truth* does an excellent job of making the threat we face understandable and dramatizes the need for emergency action. But it is precisely on what needs to be done, and how, that he falls far short.

The main solutions Gore offers are individual actions: that we all install long-life light bulbs, insulate our homes, drive hybrid cars, vote for the "right" respectable candidates. Beyond that, Gore makes few serious demands on big business, and endorses the largely voluntary market-based measures, such as emissions trading, contained in the Kyoto treaty. Gore also mentions, in passing and approvingly, "geosequestration," so-called clean coal, and nuclear power.

Unfortunately, such an approach is both inadequate and politically misleading, given the magnitude and source of the global environmental crisis. Gore and others urge us to lead "carbon-neutral" lives – but how is that possible, if the Australian and world economy is not carbon neutral because the unaccountable, unelected giant multinational car makers, fossil fuel combines, huge mineral processors and the major power generating corporations and corporatized public utilities spew greenhouse gases into the air at increasing rates?

However well intentioned, appeals to people to change their individual habits – "Don't drive a car," "Don't keep your appliances on stand-by," "Stop being a consumer" – bring trivial results when measured against the problem. If there's no adequate public transportation, if there's no adequate city planning that lets workers live close to jobs, schools, hospitals and recreation, how can they stop driving cars? If every appliance the big corporations churn out is designed be on standby by default, it makes it bloody difficult.

As a leading liberal wealthy capitalist politician who so recently sought to take the political reins of the world's most powerful capitalist government, someone who believes that capitalism and the market can solve the world's problems, Gore is unwilling to and sees no reason to confront the world's most powerful corporations, and the ruling capitalist class. He doesn't blame the political and economic system run for and by the tiny minority class of capitalists who are prepared to gamble with the fate of the Earth in order to maximize their profits.

Of course, Gore is not alone in pushing the onus of solving global warming and other manifestations of the broader environmental crisis onto individuals, while also relying on the capitalist market, nudged along by so-called "green" taxes and legislative regulations. This is also the underlying approach of most mainstream environmental groups and the major Greens parties. Even Monbiot's otherwise radical proposals include a form of carbon trading, albeit much more egalitarian. As a result, this consensus is accepted by most environmental activists.

Such views among genuine environmental activists reflect a well-meaning but ultimately utopian belief that if only enough of us decide to drastically reduce our demand on the world's resources – via greatly reduced personal consumption, purchasing from firms with sustainable production techniques and non-polluting technologies – big business and governments will respond to "market signals" and accept and adapt to a slow-growth or no-growth economy.

Of course, we should not dismiss the importance of environmental consciousness and radicalization, which is often expressed in attempts to live in ways consistent with sustainability. It is a good thing if people try to organize their lives so that they live more ecologically.

But we have to be clear that that alone will not be enough to halt the crisis. It certainly cannot be the main strategy of the mass environment movement, as it will let the real culprits off the hook and divert precious activist energy away from the underlying systemic dynamic that is driving ecological degradation. As Marxist ecologist John Bellamy Foster explained in a very useful and accessible article published in the *Monthly Review* magazine in February 1995, behind most appeals for individual "ecological morality,"

> there lies the presumption that we live in a society where the morality of the individual is the key to the morality of society. If people as individuals could simply change their moral stance with respect to nature and alter their behaviour in areas such as propagation, consumption, and the conduct of business, all would be well.

However, Foster continues: "What is all too often overlooked in such calls for moral transformation is the central institutional fact of our [capitalist] society: what might be called the global 'treadmill of production'."[1]

Foster draws directly from the scientific socialist analysis of capitalism first made by Karl Marx and Frederick Engels to illustrate how, despite the assertions of many environmental movement theorists over the years, Marxism not only provides essential insights into the fundamental cause of the environmental crisis, but also offers the best political guide to its solution. Only far-reaching social revolution aimed at replacing the anti-environmental capitalist system can pull the planet back from the brink of disaster.

Foster breaks down the logic of the capitalist "treadmill" into six elements.

First ... constituting its central rationale, is the increasing accumulation of wealth [capital] by a relatively small section of the population at the top of the social pyramid.

Second, there is a long-term movement of workers away from self-employment and into wage jobs that are contingent on the continual expansion of production.

Third, the competitive struggle between businesses necessitates, on pain of extinction, the allocation of accumulated wealth to new, revolutionary technologies that serve to expand production.

Fourth, wants are manufactured in a manner that creates an insatiable hunger for more.

Fifth, government becomes increasingly responsible for promoting national economic development ...

[and] Sixth, the dominant means of communication and education are part of the treadmill, serving to reinforce its priorities and values.

Capitalism is a system that pursues accumulation and growth for its own sake, whatever the consequences. It is a juggernaut driven by the single-minded need on the part of business for ever-greater accumulation of capital. "Accumulate, accumulate! That is Moses and the Prophets!" wrote Marx in *Capital*.[2] Capitalism is like the proverbial scorpion, who, after stinging the frog as he was being carried across the river on its back, meaning the death of both, could only say: "I could not help myself. It is my nature."

This is why all schemes based on the hope of a no-growth, slow-growth or sustainable-growth form of capitalism are pipe dreams. As too are strategies based on a critical mass of individual consumers deciding to go "green" in order to reform the system.

For capitalists, profit is an end in itself. It does not matter to them whether the commodities they produce satisfy fundamental human needs – such as food, clothing, shelter – or are devoted to pointless or ostentatious consumption, or are even destructive to human beings and the planet. A buck is a buck whether it comes from mung beans, Lamborghinis or cigarettes.

People are not "consumers" by nature. A multi-billion-dollar capitalist industry called advertising constantly plays with our minds to convince us that happiness comes only through buying more and more "stuff," to keep up with endless wasteful fads, fashions, upgrades, new models and built-in obsolescence. The desire for destructive and/or pointless goods is manufactured along with them.[3]

In 2003 alone, US big business spent more than US$54.5 billion on advertising to convince people to consume more and more goods and services.[4] This compares to the US government's total education budget of US$76 billion in 2003. In 1995, the average adult in the United States watched 21,000 television commercials a year, about 75% of them paid for by the 100 largest corporations. In Australia, annual ad spend passed the A$10 billion mark in 2004.[5] Worldwide more than US$298 billion is expected to be spent on advertising in 2007.[6]

But surely, it would be in the capitalists' own interests to shift to more energy-efficient production and replace dirty fossil fuels with cleaner, more efficient renewable sources?

Many in the environmental movement argue that with the right mix of taxes, incentives and regulations, everybody would be winners. Big business will have cheaper, more efficient production, and therefore be more profitable, and consumers will have more environment-friendly products and energy sources. In a rational society, such innovations would lower the overall environmental impact in terms of materials and energy used per unit of output, when substituted for more harmful technology. Unfortunately, we don't live in a rational society.

Capitalism approaches technology – in the production process or in the final commodity – in the same way as it does everything else. What will generate the most profits? Whether it is efficient, clean, safe, environmentally benign or rational has little to do with it. The technologies that could tackle global warming have long existed. Even though research into them has been massively under funded, renewable energy sources are even today competitive with coal and nuclear power (if the negative social and environmental costs are factored in). Public transport systems, such as trams and trains, have been around since the late 1800s (the first underground railway, London's Tube system, began operation in 1863).

Yet, huge private vested interests have ensured that, for example, the vastly more wasteful, inefficient and polluting private motor vehicle has come to dominate the industrialized capitalist countries. US Marxist economist Paul Sweezy has described how what he calls the "automobile-industrialization complex" – the major car companies, the oil industry, the steel, glass and rubber corporations, the highway builders, the trucking combines and the real-estate and construction interests tied to suburban sprawl – have been the axis "around which [capital] accumulation in the 20th century largely turned." This "automobile-industrialization complex" remains at the heart of the dependence of the major capitalist economies on oil today.8 Transportation accounts for the largest proportion of CO_2 emissions in the US and the third largest in Australia.

Today, following Henry Ford II's famous maxim, "minicars make mini-profits," car manufacturers make the bulk of their profits from making and selling big cars, 4X4s and minivans.

Toxic vandalism

Fundamental to capitalism's development has been its power to shift the cost of its ecological and social vandalism onto society as whole, by using the biosphere as a giant dunny down which it can flush its toxic wastes. More profits can accrue if the big capitalists don't have to bother themselves with the elimination, neutralization or recycling of industrial wastes. It's much

---

For capitalists, profit is an end in itself.
It does not matter to them whether the commodities
they produce satisfy fundamental human needs – such
as food, clothing, shelter – or are devoted to pointless
or ostentatious consumption, or are even destructive to
human beings and the planet.

---

cheaper to pour toxic waste into the air or the nearest river. Rather than the profiteers paying the real costs of production, society as a whole subsidizes corporate profit-making by cleaning up some of the mess or suffering the environmental and/or health costs.

Or the whole messy business can simply be exported to the Third World. In August, a Dutch company with revenues of US$28 billion last year dumped 500 tonnes of toxic waste in the Ivory Coast, West Africa, because it did not want to pay the $250,000 disposal fee in the Netherlands. At least 10 people died from the fumes, 69 were hospitalized, more than 100,000 needed medical attention.

At the same time, the impact of systematic polluting has been magnified by the profit-driven development of synthetic chemicals associated with the growth of the petrochemical and agribusinesses, and synthetic products (like plastics, pesticides and detergents) that have been substituted for natural ones (like wood, leather and soap). The result is much more toxic waste, such as that from chlorine-related (organochlorine) production – creating

Frankenstein substances such as dioxin, PCBs and CFCs. The degree of toxicity associated with a given level of production has risen steadily since the middle of last century.

Renowned pioneer of radical environmentalism Barry Commoner, in his 1992 book *Making Peace with the Planet,* reported that the petrochemical industry alone up to that point had introduced 70,000 alien synthetic chemical compounds into the biosphere. He wrote that these compounds, "disrupt normal biochemistry, leading to mutations, cancer, and in many different ways, to death. In effect, the petrochemical industry produces substances that ... cunningly enter the chemistry of life, and attack it."

In general, there is no natural feedback mechanism that works to trigger the great god "the market" to rein in this sort of environmental destruction by increasing costs for capital, no matter how severe the cost to nature and society. Attempts to manage the damage by "regulating" capitalism with "green taxes" have had limited successes, precisely because pro-capitalist governments are run by corporate-funded political parties and politicians, with bureaucracies headed by loyal establishment figures, who see their role as defenders of the status quo.

Tax rates, charges or fines are set well below the level that would impact seriously on profits; so more often than not it is cheaper for big business to go on polluting until the next scheduled refit than to immediately put a stop to it. Taxes tend to be set at rates that can be passed on to consumers, the goal being to influence demand for certain products, rather than at a level that forces a fundamental and rapid redirection of investment into non-polluting or renewable technology.

Capitalism, an economic and political system based on the never-ending expansion of production of commodities for sale, is incompatible with the basic ecological cycles of the planet. As is becoming abundantly clear today, the Earth cannot sustain this system's plundering and poisoning without humanity sooner or later experiencing a complete ecological catastrophe.

To have any chance of preventing this, within the 30-to 50-year window that we have in relation to global warming, humanity must take conscious, rational control of its interactions with the planet and its ecological processes, in ways that capitalism is inherently incapable of providing.

Marx and Engels on ecology

Contrary to the repeated assertions by some environmental movement theorists, Marx and Engels were personally well aware of and respectful of humanity's interconnectedness with the environment, and they recognized that it was essential for socialism to be ecologically sustainable. John Bellamy Foster and fellow Marxist Paul Burkett have discussed this in their articles and books on Marx and Engels' neglected writings on the subject.

But let's touch on their findings briefly. Marx in several places noted how capitalism had created a "metabolic rift" between human beings and the earth. The wrenching of the mass of people from the soil, forced to work in the factories of the cities, was one of the preconditions for the development of industrial capitalism. Before long the fields were being starved of nutrients, while city streets and rivers stunk of human effluent and associated filth.

Marx referred to capitalist farming as "an art, not only of robbing the labourer, but of robbing the soil" that sapped the everlasting sources of wealth – the soil and the worker. He argued in effect for the return to ecological sustainability, which had been destroyed by, and was not possible under, capitalism.

To simultaneously put an end to the capitalist plunder of the environment and the working people, to "systematically restore" the "metabolism," Marx urged a social revolution that would abolish private ownership. Marx wrote in *Capital* that only "the associated producers [can] govern the human metabolism with nature in a rational way, bring it under their collective control instead of being dominated by it as a blind power."[9] This symbiotic relationship between humanity and the environment must again become "a regulative law of social production." He declared that the "conscious and rational treatment of the land as eternal communal property" is "the inalienable condition for the existence and reproduction of the chain of human generations," i.e., sustainable development.[10]

Engels in *Dialectics of Nature* agreed. To "regulate" our relationship with nature "requires something more than mere knowledge. It requires a complete revolution in our hitherto existing mode of production, and simultaneously a revolution in our whole contemporary social order."[11]

Only a socialist society can build an ecologically sustainable world

A plethora of "blueprints" for an ecologically sustainable world have been produced by the dozens by Green groups here and around the world, containing logical and commonsense solutions to global warming and the general environmental crisis. They fail not because their proposals for a rapid conversion to renewable energy and the rational reorganization of production and consumption are far-fetched. They fail because they do not accept that capitalism is incapable of bringing them into being. Only a society that places the "associated producers" at its head and at its heart can open the way for the building of a genuinely feasible sustainable society.

As the Democratic Socialist Perspective's essential 1999 document *Environment, Capitalism and Socialism* succinctly puts it:

> Any proposal to save the environment that doesn't adopt this approach ... is
> doomed to be reduced to a set of 'interesting proposals' in speedy transit to

irrelevance, or to providing the newest wave of bamboozling eco-chatter, or to supplying the next menu items for futile gradualism that falls further and further behind in its tasks.[12]

A society run by and for the "associated producers" – a socialist society – would allow the controlling levers of the "treadmill" to be seized, bringing it to a halt so we can all get off and begin to think about, discuss and rationally plan the best way forward for both the planet and all its inhabitants. Profit will no longer dictate what is produced and how, or determine the relationships of rich-country governments with the Third World.

Almost immediately, huge material and human resources would be released to begin to rapidly reverse problems like global warming and the destruction of the oceans, as well as the wider global environment crisis, as well making a start on ending the poverty, hunger and disease that affect billions in the Third World.

Where from? For a start from capitalism's war spending. Global direct military spending is running at more than US$1 trillion a year, of which the US accounts for almost 50%.[13] When related spending is factored in, US military spending is set to be above $900 billion in 2008. The Australian defence budget is $22 billion a year and since 9/11 another $20 billion has been spent on the bogus "war on terror."[14]

Just a fraction of these sums could eliminate starvation and malnutrition globally, provide education for every child on Earth, provide access to water and sanitation and reverse the spread of AIDS and malaria.

It would also enable the massive transfer of new and clean technologies to the Third World, to allow poor countries to skip the stage of dirty industrial development. With the end of capitalist domination, the plunder of Third World resources would end and genuine development could ensue. With the cancellation of the Third World debt, the now poor countries would retain vast sums to kick start their clean development.

On top of that, the "ecological debt" – described by the Ecuador-based *Acción Ecológica* as the debt owed to the Third World as a result of the "Northern" countries' plundering of their natural resources, environmental damage and the dumping of wastes, including greenhouse gases – would begin to be repaid. This was estimated in 2004 to be at least $1.6 trillion a year, three times the $523 billion "owed" by the poorest countries.[15]

The wealth of the former ruling class and the ending of its rule would also provide immense resources for the tasks at hand. According to a UN report released in late November, the richest 2% of adults in the world own more than half of all household wealth. The poorest 50% of the world's population own barely 1% of global wealth. Europe, the United States and Japan account for most of the extremely wealthy. More than a third live in the US. Japan accounts for 27% of the total, and Britain and France 5-6% each.[16]

Genuine democratic socialist planning will allow priorities to be set on the production of certain items and limit or eliminate others. Just imagine the vast amounts of wasteful production of pointless commodities produced solely for sale that could be eliminated. Without the cynical manipulation of people's insecurities and vanities by the billion-dollar advertising and marketing industries, not to mention its outright dishonesty, needless and wasteful consumption would plummet.

The marketing-driven over-packaging of products could end, saving entire forests, and banishing billions of tonnes of "disposable" but environ-

---

Capitalism as a system thrives on the cultivation and celebration of the worst aspects of human behaviour; selfishness and self-interest; greed and hoarding; the dog-eat-dog mentality.

---

mentally indigestible plastic fast-food containers and beverage bottles from the rubbish dumps. The triumphant return of the humble but eminently sensible – and recyclable – glass bottle would be at hand!

Inbuilt obsolescence would end, and the corporate creation of fads and fashions would become a thing of the past. No more "this year's new model." Products would be built to last for a very long time, and when they were due for replacement they would be as totally recyclable as possible. Such basic reforms would save massive amounts of materials and energy, all along the production chain.

We could collectively redirect the investment of society's created wealth into research and development of existing and new technologies to meet society's needs while operating as cleanly as possible, and well within the environment's capacity to absorb any waste products. We could rapidly bring forward the expansion of renewable energy and speedily phase out coal and nuclear power stations.

With a huge boost to socially directed investment in research and development, reliable solar energy and wind power, other forms of alternative energy, could very soon become much cheaper than traditional sources, without many of the currently costly society-borne side-effects. We could begin to harness the sun's energy, which every day delivers to the Earth 17,000 times as much energy as the entire population uses.

Right now, the technology is available to generate all the clean electricity we need. Combined with energy-efficiency targets throughout the economy, from the industrial level to house designs and household appliances, and socially organized recycling, greenhouse gas emissions could be not only slashed but reversed.

If society so chose, entire branches of industry could be subsidized as they were force-marched into environmentally friendliness, or closed down overnight and the workers' skills and talents utilized almost immediately in other industries, or retrained on full pay.

Capitalism's dependence on the private car and truck would begin be reversed with the rapid proliferation of mass, free public transport systems. High on the agenda will be the reintroduction of extensive passenger and freight rail networks in rural, regional and remote areas. The reintroduction and expansion of coastal freight shipping will also be important. In time, cities will be no longer be designed around the private car, but around residential, community and work hubs linked by fast, efficient public transport.

And as the "associated producers" build the new society, wants and needs will inevitable alter, and so too will consumption habits. Capitalism as a system thrives on the cultivation and celebration of the worst aspects of human behaviour; selfishness and self-interest; greed and hoarding; the dog-eat-dog mentality. Capitalism's warped view of normal human interaction is summed by the Orwellian-titled unreality show, *Survivor*. In this twisted vision of the workings of society, the last person standing is the victor! But all societies survive – even capitalist societies – not by bumping each other off to get the cash, but by cooperating.

In a society that is organized first and foremost to work together to produce enough to comfortably ensure people's physical and mental wellbeing and social security – abundant food, clothing, housing, furniture and appliances, cultural pursuits, and lifelong education and training, and healthcare – and in which technological advances benefit everybody without costing the environment, a new social definition of wealth will evolve. It won't be measured by personal wealth, or by how much "stuff" you've got.

In the words of Marx and Engels, social wealth will be defined by the degree to which it provides the means for "all members of society to develop, maintain and exert their capacities in all possible directions," so that "the old bourgeois society, with its classes and class antagonisms," is replaced "by an association [society] in which the free development of each is a condition of the free development of all."[17]

Social wealth – human development – will be not be measured by an ever-increasing consumption of goods and services, or expanding indices of "economic growth," but in the shortening of the work day. In the words of Marx, "free time, [or] disposable time, is wealth itself ... free time ... for the free development , intellectual and social, of the individual."

As society's total disposable time – social wealth – expands, so too does the ability of all members of society to increasingly participate in running, planning and solving its problems, including finding solutions to the more intractable environmental or technological problems. Lifelong theoretical and practical education, made possible by this expanding disposable time, Marx states, will "convert science from an instrument of class rule into a popular force."

Only a socialist system, based on public ownership, popular democracy and planning, and a new definition of wealth based not on individual personal enrichment and consumption, can possibly meet the challenge. It would not be too extreme to declare that humanity in the next 50 or so years faces a stark choice: capitalism – or socialism and human survival.

Notes

1 John Bellamy Foster. "Global Ecology and the Common Good." http://clogic.eserver. org/3-1&2/foster.html.

2 Karl Marx, *Capital*, Vol. 1 (Penguin Books: Harmondsworth, 1976), Chapter 24, section 3, p. 742.

3 Paul M. Sweezy, "Capitalism and the Environment," *Monthly Review*, June 1989.

4 "Ad recovery gains momentum in US and Asia, lags in Europe", http://zenuthoptime-dia.com.

5 Christian Catalano, "Ad Spend Tipped to Top $10 Billion This Year," *Melbourne Age*, April 15, 2005.

6 World Advertising Research Center, November 29, 2006, http://www.warc.com.

7 *Monthly Review*, December 2000.

8 John Bellamy Foster, *Monthly Review*, December 2000.

9 Ibid., p. 959.

10 Ibid., pp. 948-949; see also John Bellamy Foster, "The Communist Manifesto and the Environment," *Socialist Register* 1998, pp. 169-189.

11 Friedrich Engels, *Dialectics of Nature* (Progress Publishers: Moscow, 1976), p. 182.

12 DSP, *Environment, Capitalism and Socialism* (Resistance Books: Chippendale, 1999), p. 19.

12 Aaron Gleans, "Democrats Expected to Increase US Military Spending," *One World*, December 13, 2006,http://us.oneworld.net/article/view/143817/1/.

14 *Melbourne Age*, Saturday, November 25, 2006.

15 John Bellamy Foster and Brett Clark, "Ecological Imperialism: The Curse of Capitalism," *Socialist Register* 2004, pp. 193-196.

16 "Richest 2% own half the wealth," BBC, December 5, 2006, http://news.bbc.co.uk/go/pr/fr/-/2/hi/business/6211250.stm.

17 Paul Burkett, "Ecology and Marx's Vision of Communism," *Socialism and Democracy Online*, http://www.sdonline.org/34/paul_burkett.htm.

5: PRIVATIZING THE ATMOSPHERE

"Multinational corporations are trying to commodify the air, really, and the pollution in the air. They want the right to do that, and they want to codify it with the legal language of contracts and put a price on it and get credit for having already polluted."
—Patrick Bond—

Many sincere environmentalists favor creating a carbon market in which polluters can buy and sell emission credits. But capitalist methods can't solve problems that are caused by capitalism – carbon trading not only won't do the job, it makes things worse.

In Part Five:

▸ **Durban Declaration on Carbon Trading.** *The Durban Group for Climate Justice was formed in South Africa in October 2004, by representatives from grassroots organizations and peoples' movements from around the globe: the founding meeting issued this statement.*

▸ **Cap and Trade Schemes.** *Chris Williams provides an overview of carbon trading, explaining why its failures are not just a result of accident or incompetent planning.*

▸ **The Obscenity of Carbon Trading,** *Kevin Smith of Carbon Trade Watch says that carbon trading is a massive public concession to dirty industries.*

▸ **Six Arguments Against Carbon Trading** , *Larry Lohmann of Corner House oshows why existing cap and trade plans don't work, and why fine-tuning them won't help.*

▸ **Why Carbon Markets Can't Save the World.** *Andrew Simms shows that all attempts to use the market to fix the climate are based on pricing mechanisms that are "too vague, imperfect, and frequently socially unjust."*

The Durban Declaration on Carbon Trading

Durban Group for Climate Justice

October 2004

As representatives of people's movements and independent organizations, we reject the claim that carbon trading will halt the climate crisis. This crisis has been caused, more than anything else, by the mining of fossil fuels and the release of their carbon to the oceans, air, soil and living things. This excessive burning of fossil fuels is now jeopardizing Earth's ability to maintain a liveable climate.

Governments, export credit agencies, corporations and international financial institutions continue to support and finance fossil fuel exploration, extraction and other activities that worsen global warming, such as forest degradation and destruction on a massive scale, while dedicating only token sums to renewable energy. It is particularly disturbing that the World Bank has recently defied the recommendation of its own Extractive Industries Review which calls for the phasing out of World Bank financing for coal, oil and gas extraction.

We denounce the further delays in ending fossil fuel extraction that are being caused by corporate, government and United Nations' attempts to construct a "carbon market," including a market trading in "carbon sinks."

History has seen attempts to commodify land, food, labour, forests, water, genes and ideas. Carbon trading follows in the footsteps of this history and turns the earth's carbon-cycling capacity into property to be bought or sold in a global market. Through this process of creating a new commodity – carbon – the Earth's ability and capacity to support a climate conducive to life and human societies is now passing into the same corporate hands that are destroying the climate.

People around the world need to be made aware of this commodification and privatization and actively intervene to ensure the protection of the Earth's climate.

Carbon trading will not contribute to achieving this protection of the Earth's climate. It is a false solution which entrenches and magnifies social inequalities in many ways.

The carbon market creates transferable rights to dump carbon in the air, oceans, soil and vegetation far in excess of the capacity of these systems to hold it. Billions of dollars worth of these rights are to be awarded free of charge to the biggest corporate emitters of greenhouse gases in the electric power, iron and steel, cement, pulp and paper, and other sectors in industrialized nations who have caused the climate crisis and already exploit these systems the most. Costs of future reductions in fossil fuel use are likely to fall disproportionately on the public sector, communities, indigenous peoples and individual taxpayers.

The Kyoto Protocol's Clean Development Mechanism (CDM), as well as many private sector trading schemes, encourage industrialized countries and their corporations to finance or create cheap carbon dumps such as large-scale tree plantations in the South, as a lucrative alternative to reducing emissions in the North.

Other CDM projects, such as hydrochlorofluorocarbons (HCFC) reduction schemes, focus on end-of pipe technologies and thus do nothing to reduce the fossil fuel industries' impacts on local communities. In addition, these projects dwarf the tiny volume of renewable energy projects which constitute the CDM's sustainable development window-dressing.

Impacts from fossil-fuel industries and other greenhouse-gas producing industries such as displacement, pollution, or climate change, are already disproportionately felt by small island states, coastal peoples, indigenous peoples, local communities, fisherfolk, women, youth, poor people, elderly and marginalized communities. CDM projects intensify these impacts in several ways. First, they sanction continued exploration for, and extraction, refining and burning of fossil fuels. Second, by providing finance for private sector projects such as industrial tree plantations, they appropriate land, water and air already supporting the lives and livelihoods of local communities for new carbon dumps for Northern industries.

The refusal to phase out the use of coal, oil and gas, which is further entrenched by carbon trading, is also causing more and more military conflicts around the world, magnifying social and environmental injustice. This in turn diverts vast resources to military budgets which could otherwise be utilized to support economies based on renewable energies and energy efficiency.

In addition to these injustices, the internal weaknesses and contradictions of carbon trading are in fact likely to make global warming worse rather than "mitigate" it. CDM projects, for instance, cannot be verified to be "neutralizing" any given quantity of fossil fuel extraction and burning. Their claim to be able to do so is increasingly dangerous because it creates the illusion that consumption and production patterns, particularly in the North, can be maintained without harming the climate.

In addition, because of the verification problem, as well as a lack of credible regulation, no one in the CDM market is likely to be sure what they are buying. Without a viable commodity to trade, the CDM market and similar private sector trading schemes are a total waste of time when the world has a critical climate crisis to address.

In an absurd contradiction, the World Bank facilitates these false, market-based approaches to climate change through its Prototype Carbon Fund, the BioCarbon Fund and the Community Development Carbon Fund at the same time it is promoting, on a far greater scale, the continued exploration for, and extraction and burning of fossil fuels – many of which are to ensure increased emissions of the North.

In conclusion, "giving carbon a price" will not prove to be any more effective, democratic, or conducive to human welfare, than giving genes, forests, biodiversity or clean rivers a price.

We reaffirm that drastic reductions in emissions from fossil fuel use are a pre-requisite if we are to avert the climate crisis. We affirm our responsibility to coming generations to seek real solutions that are viable and truly sustainable and that do not sacrifice marginalized communities.

We therefore commit ourselves to help build a global grassroots movement for climate justice, mobilize communities around the world and pledge our solidarity with people opposing carbon trading on the ground.

Cap and Trade Schemes

Chris Williams

International Socialist Review, November-December 2008
The international proposals to tackle climate change that get the most discussion all revolve around allowing the market to alter patterns of production and consumption. These so-called market-based solutions, such as carbon trading or carbon taxes, fit neatly with the needs of those who run the world economy – the corporations and their paid enablers in government. But politicians aren't the only ones seduced by the free market mantra, which decries state intervention and extols the self-healing powers of the market; the idea that the market is the best arbiter of change is accepted by many people – both within and outside the green movement – who are genuinely concerned with reducing the impact of humans on the environment.

Under the "cap and trade" system or Emissions Trading Scheme (ETS) – the first phase of which has been in place in the EU since January 2005 – a maximum or cap is placed on the amount of carbon that companies in participating countries are allowed to produce annually. If individual companies exceed their quota, they can buy carbon credits from other companies, including those outside the EU, in order to carry on with their own business. The idea is to create a market in carbon trading that will serve as an incentive for companies to reduce their carbon emissions or be forced to pay other companies and so incur additional production costs.

Capitalism has only two uses for the "environment" – it is either a source of raw materials or a sink. Resources – such as oil, coal, metals, etc. – are extracted from the environment and waste products are dumped back in. Capitalists define as waste any by-products they can't reuse or sell and therefore must dump. Since each capitalist firm, in its competition for market share, attempts to drive down costs and maximize profits, there is a built-in tendency to exclude from expense anything that falls outside the immediate process of production, which leads to capitalists' insistence on dumping for free.

Green economists have long argued that the environmental cost of waste should be included in the overall expense for any given product and noted early on the market's inability to properly take account of "externalities" like production-generated pollution. Carbon trading represents an attempt by economists and governments committed to economic expansion to respond to these criticisms by "internalizing" environmental costs or bringing them into the market. According to their logic, assigning a price to some measurable form of pollution (carbon dioxide in this case) creates market incentives for companies to move capital investment into less-polluting (in this case, less carbon-intensive) technologies – in other words, carbon trading turns what was previously regarded as a useless and potentially hazardous by-product into a valuable commodity to be bought and sold like any other.

There are a number of problems with this approach. One of the most obvious is the impossibility of putting a price on clean air, drinkable water, and a stable climate. Another is that there is currently no way to prevent companies who are made to pay to pollute (the "polluter pays" principle) from simply passing the extra costs on to the consumer at the same time that they are merely passing the problem from one capitalist or industry to another. Another major problem is that some very large and significant economic actors – airlines and cement and aluminum manufacturers, for example – are exempted from participating in the scheme.

But the most significant problem of all is that carbon trading hasn't worked. The "cap" set by the EU was well above any requirement by companies and certainly well above any level that would do anything about climate change. At one point, this led to a fall in the price of carbon emissions (traded per ton) to less than a dollar – hence producing no incentive to anyone to make any kind of switch. When the price rose, companies simply put off applying for carbon credits and used their stored bank (unlike vacation days carbon credits carry over year to year) to continue to pollute. Or, according to a study reported in the *Guardian*, December 7, 2005, they resorted to the tried-and-true capitalist response known as cheating.

A *Financial Times* investigation published April 25, 2007, outlined succinctly the problems with Europe's carbon trading program. It found:

▸ Widespread instances of people and organizations buying worthless credits that do not yield any reductions in carbon emissions.

▸ Industrial companies profiting from doing very little – or from gaining carbon credits on the basis of efficiency gains from which they have already benefited substantially.

▸ Brokers providing services of questionable or no value.

▸ A shortage of verification, making it difficult for buyers to assess the true value of carbon credits.

▸ Companies and individuals being charged over the odds for the private purchase of European Union carbon permits that have plummeted in value because they do not result in emissions cuts.'

As a result, there has been no net reduction in EU carbon emissions and the ETS scheme is thoroughly discredited:

> Europe's big polluters pumped more climate-changing gases into the atmosphere in 2006 than during the previous year, according to figures that show the EU's carbon trading system failing to deliver curbs. Critics said the data underlined the gap between the rhetoric of European leaders, who have promised to cut CO2 emissions by one-fifth by 2020, and the reality of delivering reductions. (*Guardian*, April 3, 2007)

Even the architects of ETS realize it has been an exercise in futility, but promise a new and improved "Phase 2." However, power corporations, those responsible for producing most emissions in the first place, are expected to benefit from the latest incarnation of the scheme, to the tune of $6 billion dollars. (*Independent*, Jan. 2, 2008) Indeed, according to Faisal Islam, Phase 2 allows many permits to be handed out for free, and power corporations have made an extra $100 billion dollars in "windfall profits." This is because they have passed on to consumers all increases in cost through emissions charges, thereby recouping all losses to profitability. Having been given free polluting permits that they can then sell, some of the biggest polluters end up being rewarded twice:

> A ton of carbon saved above Beijing is the same as a ton saved above 'Birmingham' is the free market mantra, but free permits have, in essence, been a rather expensive bribe to get power companies to participate in the scheme. It's an entire field of juicy carrots, with little threat of a stick. (*Ecologist*, June 2008)

The failure of the carbon-trading scheme could be put down to accident or incompetence – maybe the politicians and think tanks that dreamt up this plan just didn't think it through in enough detail, and the next version will be more effective. But this really lets them and capitalism off the hook. The ETS charade is the predictable outcome of an economic system that relies on fossil fuels for energy and has the profit motive as its prime directive. This explains why U.S.-based corporations, having studied the results of the European experiment, have suddenly become very enthusiastic about cap and trade schemes, lobbying hard to ensure that any plan considered allows at least some portion of the permits to be given away rather than auctioned.

Unless politicians are prepared to challenge this dynamic with meaningful regulations and laws – and there is no evidence that they are – any new cap and trade scheme will be as useless in procuring its stated aims as the previous one. Indeed, despite the failure of the first carbon trading system, the EU's updated version is their only major regulatory policy initiative directed at emissions reduction. Admittedly, there are some improvements, such as a larger share of auctions and the addition of previously exempt industries. However, the airline industry has already vowed to fight "all the way" against their inclusion. (*Guardian*, Nov. 19, 2007)

Meanwhile, corporations have found new and creative ways of dumping costs onto consumers. In the near future, people should expect to hear more about, and pay, so-called green taxes, yet another subsidy to the corporations; we pay for them to upgrade their technology and make it less polluting while they continue to make huge profits.

Ideologically, there is something very significant going on. Carbon trading supports the concept that it's okay to keep polluting by creating, of all things, a market in pollution. Trading pollution and earning pollution credits for carbon offsetting in order to reduce CO_2 emissions has been well satirized by the website *cheatneutral.com*:

> When you cheat on your partner you add to the heartbreak, pain and jealousy in the atmosphere. Cheatneutral offsets your cheating by funding someone else to be faithful and NOT cheat. This neutralizes the pain and unhappy emotion and leaves you with a clear conscience...
>
> When you use Cheatneutral, we'll email you a Cheatneutral Offset Certificate, so you can prove to your loved one that your playing away has been successfully offset. Then you and your partner are both happy, a broken heart is mended, and you can feel good about yourself again, all thanks to Cheatneutral.

Ultimately, these market schemes fail because they are based on an untenable contradiction: the idea that the cause of global warming – the unplanned and unfettered capitalist market – can also be its solution.

The Obscenity of Carbon Trading

Kevin Smith

Carbon Trade Watch November 2006
In 1992, an infamous leaked memo from Lawrence Summers, who was at the time Chief Economist of the World Bank, stated that "the economic logic behind dumping a load of toxic waste in the lowest wage country is impeccable, and we should face up to that."

The recently released *Stern Review* on climate change, written by a man who occupied the same position at the World Bank from 2000 to 2003, applies a similar sort of free market environmentalism to climate change.

Sir Nicholas Stern argues that the cost-effectiveness of making emissions reductions is the most important factor, advocating mechanisms such as carbon pricing and carbon trading.

While dumping toxic waste in the global South might look like a great idea from the perspective of the market, it ignores the glaringly obvious fact of it being hugely unfair on those getting dumped upon.

In a similar way, Stern's cost-benefit analysis reduces important debates about the complex issue of climate change down to a discussion about numbers and graphs that ignores unquantifiable variables such as human lives lost, species extinction and widespread social upheaval.

'Junk economics'

Cost-benefit analysis can be a useful tool for making choices in relatively simple situations when there are a limited number of straight-forward options to choose from. But as Tom Burke, visiting professor at Imperial College London, has observed:

> The reality is that applying cost-benefit analysis to questions such as [climate change] is junk economics... It is a vanity of economists to believe that all choices can be boiled down to calculations of monetary value.

Some commentators have applauded the *Stern Review* for speaking in the economics language that politicians and the business community can understand. But by framing the issue purely in terms of pricing, trade and economic growth, we are reducing the scope of the response to climate change to market-based solutions.

These "solutions" take two common forms:

▸ under emissions trading, governments allocate permits to big industrial polluters so they can trade "rights to pollute" amongst themselves as the need arises.

▸ another approach involves the generation of surplus carbon credits from projects that claim to reduce or avoid emissions in other locations, usually in Southern countries; these credits may be purchased to top up any shortfall in emissions reduction.

Such schemes allow us to sidestep the most fundamentally effective response to climate change that we can take, which is to leave fossil fuels in the ground. This is by no means an easy proposition for our heavily fossil fuel dependent society; however, we all know it is precisely what is needed.

What incentive is there to start making these costly, long-term changes when you can simply purchase cheaper, short-term carbon credits?

Forcing the market

In the current neo-liberal economic environment, trading rules inevitably succumb to the pressures of corporate lobbying and deregulation in order to ensure that governments do not "interfere" with the smooth running of the market.

We have already seen this corrosive influence in the European Union's Emissions Trading Scheme (ETS), when under corporate pressure, governments massively over-allocated emissions permits to the heaviest polluting industries in the initial round.

This caused the price of carbon to drop by more than 60%, creating even more disincentive for industries to lower their emissions at source.

There are all manner of loopholes and incentives for industry to exaggerate their emissions in order to receive more permits and thereby take even less action. Market analyst Franck Schuttellar estimated that in the scheme's first year, the UK's most polluting industries earned collectively £940m (US$1,792m) in windfall profits from generous ETS allocations.

Given all we know about the link between pollution and climate change, such a massive public concession to dirty industries borders on the obscene. We are being asked to believe that the flexibility and efficiency of the market will ensure that carbon is reduced as quickly and as effectively as possible, when experience has shown that lack of firm regulation tends to create environmental problems rather than solve them.

Community interest

There is a groundswell of opinion that the "invisible hand" of the market is not the most effective way of facing the climate challenge.

The Durban Declaration for Climate Justice, signed by civil society organizations from all over the world, asserts that making carbon a commodity represents a large-scale privatization of the Earth's carbon cycling capacity, with the atmospheric pie having been carved-up and handed over to the biggest polluters.

Effective action on climate change involves demanding, adopting and supporting policies that reduce emissions at source as opposed to offsetting or trading. Carbon trading isn't an effective response; emissions have to be reduced across the board without elaborate get-out clauses for the biggest polluters.

There is an urgent need for stricter regulation, oversight, and penalties for polluters on community, local, national and international levels, as well as support for communities adversely impacted by climate change. But currently such policies are nigh-on invisible, as they contradict the sacred cows of economic growth and the free market.

There is, unfortunately, no "win-win solution" when it comes to tackling climate change and maintaining an economic growth based on the ever increasing extraction and consumption of fossil fuels.

Market-based mechanisms such as carbon trading are an elaborate shell-game of global creative accountancy that distracts us from the fact that there is no viable "business as usual" scenario.

Climate policy needs to be made of sterner stuff.

Why Carbon Markets Can't Save the World

Andrew Simms

New Scientist, April 20, 2009

One day renewable energy looks like a sunrise industry, the next, tumbleweeds are blowing around a setting solar panel. What has changed? The price of emitting carbon dioxide.

In 2005 the European Union created the world's first proper carbon market, the EU Emissions Trading Scheme (ETS), which compels highly polluting industries to buy permits to emit CO_2. The number of permits is limited, so the idea is that supply and demand set a price that encourages the development of a low-carbon economy. A rising price with no wild fluctuations sends an economic signal to invest in clean energy. But it's not working.

The price of a tonne of CO_2 on the ETS has had a roller-coaster ride — soaring one minute, plummeting the next. In the past year it has lurched from over €30 to €8, and now languishes at around €10. Disastrously, such low and unpredictable prices for CO_2 remove the economic incentive to decarbonize economies.

This is the partly the result of the economic downturn. As heavy industries mothball factories, energy use drops and demand for permits goes down. At the same time businesses try to raise cash by selling their unused permits, flooding the market and further depressing prices. French energy company EDF recently complained that carbon markets were failing just like the market for subprime mortgages. As a result, all kinds of green energy schemes are grinding to a halt.

So how do you set a meaningful price for carbon? The reality is more complicated than the ETS might suggest, which is a problem for those who advocate using market forces to reduce emissions. As NASA climate scientist James Hansen points out, getting it right or wrong could determine whether or not we can avert irreversible climate change.

Apart from the ETS, there are many ways to put a value on carbon. You can, for example, work out what it costs per tonne to reduce emissions. But calculating this "marginal abatement cost" is complicated by doubts over the effectiveness of carbon offsetting and the true impact of some supposedly green technologies.

Another method is the "social cost of carbon," which estimates the cost of the damage from emitting a tonne of carbon over its whole lifetime in the atmosphere. This has been used by the UK treasury, and the Dutch government and the World Bank have experimented with it. But with so many variables to account for, estimates range from £35 to £140 per tonne. The UK has now dropped it for a new "shadow price of carbon," an approach supported by the French government and some members of the European Commission.

The shadow price is similar to the social cost but includes "other factors that may affect willingness to pay for reductions," to use the UK government's own words. It is "a more versatile concept." In other words, it gives politicians some scope to rig the price. Although well intentioned, it is vulnerable to abuse.

Each of these methods has its advantages and disadvantages, but there is one problem that none can solve. I'll call it the paradox of environmental economics, in which worthy attempts to value natural resources hit a wall.

The paradox is this. All these methods of pricing carbon permit the creation of a carbon market that will allow us to pollute beyond a catastrophic tipping point. In other words, they require us to put a price on the final "killing" tonne of CO_2 which, once emitted, tips the balance and triggers runaway global warming. How can we set such a price? It's like saying, how much is civilization worth? Or, if you needed a camel to cross a desert alive, what is a fair value for the straw that breaks its back?

The paradox reveals the fatal shortcoming of market solutions to environmental problems. Unless the parameters for carbon markets are set tightly in line with what science tells us is necessary to preventing runaway warming, they cannot work. That palpably did not happen with the ETS, which initially issued more permits to pollute than there were emissions and now, in the recession, is trading emissions that don't exist – so-called hot air.

Carbon markets cannot save us unless they operate within a global carbon cap sufficient to prevent a rise of more than 2°C above pre-industrial temperatures.

Governments are there to compensate for market failure but seem to have a blind spot about carbon markets. They could counteract the impact of low carbon prices by spending on renewable energy as part of their economic stimulus packages, yet they have not done so. The UK, for example, has spent nearly 20 per cent of its GDP to prop up the financial sector, but just 0.0083 per cent in new money on green economic stimulus.

Price mechanisms alone are unable to do the vital job of reducing carbon emissions. They are too vague, imperfect, and frequently socially unjust. To prevent over-consumption of key resources such as fuel during the second world war, the UK government rejected taxation in favour of rationing because taxation unfairly hit the poor and was too slow to change behaviour. Rationing was the quicker, more equitable option. Carbon rations calculated in line with a safe cap on overall emissions provide a more certain way of hitting emissions targets.

Is there an answer to the paradox of environmental economics that could make the market approach workable? I can't imagine one, but am open to suggestions. Even if you could price the killing tonne, it is a transaction that should never be allowed. Economics becomes redundant if it can rationalize an exchange that sells the future of humankind.

Six Arguments Against Carbon Trading

Larry Lohmann

Opposing Views, August 2008

1. Carbon trading is aimed at the wrong objective

Carbon trading is aimed at the wrong target. It doesn't address global warming. Solving global warming means figuring out how to keep most remaining fossil fuels in the ground. It means reorganizing industrial societies' energy, transport and housing systems – starting today – so that they don't need coal, oil and gas.

Carbon trading isn't directed at that goal. Instead, it's organized around keeping the wheels on the fossil fuel industry as long as possible. Carbon trading allocates industries generous short-term numerical emissions budgets and then tries – through trading – to make it cheap and easy for them to continue business as usual within those budgets.

Emissions budgets are numerical because that's the way a market works. You can't trade what you can't measure. Industry needs to know how much pollution it is trading around or it won't know what it's getting for its money.

Emissions budgets are generous because if you set tough targets right away your carbon price will go through the roof. Business and consumers will revolt if they haven't been given any technological and social alternatives that would keep them from having to pay that price. Emissions budgets are also generous because big market players, once they recognize that the earth's carbon-cycling capacity has become a lucrative asset, will lobby governments in order to pull in as much gravy as they can.

Emissions budgets are short-term because no government has the power to enforce a target to cut emissions drastically by 2050 – or even 2025 – without immediately starting to redirect subsidies from fossil fuels to renewable energy, undertake big programs of public investment in rejiggered energy, transport and consumption systems, and so forth. It won't do these things if it's committed to the ideology that carbon prices will be the main mechanism for change.

2. Carbon trading squanders resources and ingenuity on the wrong things

It's bad enough that carbon trading is aimed at the wrong goal. What's worse is that to try to achieve that goal, it has to set up an apparatus that ties up so many resources that it leaves little room for anything else.

Vast bureaucracies are created to measure, monitor, register, certify, validate and enforce millions of separate emissions cuts. Thousands of bright technical people go to work inventing ways of achieving those cuts as cheaply as possible.

Regulators try to keep market players happy, with little time left to think about the long-term future. Carbon buyers, sellers and consultants concentrate on finding cunning means of producing carbon permits for short-term profit. Wall Street gets into the act to cash in on opportunities for speculation and market-making. Ingenuity goes into milking the system, not into weaning the world off fossil fuels.

Rhodia, a French chemical firm, makes adipic acid at a factory in South Korea. By investing $15 million in equipment that destroys nitrous oxide – an unwanted by-product – the company is set to produce $1 billion in UN-approved carbon credits for sale to polluting industries in industrialized countries. Nitrous oxide is a greenhouse gas said to be 310 times more potent than carbon dioxide, so Rhodia can generate 310 tons of carbon credits just by burning one ton of the compound.

Clever. But does the trade reduce overall greenhouse gases? No. Customers buy Rhodia's credits only so that they can continue to invest in fossil fuels. Does the trade help Korea decarbonize? No. At best, it's irrelevant; at worst, it encourages the country to build more dirty industries so that it can make money cleaning up later. Rhodia already makes 35 times more money selling carbon credits than it does from the adipic acid market.

Nor does the deal promote green innovation: the technology Rhodia uses dates from the 1970s.[1]

Rhodia makes out very well. The struggle to keep fossil fuels in the ground gains nothing.

Such schemes are the rule in carbon trading, not the exception. Does the world have time for this charade?

3. Carbon trading requires knowledge we don't have

Carbon trading assumes that the climate doesn't care where we make a one million ton cut in carbon dioxide emissions. If Lahore can cut a million tons more cheaply than LA, then let Lahore do the work and LA can pay for it. The market saves everybody money by abstracting from how and where emissions cuts are made, and by whom.

The problem is that no one can actually know whether the cut in Lahore is going to be as climatically effective in the long term or not. The more expensive cut in LA might be just the one you want from the perspective of 20 years hence, because it helps lead to a step change away from fossil fuels, whereas the easy cut in Lahore does nothing of the kind. The calculations can't be made.

It gets worse. Suppose you want to delay or avoid reducing your fossil fuel use. Carbon trading allows you instead to buy pollution rights from companies planting trees in Uganda, building dams in India, burning off methane from coal mines in China, or setting up wind farms in Argentina. All these "carbon offsets" are supposed to be climatically equivalent to cutting your coal, oil or gas use.

But you can't prove that. You can add up how much greenhouse gas your offset "saves" only if you assume the emissions you produce are equal to emissions that don't happen elsewhere. This assumption has no scientific basis. Researcher Dan Welch sums up the difficulty: "Offsets are an imaginary commodity created by deducting what you hope happens from what you guess would have happened."[2]

Another dirty little secret: carbon trading needs exact measurements of emissions at hundreds of thousands of locations. Few countries are capable of making these measurements. In fact, they're not being made even in Europe. No one knows for sure how far European countries really are from meeting their Kyoto Protocol targets.

4. Carbon trading is antidemocratic

In the carbon markets, both buyers and sellers have an incentive to conceal from the public whether emissions reductions have actually been made. Buyers want to snap up cheap pollution rights; sellers want to make money flogging them. It doesn't matter to either whether the setup actually does any good for the climate or not. And because measurement and enforcement is inadequate or impossible, they can get away with it.

Who's going to be the watchdog for a public increasingly concerned about the climate crisis? It's not clear. For example, UN carbon market regulators and expert bodies are heavily populated by individuals with conflicts of interest: technical experts who have set up their own carbon consultancies to cash in on the market, investment bankers, heads of government offset purchase programs, and so on.

Raise questions about the arrangement and you often get the response that we have to trust the traders, economists and carbon nerds because no one else understands the dizzying complexities of carbon trading.

We've heard that one before – with ENRON, WorldCom, LTCM and the subprime mortgage market.

Who benefits from carbon trading? Big fossil fuel-using companies. Governments that want to delay climate action. Energy traders. The nuclear industry. Polluting companies that are rich enough to hire the consultants and grease the wheels that enable them to sell certified carbon credits. Hedge funds and commodities traders. Banks and law firms.

Who loses? People fighting polluting fossil fuel developments in their local areas. Communities in countries like India or Brazil who find that their local corporate bad citizens have just gotten an extra cash injection from carbon trading. Communities trying to preserve or develop low-carbon ways of life. Renewable energy developers. Consumers who are charged for carbon permits generators have gotten cheaply or for free. And a global public increasingly at risk from climate change.

5. Carbon trading interferes with positive solutions to global warming

On India's Bhilangana river, local farmers run a finely-tuned terraced irrigation system that provides them with rice, wheat, mustard, fruits and vegetables. This ingenious, extremely low-carbon system of agriculture is threatened by a new hydroelectric project designed to help power India's heavy industry. Villagers may have to leave the valley, losing not only their livelihoods but also their knowledge of a uniquely sustainable modern technology.

Is carbon trading stepping in to support the villagers' piece of the solution to global warming? On the contrary. It's supporting the hydropower company, which has hired consultants to argue that their dam will result in fewer carbon emissions than would have been the case if it had not been built. The firm plans to sell the resulting carbon emission rights to polluting companies in Europe.

The example is typical of the way carbon markets are undermining positive approaches to climate change everywhere. The bulk of carbon credit sales under the Kyoto Protocol benefit chemical, iron and steel, oil and gas, electricity and other companies committed to a fossil fuel-intensive future, not communities, organizations or firms working to overcome fossil addiction.

In California, the environmental justice movement opposes carbon trading as a "charade to continue business as usual." One reason: carbon trading would help facilitate the construction of 21 new fossil fuel-fired power plants there. Local activists want the money to be spent instead on building a green economy that would provide new jobs for the poorer communities of colour that now suffer the most from fossil fuel pollution.[3]

Carbon trading obscures the real solutions to global warming. Chicago derivatives trader and economics professor Richard Sandor – one of carbon trading's architects – claims, for instance, that forests in less industrialized countries can be saved from "slash and burn" agriculture by turning them into production zones for carbon credits.[4]

More experienced observers of the plantation, dam, logging and oil industries know, however, that such forests are threatened not principally by poor farmers, but by precisely the type of land grab that Sandor advocates. Saving forests – and their moderating effects on climate – means respecting local people's needs, not trying to evict them or turn them into workers on a carbon production line.

6. Carbon trading is based on faith, not experience

The case for carbon trading is based largely on stirring, lofty abstractions.

Here's one, from Matthew Whittell of Climate Exchange: "None of us is clever enough to work out what is the best way to tackle climate change, but if we have a global carbon price, the market sorts it out."[5]

Here's another, from Oliver Tickell: "Markets are generally the best means of allocating finite resources without unnecessary waste, while keeping as many people happy as possible."[6]

The near-religious faith of such sentiments might almost be enough to move you to tears.

But the response to a crisis that threatens human civilization needs to be grounded not on unsupported faith in vague slogans but in a sober review of historical experience and a hard empirical understanding of the problem.

Carbon trading is the centrepiece of the Kyoto Protocol; Kyoto has failed. Carbon trading is the centrepiece of Europe's response to climate change; the EU Emissions Trading Scheme has failed. Before Kyoto, pollution trading had also largely failed in the US, the only country in which it had ever previously been tried.

These failures were not accidental. The reasons for them go deep and can't be overcome by economists twiddling a few dials – auctioning a few more pollution rights here, tightening up carbon offset regulation there. The failures will be repeated if carbon trading comes to dominate the North American climate agenda – as both major US presidential candidates, having received some singularly bad advice, assure us it will.

Prices can do many things, but one thing they have never done is solve problems that require structural change in so many fundamental areas of industrial life. If disaster is to be staved off, it will not be by letting technicians and Wall Street investment firms try to turn the world's carbon-cycling capacity into a resource to make money out of, but by a democratic resolve to enter into a new kind of discussion worldwide about the kind of societies that people want in a post-fossil fuels age.

Notes

1 Charles Forelle, "French Firm Cashes in under UN Warming Program", *Wall Street Journal*, 23 July 2008, p. 1A.

2 Dan Welch, "A Buyer's Guide to Offsets", *Ethical Consumer* 106, May/June 2007. See also Larry Lohmann, "Marketing and Making Carbon Dumps: Commodification, Calculation and Counterfactuals in Climate Change Mitigation", *Science as Culture* 14, 3, 2005, pp. 203-235; "Toward a Different Debate in Environmental Accounting: The Cases of Carbon and Cost-Benefit," forthcoming in *Accounting, Organisations and Society*.

3 See www.ejmatters.org.

4 Michael Specter, "Big Foot", *The New Yorker*, 25 February 2008.

5 Mike Scott, "Market Meltdown? Carbon Trading is just Warming up", *Independent on Sunday Business*, 27 July 2008, p. 4.

6 Oliver Tickell, *Kyoto 2: How to Manage the Global Greenhouse*, Zed Books, London, p. 9.

6: VOICES FROM THE GLOBAL SOUTH

*"The future of the north depends on the south ...
even before the polar caps melt and entire countries
become submerged under the waters, the planet will see
hundreds of violent rebellions."*
—Hugo Chávez—

*The principal victims of climate change are the people of the Global South
and indigenous peoples from all parts of the world — are they are also
leading the way in resisting environmental destruction.*

In Part Six:

▸ **Respect Mother Earth.** *Three statements by Bolivian president Evo
Morales, the first indigenous head of state in the Americas.*

▸ **A New Era is Beginning, We Demand Full and Effective Participation;** and **Mother Earth is in Crisis.** *Three statements from
the growing world movement of indigenous peoples fighting to save
Mother Earth.*

▸ **Two Statements by Climate Justice Now!** *CJN is an international
coalition of more than 160 peasant, indigenous and grassroots organizations that was formed during the UN climate negotiation conference
in Bali in 2007.*

▸ **ALBA Statement at the 2009 Americas Summit** *As a word, "alba"
means "dawn" in Spanish. As an acronym, it stands for the Bolivarian Alternative for the Americas, an anti-imperialist alliance that includes Bolivia, Cuba, Dominica, Ecuador, Honduras, Nicaragua and Venezuela.*

▸ **Rich Nations Must Pay Their Ecological Debt.** *A position paper
submitted by the government of Bolivia in April 2009, under the UN
Framework Convention on Climate Change.*

▸ **To Save Humanity We Must Return to Our Roots.** *Peruvian peasant leader Hugo Blanco argues that the path forward lies in a return to
the ethical values of our origins.*

Respect Mother Earth!

Three statements by Evo Morales

'LET US RESPECT OUR MOTHER EARTH'
(Letter to the United Nations, September 25, 2007)
The world is suffering from a fever due to climate change, and the disease is the capitalist development model.

While over 10,000 years the variation in carbon dioxide (CO_2) levels on the planet was approximately 10%, during the last 200 years of industrial development, carbon emissions have increased by 30%. Since 1860, Europe and North America have contributed 70% of the emissions of CO_2. 2005 was the hottest year in the last one thousand years on this planet.

Various studies have demonstrated that out of the 40,170 living species that have been studied, 16,119 are in danger of extinction. One out of eight birds could disappear forever. One out of four mammals is under threat. One out of every three reptiles could cease to exist. Eight out of ten crustaceans and three out of four insects are at risk of extinction. We are living through the sixth crisis of the extinction of living species in the history of the planet and this time the rate of extinction is 100 times more accelerated than in geological times.

Faced with this bleak future, transnational interests are proposing to continue as before, and paint the machine green, that is, to continue with growth and irrational consumerism and inequality, generating more and more profits, without realizing that we are currently consuming in one year what the planet produces in one year and three months. Faced with this reality, the solution can not be an cosmetic change.

I read in the World Bank report that in order to mitigate the impacts of climate change we need to end subsidies on hydrocarbons, put a price on water and promote private investment in the clean energy sector. Once again they want to apply market recipes and privatization in order to carry on withbusiness as usual, and thus with the same illnesses that these policies produce. The same occurs in the case of biofuels, because to producing one litre of ethanol requires 12 litres of water. Similarly, to process one ton of agrofuels you need, on average, one hectare of land.

Faced with this situation, we – the indigenous peoples and humble and honest inhabitants of this planet – believe that the time has come to put a stop to this, in order to rediscover our roots, with respect for Mother Earth; with the Pachamama as we call it in the Andes. Today, the indigenous peoples of Latin America and the world have been called upon by history to convert ourselves into the vanguard of the struggle to defend nature and life.

I am convinced that the United Nations Declaration on the Rights of Indigenous Peoples, recently approved after so many years of struggle, needs to pass from paper to reality so that our knowledge and our participation can help to construct a new future of hope for all. Who else but the indigenous people, can point out the path for humanity in order to preserve nature, natural resources and the territories that we have inhabited from ancient times.

We need a profound change of direction, at the global level, so as to stop being the condemned of the earth. The countries of the North must reduce their carbon emissions by between 60% and 80% if we want to avoid a temperature rise of more than 2° in what is left of this century, which would provoke global warming of catastrophic proportions for life and nature.

We need to create a World Environment Organization which is binding, and which can discipline the World Trade Organization, which is propelling us towards barbarism. We can no longer continue to talk of growth in Gross National Product without taking into consideration the destruction and wastage of natural resources. We need to adopt an indicator that allows us to consider, in a combined way, the Human Development Index and the Ecological Footprint in order to measure our environmental situation.

We need to apply harsh taxes on super concentrations of wealth, and adopt effective mechanisms for its equitable redistribution. It is not acceptable for three families to have incomes greater the combined GDP of the 48 poorest countries. We can not talk of equity and social justice whilst this situation continues.

The United States and Europe consume, on average, 8.4 times more that the world average. They must reduce their level of consumption and recognize that all of us are guests on this same land; of the same Pachamama.

I know that change is not easy when an extremely powerful sector has to renounce its extraordinary profits for the planet to survive. In my own country I suffer, with my head held high, constant sabotage because we are ending privileges so that everyone can "Live Well" but not better than others. I know that change in the world is much more difficult than in my country, but I have absolute confidence in human beings, in their capacity to reason, to learn from mistakes, to rediscover their roots, and to change in order to forge a just, diverse, inclusive, egalitarian world in harmony with nature.

* * *

'CAPITALISM IS THE WORST ENEMY OF HUMANITY'

Speech to the United Nations. September 24, 2007

I would like to greet the panel, and on behalf of the Bolivian peoples I want to say that I am pleased that there is such a great gathering to debate global warming and climate change.

Today in our discussions, we must be very sincere and very realistic about the problems faced by our peoples, humanity and the entire planet.

I feel that we are not speaking truthfully if we talk about life and the future of humanity, while each day we are destroying the future of humanity. It is important to pinpoint who our enemies are, what the causes are of the damage being done to the planet, damage that may put an end to humanity.

I'd like to sincerely apologize if some countries or some groups are bothered by the survival of my country, the survival of the indigenous people. I think that that capitalism is the worst enemy of humanity and if we do not change the model, change the system, then our presence, our debate, our exchange, and the proposals that we make in these meetings at the United Nations will be totally in vain.

Capitalism has twins, the market and war. The market converts life into commodities, it converts land into a commodity. And when capitalists cannot sustain this economic model based on looting, on exploitation, on marginalization, on exclusion and, above all, on the accumulation of capital, they turn to war, to the arms race. If we ask ourselves how much money is spent on the arms race — we are not supposed to be concerned about that.

This is why I feel that it is important to change economic models, development models, and economic systems, particularly those in the western world. And if we do not understand and thoroughly discuss the very survival of our peoples, then we certainly not will will not be addressing the problem of climate change, the problem of life, the human problems.

It is important that we learn lessons from other groups, from other regions. Let me avail myself of this opportunity: I come from a culture based on peace, from a lifestyle based on equality, of living not only in solidarity with all people, but also living in harmony with Mother Earth. For the indigenous movement, land cannot be a commodity; it is our mother who gives us life, so how could we treat it as a commodity as the western model does?

This is a profound lesson which we must learn in order to resolve the problems of humanity that are being discussed here, climate change and pollution. Where does this pollution come from? It comes from, and is generated by, the unsustainable development of a system which destroys the planet: in other words, capitalism.

I want to use this opportunity to call on sectors, groups and nations to abandon luxury, to abandon over-consumption, to think not only about money but about life, to not only think about accumulating capital but to think in wider terms about humanity. Only then can we begin to solve the root causes of these problems facing humanity.

Because if we don't think that way, if we do not change, it won't matter if business owners have a lot of money, no matter if they are a multinational or even a country — no one can escape these ecological problems, environment problems, and climate change. No one will be spared, and the wealth that some country, some region or some capitalist may have will be useless.

I feel that it is important to organize an international movement to deal with the environment, a movement that will be above institutions, businesses and countries that just talk about commerce, that only think about accumulating capital. We have to organize a movement that will defend life, defend humanity, and save the earth.

I think that it is important to think about some regions, some sectors and some countries repaying what has often been called the ecological debt.

If we do not think about how this ecological debt will be paid, how are we going to solve the problems of life and humanity?

I want to say, dear colleagues and friends, that we must assume the responsibility as leaders or as presidents, as governments — we must save life, we must save humanity, we must save the entire planet.

* * *

10 COMMANDMENTS TO SAVE THE PLANET

Message to the Continental Gathering of Solidarity
with Bolivia in Guatemala City, October 9, 2008

Sisters and brothers, on behalf of the Bolivian people, I greet the social movements of this continent participating in this event of continental solidarity with Bolivia.

We have just suffered the violence of the oligarchy, whose most brutal expression was the massacre in Panda, a deed that teaches us that an attempt at power based on money and weapons in order to oppress the people is not sustainable. It is easily knocked down, if it is not based on a program and the consciousness of the people.

We see that the re-founding of Bolivia affects the concealed interests of a few families of large landholders, who reject as aggression measures that are enacted in the peoples' interes, such as more balanced distribution of the natural gas resources we inherited from our ancestors, such as land distribution, health and literacy campaigns, and others.

To protect their power and privileges and to escape the process of change, the ruling elite of large landholders of the so-called Half Moon (Media Luna) dress themselves up as movements for departmental autonomy and rupture national unity, allying themselves with the Yankee objective of stopping the re-founding of Bolivia.

However, in the revocation referendum of August 10, we received a mandate from two-thirds of the Bolivian people to consolidate this process of change, to continue advancing in the recovery of our natural resources, to ensure the well being of all Bolivians, and to unite the different sectors of society of the countryside and the city, of the east and the west.

---

10 Commandments to Save the Earth

Speaking at the United Nations on April 21, 2008, Evo Morales proposed 10 commandments to save the planet, life and humanity.

1. Acabar con el sistema capitalista. *Put an end to the capitalist system.*
2. Renunciar a las guerras. *Renounce wars.*
3. Un mundo sin imperialismo ni colonialismo. *A world without imperialism or colonialism.*
4. Derecho al agua. *Right to water.*
5. Desarrollo de energías limpias. *Development of clean energy.*
6. Respeto a la madre tierra. *Respect Mother Earth.*
7. Servicios básicos como derechos humanos. *Treat basic services as human rights.*
8. Combatir las desigualdades. *Fight inequality.*
9. Promover la diversidad de culturas y economías. *Promote cultural and economic diversity.*
10. Vivir buen, no vivir mejor a costa del otro. *Live well, not better at the expense of others.*

Sisters and brothers, what happened with this referendum in Bolivia is important not only for Bolivians but for all Latin Americans. We dedicate it to the Latin American revolutionaries and those throughout the world, reaffirming the struggle for all processes of change.

I want to stress our desire to recover the traditional values of our peoples, called Living Well (*Buen Vivir*), to recover our vision of the Mother Earth, that for us is life, because it is not appropriate to convert Mother Earth into a commodity as capitalism does. Once again we see the profound correlations between the indigenous movement and the social movements that also support Living Well. We greet them so that together we can seek balance in the world.

In that respect, I want to share and propose for debate 10 commandments to save the planet for humanity and for life, not just for discussion at this meeting but also in our communities and rganizations.

First, if we want to save the planet earth, to save life and humanity, we must end the capitalist system. The grave effects of climate change, of the energy, food and financial crises, are not products of human beings in general, but rather of the inhuman capitalist system, with its objective of unlimited industrial development.

Second, we must renounce war, because the people do not win in war, but only the imperial powers; the nations do not win, but rather the transnational corporations. Wars benefit a small group of families and not the people. The trillions of millions of dollars used for war should be used to repair and cure the wounds inflicted on Mother Earth by climate change.

Third proposal for debate: a world without imperialism nor colonialism. Our relationships should be based the principle of complementarity, and take into account the profound inequalities that exist between families, between countries, and between continents.

And the fourth point about the issue of water, which ought to be guaranteed as a human right, and which should not be privatized, because water is life.

As the fifth point, I would like to say that we must end the energy debacle. In 100 years we have used up fossil fuel that was created over millions of years. While some executives set aside land for luxury automobiles and not for human beings, we need to implement policies that block the use of agro-fuels, to prevent hunger and misery among our peoples.

As a sixth point, in relationship to Mother Earth: the capitalist system treats our Mother Earth as raw material, but the Earth must not be treated as a commodity. Who could privatize, rent or lease their own mother? I propose that we organize an international movement in defence of Mother Nature, to rebuild her health and re-establish a harmonious and responsible life with her.

A central theme of the seventh point for debate is that access to basic services, whether they be water, electricity, education or health, must be treated as human rights.

As the eighth point, for essential consumption, we should give priority to what we can produce and consume locally. End consumerism, decadence and luxury. We need to prioritize local production for local consumption, stimulate self-reliance and community sovereignty, as much as possible within the limits permitted by the health and remaining resources of the planet.

As the next to last point, we must promote cultural and economic diversity of cultures. We must live together respecting not only physical differences, but also economic differences, managing our economies through our communities and their associations.

Sisters and brothers, as the tenth point, we propose to Live Well, to live good lives based on our peoples' traditions, not at the expense of others but based on the riches of our communities, fertile lands, water and clean air. Socialism is talked about a lot, but we need to improve it, to build on proposals for socialism in the 21st century, building a communitarian socialism, or simply good living, in harmony with Mother Earth, respecting the shared ways of life in our community.

Finally, sisters and brothers, I know you will work on the existing problems. I have reached the conclusion that there will always be problems. But I want to assure you that I am very happy, I am not not disappointed or upset that the families who enslaved our families during colonial times, during the republic and during this period of neoliberalism, are resisting us today.

We struggle to confront these groups who live in luxury and who do not wish to lose their privileges or lands. This is a historic struggle and it will continue.

Sisters and brothers, I hope that the Continental Gathering of the Social Forum of the Americas culminates with strong bonds of unity among you and a strong action plan in suppport of Bolivia and of our peoples. I repeat my fraternal greeting.

'A New Era Is Beginning'

Cochabamba Statement

America Latina en Movimiento, October 12, 2007.
Translated by Richard Fidler for Bolivia Rising

A formal summons to world states
by indigenous first nations and peoples

(Chimoré, Cochabamba, Bolivia) From the heart of South America, on this 12th day of October, 2007, the delegates of the indigenous first nations and peoples of the world, meeting in the World Encounter "For the Historic Victory of the Indigenous Peoples of the World," to celebrate the adoption of the United Nations Declaration on the Rights of Indigenous Peoples, hereby declare:

That, after 515 years of oppression and domination, here we stand. They have been unable to eliminate us. We have confronted and resisted the policies of ethnocide, genocide, colonization, destruction and plunder, and the imposition of such economic systems as capitalism, characterized by interventionism, wars and socio-environmental disasters, a system that continues to threaten our ways of life as peoples.

That as a consequence of the neoliberal policy of domination of nature, the search for easy profits from the concentration of capital in a few hands and the irrational exploitation of natural resources, our Mother Earth is mortally wounded, while the indigenous peoples are still being displaced from our territories. The planet is warming up. We are experiencing an unprecedented change in climate with ever-stronger and more frequent socio-environmental disasters, affecting all of us without exception.

That we are trapped in a great energy crisis, with the Age of Petroleum coming to an end, and without having found a clean alternative energy that can substitute for it in the quantities necessary to maintain that Western civilization that has made us totally dependent on hydrocarbons.

That this situation may be a threat that will leave us exposed to the danger that neoliberal and imperialist policies will trigger wars for the last drops of the so-called black gold and blue gold, but may also give us the opportunity to make this new millennium a millennium of life, a millennium of balance and complementarity, without having to take advantage of energies that destroy Mother Earth.

That both the natural resources and the lands and territories we inhabit are ours for history, for birth, in law and for ever, and that the power to determine their use is fundamental to our ability to maintain our life, sciences, learning, spirituality, organization, medicines and food sovereignty.

That a new era is beginning, promoted by the original indigenous peoples and bringing again times of change, times of Pachakuti,[1] in the times of the culmination of the Quinto Sol.[2]

That we welcome the adoption of the United Nations Declaration on the Rights of Indigenous Peoples, which is essential for the survival and well-being of the more than 370 million native peoples in some 70 countries of the world. After more than twenty years of struggle, it is responsive to our historical demand for self-determination of the peoples and recognition of ourselves and our collective rights.

The adopted Declaration contains a set of principles and norms that recognize and establish in the international regulatory system the fundamental rights of the Indigenous Peoples, those that must be the basis of the new relationship between the Indigenous Peoples, States, societies and cooperation throughout the world. In addition, therefore, to the other existing juridical instruments governing human rights, the Declaration is the new regulatory and practical basis for guaranteeing and protecting indigenous rights in various spheres and at various levels.

We call on the member countries of the United Nations and encourage the indigenous peoples to implement and comply with this important instrument of historical significance. We censure those governments that have voted in opposition to the Declaration on the Rights of the Indigenous Peoples, and condemn their double standards.

That we pledge to support the historical effort being led by our brother Evo Morales, President of the Indigenous Peoples of Abya Yala,[3] in the construction of a new plurinational State. We will be vigilant in the face of any threat, internal or external, to the process in Bolivia and we call on the peoples of the planet to lend their support and solidarity to this process, which ought to serve as an example so that the Peoples, Nations and States of the world continue along this path.

Accordingly, the Indigenous Peoples and Nations of the world demand that the States fulfil the following mandates:

1. To construct a world based on the Culture of Life, in the identity, philosophy, world view and age-old spirituality of the original indigenous peoples, applying the aboriginal knowledge and skills, strengthening the processes of interchange and brotherhood among the nations and respecting self-determination.

2. To make national and international decisions to save Mother Nature from the disasters that are being brought about by capitalism in its decline, as manifested in global warming and the ecological crisis; reaffirming that the original indigenous culture is the only alternative means of saving our planet earth.

3. To replace the present models of development based on capitalism, commodities, the irrational exploitation of humanity and natural resources, the squandering of energy, and consumerism, with models that establish life, complementarity, reciprocity, respect for cultural diversity and the sustainable use of natural resources as the principal priorities.

4. To implement national policies governing Food Sovereignty as a principal basis of National Sovereignty, in which the community guarantees respect for its own culture as appropriate spaces and modes of production, distribution and consumption consistent with the nature of healthy pollutant-free foods for the entire population, eliminating hunger, because food is a right to life.

5. To repudiate schemes and projects for the generation of energy such as biofuel, which destroy and deny food to the peoples. Likewise, we condemn the use of transgenic seeds because it replaces our ancient seeding process and makes us dependent on agro-industry.

6. To recognize and re-evaluate the role of indigenous women as the vanguard of the emancipatory struggles of our peoples in accordance with the principles of duality, equality and equity of relationships between men and women.

7. To adopt the Culture of Peace and Life as a guide for resolving the world's problems and conflicts, renouncing the arms race, and to initiate disarmament in order to guarantee the preservation of life on this planet.

8. To adopt the just legal transformations that are necessary for the construction of systems and means of communication and information based on our world view, spirituality and communal philosophy, in the wisdom of our ancestors. To guarantee recognition of the indigenous peoples' right to communication and information.

9. To guarantee respect for and the right to life, health and bilingual intercultural education, incorporating policies of benefit to the indigenous first nations and peoples.

10. To declare water to be a human right, a vital element and social property of humanity and not a source of profit. Likewise, to encourage the use of alternative energies that do not threaten the life of the planet, thereby guaranteeing access to all basic services.

11. To solve cases of migration between countries in a mutually responsible way, adopting policies of free circulations of persons in order to guarantee a world without borders in which there is no discrimination, marginalization and exclusion.

13. To decolonize the United Nations and move its headquarters to a territory that dignifies and expresses the just aspirations of the Peoples, Nations and States of the world.

14. Not to criminalize the struggles of the indigenous peoples, or demonize or accuse us of terrorism when we reclaim our rights and advance our ideas on how to save life and humanity.

15. To release immediately the indigenous leaders imprisoned in various parts of the world, and in the first place Leonard Peltier in the United States.

The struggle is unceasing, we will continue our resistance until our time comes. We proclaim the 12th of October the "day of commencement of our struggles to save Mother Nature."

From our families, homes, communities, peoples, whether in government or without, we ourselves are determining and directing our destinies, we ourselves are assuming the will and responsibility to live well that has been bequeathed to us by our ancestors, to expand, from the simplest and least complicated to the greatest and most complex, to construct horizontally and mutually, each and every one, the culture of patience, the culture of dialogue and fundamentally the Culture of Life.

By the dead, the heroes and martyrs who lend meaning to our lives through their utopias and longings, we strengthen our identity, our organizational processes and our struggles to build the unity of the peoples of the world and to restore the balance, saving life, humanity and the planet earth.

We confirm our support for the award of the Nobel Peace Price to brother Evo Morales for his ongoing and unconditional dedication to the good of humanity, the peoples, the planet and world peace.

Translator's Notes

[1] "Pachakuti is a Quechua word with multiple meanings. Literally meaning turning or returning (kuti) of the earth (pacha), it is translated alternatively as 'new beginning', 'reawakening', 'revolution', or 'renovation'." – Donna Lee Van Cott, "From Exclusion to Inclusion: Bolivia's 2002 Elections", *J. Lat. Amer. Stud.* 35, 751–775, p. 764n.

[2] Literally, the Fifth Sun. See www.mexconnect.com/mex_/mysfifthsun.html.

[3] "Continent of Life." See abyayala.nativeweb.org/about.html.

'We Demand Full and Effective Participation'

Bali Statement

Indigenous Peoples' statement to the international
conference on climate change in Bali, Indonesia, December 2007

On behalf of the International Forum of Indigenous Peoples on Climate Change (IFIPCC), I would like to draw your attention to the fact that more than 80% of the world's biodiversity and most of the forests are found within our territories. Indigenous peoples also represent some 350 million individuals in the world and make up 90% of the world's cultural diversity. Yet, we are suffering the worst impacts of climate change without having contributed to its creation as is clearly evident in many parts of the Indigenous Peoples' lands, and which threatens our very survival.

We, Indigenous Peoples, have addressed our concerns to the UNFCCC [United Nations Framework Convention on Climate Change] Conference of the Parties since SBSTA 13 [Subsidiary Body for Scientific and Technological Advice] in Lyon, France, 2000. However, despite years of experience and efforts to participate in this process, and despite also the resounding support and approval this year of the United Nations Declaration on the Rights of Indigenous Peoples, we are profoundly disappointed that, even as the United Nations' Second International Decade of Indigenous Peoples begins, states are still ignoring our demands and contributions and we have even been shut out of this Bali process. This is unacceptable.

Mr. President, the IFIPCC takes this opportunity to again reaffirm the following:

a. We demand the creation of an Expert Group on Climate Change and Indigenous Peoples with the full participation and representation of Indigenous Peoples, taking into account the example of the United Nations Permanent Forum on Indigenous Issues that includes indigenous experts;

b. We demand the creation of a voluntary fund for the full and meaningful participation of Indigenous Peoples, such as that which exists in the Convention on Biological Diversity;

c. We demand that the Conference of the Parties recognize and take action to curb the adverse impacts of climate change on indigenous peoples; and to refrain from adaptation and mitigation schemes and projects promoted as solutions to climate change that devastate Indigenous Peoples' lands and territories and cause more human rights violations, like market based mechanisms, carbon trading, agrofuels and especially avoided deforestation (REDD). All adaptation and mitigation plans affecting indigenous communities must follow the principles of free prior and informed consent of Indigenous communities, especially those mostly impacted.

d. We demand full and effective participation of Indigenous Peoples in all levels of planning, decision making and implementation of the Nairobi Five Year Programs of Work, including the SBI [Subsidiary Body for Implementation] and SBSTA programs and that a human rights-based approach be used in this work and to engage the UN Human Rights Council to monitor the impacts of climate change mitigation and adaptation on Indigenous Peoples.

e. We demand that any financial mechanism agreed to here by the COP/MOP [Conference/Meeting of the Parties to the UNFCCC] must be easily accessible to, and allow direct access by Indigenous Peoples noting that the Adaptation Fund is fully funded through CDM projects which cause disastrous impacts on Indigenous Peoples lands, territories, and resources, as well as violating their rights in ways that have ended up costing many Indigenous Peoples lives, and force them from their lands.

f. We request the UNFCCC to submit its reports to the 7th Session of the UN Permanent Forum on Indigenous Issues in April 2008 as the main theme of this session is on climate change and Indigenous Peoples.

Mr. President, the IFIPCC sincerely believes that Indigenous Peoples have a role to play in this convention and the Protocol. It is time that we all co-operate in our efforts to address climate change in a manner that recognizes social justice, environmental integrity, indigenous and other human rights.

Terima Kasih!

Mother Earth is in Crisis

Anchorage Declaration

Agreed by consensus of the participants in the Indigenous Peoples'
Global Summit on Climate Change, Anchorage Alaska, April 24, 2009
From 20 to 24 April, 2009, Indigenous representatives from the Arctic, North America, Asia, Pacific, Latin America, Africa, Caribbean, and Russia met in Anchorage, Alaska for the Indigenous Peoples' Global Summit on Climate Change. We thank the Ahtna and the Dena'ina Athabascan Peoples in whose lands we gathered.

We express our solidarity as Indigenous Peoples living in areas that are the most vulnerable to the impacts and root causes of climate change. We reaffirm the unbreakable and sacred connection between land, air, water, oceans, forests, sea ice, plants, animals, and our human communities as the material and spiritual basis for our existence.

We are deeply alarmed by the accelerating climate devastation brought about by unsustainable development. We are experiencing profound and disproportionate adverse impacts on our cultures, human and environmental health, human rights, well-being, traditional livelihoods, food systems, and food sovereignty, local infrastructure, economic viability, and our very survival as Indigenous Peoples.

Mother Earth is no longer in a period of climate change, but in climate crisis. We therefore insist on an immediate end to the destruction and desecration of the elements of life.

Through our knowledge, spirituality, sciences, practices, experiences, and relationships with our traditional lands, territories, waters, air, forests, oceans, sea ice, other natural resources, and all life, Indigenous Peoples have a vital role in defending and healing Mother Earth. The future of Indigenous Peoples lies in the wisdom of our elders, the restoration of the sacred position of women, the youth of today, and in the generations of tomorrow.

We uphold that the inherent rights of Indigenous Peoples, affirmed by the United Nations Declaration on the Rights of Indigenous Peoples (UN-DRIP), must be fully respected in all decision-making processes and activities related to climate change. This includes our rights to our lands, territories, environment and natural resources as contained in Articles 25–30 of the UN-DRIP. When specific programs and projects affect them, the right to self-determination of Indigenous Peoples must be respected, emphasizing our right to Free Prior and Informed Consent, including the right to say "no." The UNFCCC agreements and principles must reflect the spirit of the UN-DRIP.

Calls for action

1. In order to achieve the fundamental objective of the United Nations Framework Convention on Climate Change (UNFCCC), we call upon the 15th meeting of the Conference of the Parties to the UNFCCC to support a binding emissions reduction target for developed countries (Annex 1) of at least 45% below 1990 levels by 2020 and at least 95% by 2050. In recognizing the root causes of climate change, participants call upon states to work towards decreasing dependency on fossil fuels. We further call for a just transition to decentralized renewable energy economies, sources and systems owned and controlled by our local communities, to achieve energy security and sovereignty.

In addition, the Summit participants agreed to present two options for action which were each supported by one or more of the participating regional caucuses. These were as follows:

a. We call for the phase out of fossil fuel development and a moratorium on new fossil fuel developments on or near Indigenous lands and territories.

b. We call for a process that works towards the eventual phase out of fossil fuels, without infringing on the right to development of Indigenous nations.

2. We call upon the Parties to the UNFCCC to recognize the importance of our Traditional Knowledge and practices shared by Indigenous Peoples in developing strategies to address climate change. To address climate change we also call on the UNFCCC to recognize the historical and ecological debt of the Annex 1 countries in contributing to greenhouse gas emissions and we call on these countries to pay this historical debt.

3. We call on the Intergovernmental Panel on Climate Change (IPCC), the Millennium Ecosystem Assessment, and other relevant institutions to support Indigenous Peoples in carrying out Indigenous Peoples' climate change assessments.

4. We call upon the UNFCCC's decision-making bodies to establish formal structures and mechanisms for and with the full and effective participation of Indigenous Peoples. Specifically we recommend that the UNFCCC:

1. Organize regular Technical Briefings by Indigenous Peoples on Traditional Knowledge and climate change;

2. Recognize and engage the International Indigenous Peoples' Forum on Climate Change and its regional focal points in an advisory role;

3. Immediately establish an Indigenous focal point in the secretariat of the UNFCCC;

4. Appoint Indigenous Peoples' representatives in UNFCCC funding mechanisms in consultation with Indigenous Peoples;

5. Take the necessary measures to ensure the full and effective participation of Indigenous and local communities in formulating, implementing, and monitoring activities, mitigation, and adaptation to impacts of climate change.

5. All initiatives under Reducing Emissions from Deforestation and Degradation (REDD) must secure the recognition and implementation of the rights of Indigenous Peoples, including security of land tenure, recognition of land title according to traditional ways, uses and customary laws and the multiple benefits of forests for climate, ecosystems, and peoples before taking any action.

6. We challenge States to abandon false solutions to climate change that negatively impact Indigenous Peoples' rights, lands, air, oceans, forests, territories and waters. These include nuclear energy, large-scale dams, geo-engineering techniques, "clean coal," agro-fuels, plantations, and market based mechanisms such as carbon trading, the Clean Development Mechanism, and forest offsets. The rights of Indigenous Peoples to protect our forests and forest livelihoods must be ensured.

7. We call for adequate and direct funding in developed and developing

States and for a fund to be created to enable Indigenous Peoples' full and effective participation in all climate processes, including adaptation, mitigation, monitoring, and transfer of appropriate technologies, in order to foster our empowerment, capacity building, and education. We strongly urge relevant United Nations bodies to facilitate and fund the participation, education, and capacity building of indigenous youth and women to ensure engagement in all international and national processes related to climate change.

8. We call on financial institutions to provide risk insurance for Indigenous Peoples to allow them to recover from extreme weather events.

9. We call on all United Nations agencies to address climate change impacts in their strategies and action plans, in particular their impacts on Indigenous Peoples, including the World Health Organization the United Nations Educational, Scientific and Cultural Organization, the United Nations Permanent Forum on Indigenous Issues, etc. We call upon the United Nations Food and Agriculture Organization and other relevant United Nations bodies to establish an Indigenous Peoples' working group to address the impacts of climate change on food security and food sovereignty for Indigenous Peoples.

10. We call on United Nations Environment Programme to conduct a fast track assessment of short-term drivers of climate change, specifically black carbon, with a view to initiating negotiation of an international agreement to reduce emission of black carbon.

11. We call on States to recognize and implement the fundamental human rights and status of Indigenous Peoples, including the collective rights to traditional ownership, use, access, occupancy and title to traditional lands, air, forests, waters, oceans, sea ice and sacred sites as well as the rights affirmed in treaties are upheld and recognized in land use planning and climate change mitigation strategies. In particular, States must ensure that Indigenous Peoples have the right to mobility and are not forcibly removed or settled away from their traditional lands and territories, and that the rights of peoples in voluntary isolation are upheld. In the case of climate change migrants, appropriate programs and measures must address their rights and vulnerabilities.

12. We call on States to return and restore lands, territories, waters, forests, oceans, sea ice and sacred sites that have been taken from Indigenous Peoples and have limited our access to our traditional ways of living, thereby causing us to misuse and expose our lands to climate conditions that contribute to climate change.

13. In order to provide the resources necessary for our collective survival in response to the climate crisis, we declare our communities, waters, air, forests, oceans, sea ice, traditional lands and territories to be "Food Sovereignty Areas," defined and directed by Indigenous Peoples according to

customary laws, and free from chemical-based industrial food production systems and extractive industries (i.e. contaminants, agro-fuels, genetically modified organisms, and deforestation).

14. We encourage our communities to exchange information while ensuring the protection and respect of intellectual property rights at the local, national and international levels pertaining to our Traditional Knowledge, innovations, and practices. These include land, water, and sea ice use, traditional agriculture, forest management, ancestral seeds, pastoralism, food plants and animals, medicines, which are essential in developing climate change adaptation and mitigation strategies, restoring our food sovereignty and food independence, and strengthening our Indigenous families and nations.

We offer to share with humanity our Traditional Knowledge, innovations, and practices relevant to climate change, provided our fundamental rights as intergenerational guardians of this knowledge are fully recognized and respected. We reiterate the urgent need for collective action.

Two Statements from Climate Justice Now!

Climate Justice Now!

WHAT'S MISSING FROM THE CLIMATE TALKS? JUSTICE!

Statement issued by the newly-formed Climate Justice Now! alliance following the UN climate negotiations in Bali, Indonesia, in December 2007

Peoples from social organizations and movements from across the globe brought the fight for social, ecological and gender justice into the negotiating rooms and onto the streets during the UN climate summit in Bali.

Inside and outside the convention centre, activists demanded alternative policies and practices that protect livelihoods and the environment.

In dozens of side events, reports, impromptu protests and press conferences, the false solutions to climate change – such as carbon offsetting, carbon trading for forests, agrofuels, trade liberalization, and privatization pushed by governments, financial institutions and multinational corporations – have been exposed.

Affected communities, Indigenous Peoples, women and peasant farmers called for real solutions to the climate crisis, solutions which have failed to capture the attention of political leaders. These genuine solutions include:

▸ reduced consumption.
▸ huge financial transfers from North to South based on historical respon-

sibility and ecological debt for adaptation and mitigation costs paid for by redirecting military budgets, innovative taxes, and debt cancellation.

▸ leaving fossil fuels in the ground and investing in appropriate energy-efficiency and safe, clean and community-led renewable energy.

▸ rights based resource conservation that enforces indigenous land rights and promotes peoples' sovereignty over energy, forests, land, and water.

▸ sustainable family farming and peoples' food sovereignty.

Inside the negotiations, the rich industrialized countries have put unjustifiable pressure on Southern governments to commit to emissions' reductions. At the same time, they have refused to live up to their own legal and moral obligations to radically cut emissions and support developing countries' efforts to reduce emissions and adapt to climate impacts. Once again, the majority world is being forced to pay for the excesses of the minority.

Compared to the outcomes of the official negotiations, the major success of Bali is the momentum that has been built towards creating a diverse, global movement for climate justice.

We will take our struggle forward not just in the talks, but on the ground and in the streets – *Climate Justice Now!*

Members of this coalition include: Carbon Trade Watch, Transnational Institute; Center for Environmental Concerns; Focus on the Global South; Freedom from Debt Coalition, Philippines; Friends of the Earth International; Gendercc–Women for Climate Justice; Global Forest Coalition; Global Justice Ecology Project; International Forum on Globalization; Kalikasan-Peoples Network for the Environment (Kalikasan-PNE); La Via Campesina; Members of the Durban Group for Climate Justice; Oilwatch; Pacific Indigenous Peoples Environment Coalition, Aotearoa/New Zealand; Sustainable Energy and Economy Network; The Indigenous Environmental Network; Third World Network; WALHI/ Friends of the Earth Indonesia; World Rainforest Movement.

* * *

THE URGENCY OF CLIMATE JUSTICE

Adopted by members of the Climate Justice Now! alliance
who attended the UN climate negotiations in Poznan in 2008.

We will not be able to stop climate change if we don't change the neo-liberal and corporate-based economy which stops us from achieving sustainable societies. Corporate globalization must be stopped.

The historical responsibility for the vast majority of greenhouse gas emissions lies with the industrialized countries of the North. Even though the primary responsibility of the North to reduce emissions has been recognized in the Convention, their production and consumption habits continue to threaten the survival of humanity and biodiversity. It is imperative that the North urgently shifts to a low carbon economy. At the same time in order to avoid the damaging carbon intensive model of industrialization, the South is entitled to resources and technology to make this transition.

We believe that any "shared vision" on addressing the climate crisis must start with climate justice and with a radical re-thinking of the dominant development model.

Indigenous Peoples, peasant communities, fisherfolk, and especially women in these communities, have been living harmoniously and sustainably with the Earth for millennia. They are not only the most affected by climate change, but also its false solutions, such as agrofuels, mega-dams, genetic modification, tree plantations and carbon offset schemes. Instead of market led schemes, their sustainable practices should be seen as offering the real solutions to climate change.

UNFCCC in Crisis

Governments and international institutions have to recognize that the Kyoto mechanisms have failed to reduce greenhouse gas emissions.

The principles of the United Nations Framework Convention on Climate Change (UNFCCC) – common but differentiated responsibilities, intergenerational equity, and polluter pays – have been undermined in favour of market mechanisms. The three main pillars of the Kyoto agreement -the clean development mechanism, joint implementation and emissions trading schemes – have been completely ineffective in reducing emissions, yet they continue to be at the center of the negotiations.

Kyoto is based on carbon-trading mechanisms which allow Northern countries to continue business as usual by paying for "clean development" projects in developing and transition countries. This is a scheme designed deliberately to allow polluters to avoid reducing emissions domestically. Clean Development Mechanism projects, which are supposed to support "sustainable development," include infrastructure projects such as big dams and coal-fired power plants, and monoculture tree plantations. Not only do these projects fail to reduce carbon emissions, they accelerate the privatization and corporate take-over of the natural world, at the expense of local communities and Indigenous Peoples.

Proposals on the table in Poznan are heading in the same direction.

In the current negotiations, industrialized countries continue to act on the basis of self-interest, using all their negotiating tactics to avoid their obligations to reduce carbon emissions, to finance adaptation and mitigation and transfer technology to the South. In their pursuit of growth at any cost, many Southern governments at the talks are trading away the rights of their peoples and resources. We remind them that a climate agreement is not a trade agreement.

The main protagonists for climate stability – Indigenous Peoples, women, peasant and family farmers, fisher folk, forest dependent communities, youth, and marginalized and affected communities in the global South and North, are systematically excluded. Despite repeated demands, Indigenous Peoples are not recognized as an official party to the negotiations. Neither are women's voices and gender considerations recognized and included in the process. At the same time, private investors are circling the talks like vultures, swooping in on every opportunity for creating new profits. Business and corporate lobbyists expanded their influence and monopolized conference space at Poznan. At least 1500 industry lobbyists were present either as NGOs or as members of government delegations.

The Reducing Emissions from Deforestation and Forest Degradation (REDD) scheme could create the climate regime's largest ever loophole, giving Northern polluters yet another opportunity to buy their way out of emissions reductions. With no mention of biodiversity or Indigenous Peoples' rights, this scheme might give a huge incentive for countries to sell off their forests, expel Indigenous and peasant communities, and transform forests into tree plantations under corporate-control. Plantations are not forests.

Privatization and dispossession through REDD or any other mechanisms must be stopped. The World Bank is attempting to carve a niche in the international climate change regime. This is unacceptable as the Bank continues to fund polluting industries and drive deforestation by promoting industrial logging and agrofuels. The Bank's recently launched Climate Investment Fund goes against government initiatives at the UN and promotes dirty industries such as coal, while forcing developing countries into the fundamentally unequal aid framework of donor and recipient. The World Bank Forest Carbon Partnership Facility aiming to finance REDD through a forest carbon mechanism serves the interest of private companies and opens the path for commodification of forests.

These developments are to be expected. Market ideology has totally infiltrated the climate talks, and the UNFCCC negotiations are now like trade fairs hawking investment opportunities.

The Real Solutions

Solutions to the climate crisis will not come from industrialized countries and big business. Effective and enduring solutions will come from those who have protected the environment – Indigenous Peoples, women, peasant and family farmers, fisher folk, forest dependent communities, youth and marginalized and affected communities in the global South and North. These include:

▸ Achieving low carbon economies, without resorting to offsetting and false solutions such as nuclear energy and "clean coal", while protecting

the rights of those affected by the transition, especially workers.
▸ Keeping fossil fuels in the ground.
▸ Implementing people's food and energy sovereignty.
▸ Guaranteeing community control of natural resources.
▸ Re-localization of production and consumption, prioritizing local markets.
▸ Full recognition of Indigenous Peoples, peasant and local community rights,
▸ Democratically controlled clean renewable energy.
▸ Rights based resource conservation that enforces indigenous land rights and promotes peoples sovereignty and public ownership over energy, forests, seeds, land and water.
▸ Ending deforestation and its underlying causes.
▸ Ending excessive consumption by elites in the North and in the South.
▸ Massive investment in public transport.
▸ Ensuring gender justice by recognizing existing gender injustices and involving women in decision making.
▸ Cancelling illegitimate debts claimed by northern governments and IFIs. The illegitimacy of these debts is underscored by the much greater historical, social and ecological debts owed to people of the South.

We stand at the crossroads. We call for a radical change in direction to put climate justice and people's rights at the centre of these negotiations.

In the lead-up to the 2009 COP 15 at Copenhagen and beyond, the Climate Justice Now! alliance will continue to monitor governments and to mobilize social forces from the south and the north to achieve climate justice.

ALBA Statement at Americas Summit

Cumana, April 17, 2009. Translation by Socialist Voice
The heads of state and governments of Bolivia, Cuba, Dominica, Honduras, Nicaragua and Venezuela, member countries of ALBA, consider that the proposed Declaration of the 5th Summit of the Americas is insufficient and unacceptable for the following reasons:
▸ It offers no answers to the issue of the Global Economic Crisis, despite the fact that this constitutes the largest challenge faced by humanity in decades and the most serious threat in the current epoch to the wellbeing of our peoples.
▸ It unjustifiably excludes Cuba in a criminal manner, without reference to the general consensus that exists in the region in favour of condemning the blockade and the isolation attempts, which its people and govern-

ment have incessantly objected to.

For these reasons, the member countries of ALBA consider that consensus does not exist in favour of adopting this proposed declaration, and in light of the above we propose to have a thoroughgoing debate over the following issues:

1) Capitalism is destroying humanity and the planet. What we are living through is a global economic crisis of a systemic and structural character and not just one more cyclical crisis. Those who think that this crisis will be resolved with an injection of fiscal money and with some regulatory measures are very mistaken.

The financial system is in crisis because it has issued financial paper valued at at six times the real value of goods and services being produced in the world. This is not a "failure of the regulation of the system" but rather a fundamental part of the capitalist system that speculates with all goods and values in the pursuit of obtaining the maximum amount of profit possible. Until now, the economic crisis has created 100 million more starving people and more than 50 million new unemployed people, and these figures are tending to increase.

2) Capitalism has provoked an ecological crisis by subordinating the necessary conditions for life on this planet to the domination of the market and profit. Each year, the world consumes a third more than what the planet is capable of regenerating. At this rate of wastage by the capitalist system, we are going to need two planets by the year 2030.

3) The global economic, climate change, food and energy crises are products of the decadence of capitalism that threatens to put an end to the existence of life and the planet. To avoid this outcome it is necessary to develop an alternative model to that of the capitalist system.

▸ A system based on solidarity and complementarity and not competition.
▸ A system in harmony with our Mother Earth, rather than one that loots our natural resources.
▸ A system based on cultural diversity and not the crushing of cultures and impositions of cultural values and lifestyles alien to the realities of our countries.
▸ A system of peace based on social justice and not on imperialist wars and policies.

In short, a system that restores the human condition of our societies and peoples, rather than reducing them to simple consumers or commodities.

4) As a concrete expression of the new reality on the continent, Latin American and Caribbean countries have begun to construct their own institutions, whose roots lie in the common history that goes back to our independence revolution, and which constitutes a concrete instrument for deepening the processes of social, economic and cultural transformation that will con-

solidate our sovereignty. The ALBA-TCP [TCP — Peoples Trade Agreement], Petrocaribe and UNASUR [Union of South American Nations], to cite only the most recently created one, are mechanisms for solidarity-based union forged in the heat of these transformations, with the manifest intention of strengthening the efforts of our peoples to reach their own liberation.

In order to confront the grave effects of the global economic crisis, the ALBA-TCP countries have taken innovative and transformational measures that seek real alternatives to the deficient international economic order, rather than strengthening these failed institutions. That is why we have set in motion a Single System of Regional Compensation, the SUCRE, that includes a Common Accounting Unit, a Payments Clearing House and a Single System of Reserves.

At the same time, we have promoted the establishment of grand national companies in order to satisfy the fundamental necessities of our peoples, implementing mechanisms of just and complementary trade, that leave to one side the absurd logic of unrestrained competition.

5) We question the G20's decision to triple the amount of resources going to the International Monetary Fund, when what is really necessary is the establishment of a new world economic order that includes the total transformation of the IMF, the World Bank and the WTO [World Trade Organization], which with their neoliberal policies have contributed to this global economic crisis.

6) The solutions to the global economic crisis and the definition of a new international financial architecture should be adopted with the participation of the 192 countries that will meet between June 1 and 3 at a United Nations conference about the international financial crisis, in order to propose the creation of a new international economic order.

7) In regard to the climate change crisis, the developed countries have an ecological debt to the world, because they are responsible for 70% of historic emissions of carbon that have accumulated in the atmosphere since 1750.

The developed countries, in debt to humanity and the planet, should contribute significant resources towards a fund so that the countries on the path towards development can undertake a model of growth that does not repeat the grave impacts of capitalist industrialization.

8) The solutions to the energy, food and climate change crises have to be integral and interdependent. We cannot resolve a problem by creating others in the areas fundamental to life. For example, generalizing the use of agrofuels can only impact negatively on the price of food and in the utilization of essential resources such as water, land and forests.

9) We condemn discrimination against migrants in all its forms. Migration is a human right, not a crime. Therefore, we demand urgent reform of the migration policies of the United States government, with the objective of

halting deportations and mass raids and allowing the reunification of families, and we demand the elimination of the wall that divides and separates us, rather than uniting us.

To that end, we demand the repeal of the *Cuban Adjustment Act* and the elimination of the discriminatory and selective wetbacks-drybacks policy, which is the cause of loss of human lives.

Those that are truly to blame for the financial crisis are the bankers who steal the money and resources of our countries, not migrant workers. Human rights come first, particularly the human rights of the most unprotected and marginalized sectors of our society, as undocumented workers are.

For there to be integration there must be free circulation of people, and equal human rights for all regardless of migratory status. Brain drain constitutes a form of looting of qualified human resources by the rich countries.

10) Basic services such as education, health, water, energy and telecommunications have to be declared human rights and cannot be the objects of private business nor be commodified by the World Trade Organization. These are essential public services and should be universally accessible.

11) We want a world where all countries, big and small, have the same rights, and where empires do not exist. We oppose intervention. Strengthen, as the only legitimate channel for discussion and analysis of bilateral and multilateral agendas of the continent, the base of mutual respect between states and governments, under the principal of non-interference of one state over another and the inviolability of the sovereignty and self-determination of the peoples.

We demand that the new government of the United States, whose inauguration has generated some expectations in the region and the world, put an end to the long and nefarious tradition of interventionism and aggression that has characterized the actions of the governments of this country throughout its history, especially brutal during the government of George W. Bush.

In the same way, we demand that it eliminate interventionist practices such as covert operations, parallel diplomacy, media wars aimed at destabilizing states and governments, and the financing of destabilizing groups. It is fundamental that we construct a world in which a diversity of economic, political, social and cultural approaches are recognized and respected.

12) Regarding the United States blockade against Cuba and the exclusion of this country from the Summit of the Americas, the countries of the Bolivarian Alternative for the Americas (ALBA) reiterate the position that all the countries of Latin America and the Caribbean adopted last December 16, 2008, regarding the necessity of putting an end to the economic, trade and financial blockade imposed by the government of the United States of America against Cuba, including the application of the denominated Helms-

Burton law and that among its paragraphs notes:

> CONSIDERING the resolutions approved by the United Nations General Assembly on the need to put an end to the economic, commercial, and financial embargo imposed by the United States on Cuba and the decisions on the latter approved at several international meetings,
>
> DECLARE that in defence of free trade and the transparent practice of international trade, it is unacceptable to apply unilateral coercive measures that will affect the well-being of nations and obstruct the processes of integration.
>
> WE REJECT the implementation of laws and measures that contradict International Law such as the Helms-Burton law and urge the U.S. Government to put an end to its implementation.
>
> WE ASK the U.S. Government to comply with the 17 successive resolutions approved at the United Nations General Assembly and put an end to the economic, commercial and financial embargo it has imposed on Cuba."

Moreover, we believe that the attempt to impose isolation on Cuba, which today is an integral part of the Latin American and Caribbean region, which is a member of the Rio Group and other organizations and regional mechanisms, which carries out a policy of cooperation and solidarity with the people of the region, and which promotes the full integration of the Latin American and Caribbean peoples, has failed. Therefore, no reason exists to justify its exclusion from the Summit of the Americas.

13) The developed countries have allocated no less than $8 trillion towards rescuing the financial structure that has collapsed. They are the same ones that do not comply with spending a small sum to reach the Millennium Goals or 0.7% of GDP for Official Development Aid. Never before have we seen so nakedly the hypocrisy of the discourse of the rich countries. Cooperation has to be established without conditions and adjusted to the agendas of the receiving countries, simplifying the procedures, making resources accessible and privileging issues of social inclusion.

14) The legitimate struggle against narco-trafficking and organized crime, and any other manifestation of the so-called "new threats," should not be utilized as excuses for carrying out acts of interference or intervention against our countries.

15) We are firmly convinced that change, which all the world is hoping for, can only come about through the organization, mobilization and unity of our peoples.

As the Liberator Simón Bolívar well stated: "The unity of our peoples is not simply the chimera of men, but an inexorable fate."

Rich Countries Must Pay Their Ecological Debt

Bolivia

Full text at www.ecologicaldebt.org/documentos/bolivia250409.pdf

We call on developed countries to commit to deep emission reductions in order to advance the objective of avoiding dangerous anthropogenic interference with the climate system and its consequences, to reflect their historical responsibility for the causes of climate change, and to respect the principles of equity and common but differentiated responsibilities in accordance with the UN Framework Convention on Climate Change (UNFCCC).

The causes and consequences of climate change

Since 1750 the emission of greenhouse gases has increased significantly as the result of human activities. These emissions have accumulated in the atmosphere leading to current atmospheric concentrations, which now far exceed levels dating back hundreds of thousands of years. These concentrations, in turn, are warming the Earth with significant and catastrophic effects.

Current levels of warming are already damaging forest, mountain and other ecosystems, melting snow and glaciers, thinning ice sheets, causing the oceans to rise and acidify, threatening coral reefs and intensifying droughts and floods, fires and extreme weather events. These adverse effects threaten to worsen the damages already produced by the current global warming on the Earth's systems.

The countries most vulnerable to the adverse effects of climate change are developing countries. Climate-induced disasters, water stress, adverse impacts on agriculture, threats to coastlines, ecosystems and infrastructure, and altered disease vectors are already imposing substantial and rising costs, damages and setbacks in development – undermining developing countries' rights and aspirations to development.

The historical cumulative emissions debt of developed countries

Responsibility for the majority of the historical emissions contributing to current atmospheric concentrations and to current and committed future warming lies with developed countries. Developed countries with less than 20% of the world's population are responsible for around three quarters of historical emissions. Their current per person emissions continue to exceed those of developing countries by a factor of four. Their accumulated historic emissions on a per person basis exceed those of developing countries by a factor of eleven.

Developed countries – which have contributed disproportionately to the causes of climate change – now seek to appropriate a disproportionate share of the Earth's remaining environmental space. By basing their future emission allowances on their past excessive level of emissions, they seek an entitlement to continue emitting at 70% or more of their 1990 levels through until 2020 (i.e. consistent with reductions of 30% or less). At the same time, they propose limiting developing countries – which most need environmental space in the course of their development – to much lower levels of per person emissions.

The excessive past, current and proposed future emissions of developed countries are depriving and will further deprive developing countries of an equitable share of the much diminished environmental space they require for their development and to which they have a right. By overconsuming the Earth's limited capacity to absorb greenhouse gases, developed countries have run up an "emissions debt" which must be repaid to developing countries by compensating them for lost environmental space, stabilizing temperature and by freeing up space for the growth required by developing countries in the future.

Quantifying developed countries' mitigation commitments

Developed countries' commitments to reduce emissions should be sufficient to address their historical emission debt, minimize their contribution to further adverse impacts on the climate and developing countries, provide sufficient environmental space for developing countries to develop, and conform with the ultimate objective of the Convention.

The scale and timing of these commitments should reflect the latest scientific information and be rooted in the objective, principles and provisions of the UNFCCC and its Kyoto Protocol. They should be quantified on the basis of a clear and objective methodology that reflects, among other factors:

▸ The historic responsibility of developed countries for current atmospheric concentrations;
▸ The historic and current per-capita emissions of developed countries; and
▸ The share of global emissions required by developing countries in order to meet their first overriding priorities which are the economic and social development and poverty eradication.

The establishment of assigned amounts of emissions for developed countries is a question of policy as well as science and must address issues of equity as well as effectiveness. The level of their assigned amounts also bears a close relationship to the extent of their obligations to provide compensation for the effects of climate change. Bearing in mind these considerations, the Annex to this document offers some possible elements of a methodology for evaluating developed countries' emission debt and associated further mitigation commitments.

Emissions and adaptation debts are components of climate and ecological debt

Despite not being responsible for the problem of global warming, developing countries are among the worst affected its adverse impacts. The historical emissions of developed countries, as well as denying developing countries the atmospheric space they need for development, are harming poor countries and people who live daily with rising costs, damages and lost opportunities for development.

These impacts are the direct result of current atmospheric concentrations, which have been caused predominantly by emissions from developed countries. Developed countries are thus responsible for compensating developing countries for their contribution to the adverse effects of climate change as part of an "adaptation debt" owed by developed countries to developing countries.

Developed countries "climate debt" – the sum of their emissions debt and adaptation debt – are part of a broader ecological debt reflecting their heavy environmental footprint, excessive consumption of resources, materials and energy and contribution to declining biodiversity and ecosystem services.

Repaying their climate debt

The climate debt of developed countries must be repaid, and this payment must begin with the outcomes to be agreed in Copenhagen.

Developing countries are not seeking economic handouts to solve a problem we did not cause. What we call for is full payment of the debt owed to us by developed countries for threatening the integrity of the Earth's climate system, for over-consuming a shared resource that belongs fairly and equally to all people, and for maintaining lifestyles that continue to threaten the lives and livelihoods of the poor majority of the planet's population. This debt must be repaid by freeing up environmental space for developing countries and particular the poorest communities.

There is no viable solution to climate change that is effective without being equitable. Deep emission reductions by developed countries are a necessary condition for stabilizing the Earth's climate. So too are profoundly larger transfers of technologies and financial resources than so far considered, if emissions are to be curbed in developing countries and they are also to realize their right to development and achieve their overriding priorities of poverty eradication and economic and social development.

Any solution that does not ensure an equitable distribution of the Earth's limited capacity to absorb greenhouse gases, as well as the costs of mitigating and adapting to climate change, is destined to fail.

Developed countries must therefore fulfill their responsibilities through deeper domestic emission reduction commitments than so far considered in the current negotiations, and through all available means to generate the opportunities required for developing countries to achieve their development.

Developing countries are willing to play their part in addressing this common challenge. But any such participation can and must be based on the provisions of the Convention, on a clear understanding of the causes of climate change and its consequences, and on an equitable approach to stabilizing the Earth's climate system and to ensuring a sustainable future.

To Save Humanity We Must Return to Our Roots

Hugo Blanco

Received from Hugo Blanco, May 2009. Translated by Richard Fidler.
The overriding principle of the present system is: "to make as much money as possible in the shortest possible time." To do this, it crushes the majority of humanity, damaging the environment and sacrificing the future of our descendants.

It produces a self-serving ethical system, some of whose principles are clearly enunciated while others are necessarily obscured by hypocrisy.

The term "democracy" is used in the same hypocritical way as it was by our predecessors who created the word. Democracy means government by the people. When it was invented in Greece, it referred to the dictatorship of the male slaveholders over women and slaves. Now it refers to the dictatorship of the big multinational companies over the vast majority of humanity.

This dictatorship is exercised through states governed by people elected in "democratic elections," participation in which requires a huge amount of money consumed in propaganda.

The major companies dominate governments, armies and the entire state apparatus: parliament, judiciary, police, education, transportation, etc.

They control the media. Through their ministries of education and the media they teach us that humanity has evolved from cultures belonging to the past and that this evolution progresses to higher levels day by day. What is "modern" is best.

Happiness is achieved by buying things, the ads tell us daily. What is important is the sale of commodities, and people are commodities.

"Modern agriculture is best." It practices monoculture over large areas, planting year after year the most commercially profitable varieties of produce, irrespective of what people need most. It doesn't matter that the soil is depleted or becomes a paradise for pests. These disadvantages are overcome with the use of chemical fertilizers, herbicides and insecticides. So what if that ruins the soil, when other soil will be available in this or some other country or continent.

The price of wood is leading to the devastation of the Amazon and other forests, and there is no reforestation because it costs too much and it is cheaper to bribe the authorities than to enforce protective laws.

What does it matter if the Amazon jungle, the lungs of the world, is being destroyed and global warming is on the rise, when the important thing is to make as much money as possible in the least possible time.

The advance of mining and the extraction of hydrocarbons are an important part of "progress." No matter that water sources are poisoned, that agriculture is harmed, or that more and more inhabitants are left without water, the important thing is the money that is provided. And in this activity it is much cheaper to elude environmental protection legislation by bribing the authorities that are supposed to enforce it.

Another feature of "progress" is the food industry. Instinct told us that we ought to like sweet things so we would consume fruit that gave us vitamins. Now we consume sweets without fruit that do not give us vitamins, and fruits without sugar since they were harvested while still green and ripened artificially.

We have to feed ourselves in the "modern" way with transgenic foods, with foods using preservatives, with McDonalds products and others of that type, eating meat from animals that have been bred not in terms of the interests of the animal or the consumer but in terms of producing more money in less time (like what are called "factory chickens" in Peru).

We have to care for our health in the "modern" way, using "modern" medicine, manufactured by the big laboratories. Here is what the Mexican ecologist Silvia Ribeiro reports about them:

> The big pharmaceutical industry has been notable since its origins for its unscrupulous search for profit. For many years it was the industrial sector with the highest percentage of earnings. As of 2008, ten companies controlled 55 percent of the global pharmaceutical market. When they don't find new markets, they invent them. They "create" ailments, fobbing off new items on situations that did not require treatment with drugs, through aggressive marketing on their supposed benefits.

The cosmetics section in "first world" supermarkets is enormous. The media tell us all about our need to consume in order to be happy, to enhance our self-esteem, to acquire social standing. Society must produce and produce, in order later to consume and consume.

Vacations, too, are being taken over by the consumer society: tourism companies, hotels, voyages, etc. "Discover Europe in 15 days," even if that only means standing with your back to Notre Dame Cathedral in Paris for 10 minutes: what counts is that you get some photos of it in order to be a hit with your friends. Those with the most money, who accumulate the most, are the most important, irrespective of whether this produces stress and increased consumption of drugs.

They manufacture wars on which three trillion dollars will be spent in a decade, financed from the taxes paid by the people, killing hundreds of thousands of innocent persons. This is done to benefit the weapons manufacturers, and, in the case of Iraq, for oil as well.

Tax havens are used to combine the money from "legal" transactions with the proceeds of drug trafficking, money stolen by the rulers, money from the "illegal" sale of weapons, etc.

In the United States a robot has been invented at a cost of $3,000 that moves about connected to tomato plants; when the plants signal that they are parched the robot sprays them with a burst of water. When the tomatoes are ripe, the machine plucks the fruit. Of course, there are millions of people prepared to do that work in order to get a meal, but that is not "progress."

Much more can be said about "progress," but let us end by saying that such "progress" is bringing about increased global warming which, combined with many other forms of environmental contamination, will mean that the human species will cease to exist within 100 years.

Building a new world

An ever-increasing number of people are looking for "another possible world," to which all the social and collective struggles with some exceptions are bringing us closer; and the electoral victories, as in Ecuador and Bolivia, are positive.

However, the construction of the new world is not initiated by "taking power," although we can get a glimpse of it in the construction or reconstruction at the base of societies that are truly democratic.

That is what Raúl Zibechi refers to in his article "The movements in the hegemonic transition."[1] As tools for change, he points to the movements which, in both countryside and city, are germinating forms of power in opposition to the system in a number of ways: factories being taken over by their workers, settlements of landless farmers, autonomous indigenous communities or more diverse collectives (young people, women, homeless, unemployed). The forms of power that ultimately emerge, he says, will serve as an inspiration for others below them who, lacking experience in the movement, will sense that there are other, collective, communitarian, non-market ways to live and experience, in which use-values replace exchange-values.

He shows that they can constitute a beginning of new ways of life, less hierarchical and oppressive than the present ones.

In another article Zibechi shows us the Colombian experience:

> In the mountains in the north of the department of Cauca, in Colombia's central mountain range, about 100 km to the south of Calí, there has been unfolding for several decades one of the most remarkable experiments in building a world unlike the hegemonic one of today....
>
> In the middle of the war a miracle appears, nourished by the Indigenous of the North of Cauca with their projects of life and hope. In a small area... they have initiated an experiment that is unique in South America, but which has much in common with the neo-Zapatismo of Chiapas and its construction of a new world.... In this region, 25,000 families live in 304 villages, small rural settlements, and govern themselves through 18 cabildos, an indigenous authority....
>
> The power structure has been built from the bottom up: village assemblies elect constables that accompany the governors of the cabildos, who in turn are elected by large assemblies in each of the indigenous defensive areas. The cabildos are forms of indigenous power deeply rooted in territories or reserves.

The best example of collective self-government is that of the Zapatista brothers in Mexico. In the area of Chiapas that is their stronghold, the Zapatista Army of National Liberation (EZLN) does not give orders, it simply serves as a defense for the indigenous society against the country's prevailing aggressive capitalism.

Here the people as a whole govern through the so-called Juntas de Buen Gobierno, which are filled in rotation by the indigenous, their mandates revocable at any time that the society chooses.

Here nature is respected. Here one is educated in accord with the necessities of life. Here children are respected when they are playing together without being inhibited, even in international political ceremonies.

In the Peruvian countryside we have many examples of the construction of autonomous and democratic power.

In 1962, in a province of Cusco, we carried out an agrarian reform, distributing land to the indigenous that was the "property" of more than one hundred landowners. Faced with violent repression by the state, we fought back and forced them to give in and today the land remains in the hands of the peasants. Years later, the indigenous communities of Puno, in the midst of a repressive internal war, recovered as communal property 1,250,000 hectares of lands that had belonged to huge bureaucratized cooperatives strung together by a military government. Today those lands continue to be held by the *comuneros*. These actions mean that Peru is today the country in America with the highest percentage of land-owning farmers working collectively or individually.

The Provincial Municipality of Datem del Marañón, whose mayor is the Awajún indigenous Emir Masengkai Tempo, announced on April 20, 2009 the implementation of the Ecological and Economic Territorial and Zoning Arrangement Plan of the indigenous peoples of the area.

The work of implementing the management plans and documents will be undertaken by representative organizations of each indigenous people.

In this sense, the plan will prioritize the protection of areas of ecological, spiritual and economic importance according to the conception of each native community. Under it, the indigenous peoples themselves will be the ones who determine what needs to be done to fulfill the objectives.

The provincial municipality authorities will ensure that this provision complies with the requirements of Convention (No. 169) concerning Indigenous and Tribal Peoples in Independent Countries of the International Labour Organization (ILO).

Datem del Marañón, a province in the Lareto region of Peru, is inhabited by the Achuar, Awajún, Cocama-Cocamilla, Chayahuita or Chawi, Shibilo, Shapra, Kandozi, Quechua and Wampis or Huambisa peoples.

A more or less democratic, more or less self-governing indigenous community subsists in most of the countryside.

In the district of Limatambo, when Wilbert Rozas was the mayor, the municipal budget was drafted by the assemblies of the indigenous communities, and not the mayor or the municipal council.

In the north of Peru, by order of the community, Rondas Campesinas (Peasant Patrols) have arisen to replace corrupt judges and police in law enforcement. After waging a fierce fight against them, which it was unable to win, the "law" had to recognize them. These institutions have to some degree spread to other areas.

In the marginal neighbourhoods of Lima and other cities, where the homeless have occupied vacant lands, they have set up collective self-government bodies that organize the work of the community, self-defense against attacks from the state, and the administration of internal justice.

Even in the midst of the capital city, Lima, juntas vecinales (neighborhood councils) have arisen to handle security and green belts.

The natives of the jungles, Shipibos and others, head up educational institutions in their own languages.

In Peru, collective "people's power" is advancing in the economic field, in native art and medicines.

The current economic crisis also brings forth some interesting opinions in the urban space of the "first world" in this regard, For example, Noam Chomsky replying to questions by RealTV interviewer Paul Jay:

... but nationalization [of the banks] is only one step towards democratization. The question is, who manages them? Who makes the decisions? Who controls them? Now in the case of nationalized institutions, it's still top-down. But, it doesn't have to be. Again, it's not a law of nature that institutions can't be democratically run.

Paul Jay: What would it look like?

Noam Chomsky: What would they look like? The participation by workers councils, by community organizations – meetings, discussions in which policies are made. That's how a democracy is supposed to work. We're very far from that.

Even in the political system – take say, primaries. The way our system works, candidates running for office, their campaign managers, go to some town in New Hampshire and they set up a meeting and the candidate comes in and says "Here's what a nice guy I am, vote for me." People either believe him or not and go home.

Suppose we had a democratic system that worked the other way around. The people in the town of New Hampshire would get together at conferences, meetings, public organizations and so on and they would work out the policies that they would like to see and then if somebody is running for office, he could come if they want. They could invite him and he would listen to them. They would say: "Look, here's the policies we want you to implement, if you can do this, we'll allow you to represent us, but we'll recall you if you're not doing it.[2]

A few days ago, when 35,000 persons came together in London to protest the G20 summit, one of the demonstrators said: "...we want the earth. Give us back our planet. We want it; you've got it. We're gonna take it, and you should be good-humored about it. You are incompetent idiots who have messed everything up, and you should step aside and let the people take over."[3]

How to avoid the early extinction of our species?

As stated, "progress" is bringing about increased global warming which, combined with many other forms of environmental contamination, will mean that the human species ceases to exist within 100 years.

With this in mind, the British magnate Richard Branson, owner of Virgin Airlines, sponsored a contest to award 25 million dollars to the scientist who came up with a commercially viable design that would eliminate greenhouse gases. People said: "But you too are contributing to global warming with your airline." To which he replied: "What do you want me to do? I could ground my airline today, but British Airways would simply take its place."

He was completely right. It is not a problem of knowledge or an individual moral problem. The solution is not in changing peoples' attitudes, or in getting everyone to turn out the lights on a particular day or stop throwing away plastic bags. That's all very good, but while we are doing that, the big companies are continuing to mount a huge and brutal assault on the planet.

The problem will not be resolved as long as businesses are free to destroy the environment.

Nor will be it be resolved until the capitalist system disappears.

That system, which holds power on a world scale, dominates not only in a material way: it has penetrated the brains of its victims, so that they share its ethic in whole or in part, an ethic that in addition to being male chauvinist and racist, makes us think that the existing system is the only one possible, that capitalist principles are eternal, undebateable and irreplaceable.

Therefore, the only possibility of salvation is to replace this system by the other possible world, the one that, as we will show later, we can already see in an embryonic form in small and different practices in various places and in different forms, in which governance is exercised from below, not above, and in which the decision makers are the community, not individuals.

If we look closely, we will see that those who come closest to this style of politics are the indigenous communities, which is not surprising since they are the ones closest to the original moral principles of humanity.

Let us read a little of what the Uruguayan writer Eduardo Galeano says:

> How could we?
>
> To be mouth or mouthful, hunter or hunted. That was the question.
>
> We deserved scorn, or at most pity. In the hostile wilderness no one respected us, no one feared us. We were the most vulnerable beasts in the animal kingdom, terrified of night and the jungle, useless as youngsters, not much better as adults, without claws or fangs or nimble feet or keen sense of smell.
>
> Our early history is lost in mist. It seems all we ever did was break rocks and beat each other with clubs.
>
> But one might well ask: Weren't we able to survive, when survival was all but impossible, because we learned to share our food and band together for defense? Would today's me-first, do-your-own-thing civilization have lasted more than a moment? (*Espejos* – Eduardo Galeano)[4]

Let us mention some of the principles of indigenous culture:
- ▸ "Living well." Happiness does not consist in the accumulation of money or property, or in the possession of "modern" things, but in living peacefully and without stress.
- ▸ In opposition to the individualism that rules the world today, communal solidarity – the collective "I" – is maintained. Issues affecting the community are resolved not by an individual or group of individuals but by the wider community.
- ▸ Mother Nature is a living being. As are all of her components, including

the hills and rivers. They are deeply loved and respected.

▸ "Command through obeying," the Zapatista slogan that has resonated around the world, applies to the indigenous communities of all countries.

▸ Also popularized by the Zapatistas is the slogan "Public servants must serve the public, not themselves." It is practiced to a greater or lesser degree by the indigenous peoples of each country in their resistance to the contamination of the system.

▸ Agreement is reached by consensus, not by majority vote.

I will elaborate briefly:

Living well. The Amazonian native – especially one who remains in voluntary isolation from "civilization," but also others to a large extent – emerges from his collective hut with a bow and arrows, and when he sees something worth hunting he does so. He passes through his parcel of cultivated land with its various species of distinct life cycles imitating nature. If he sees something that is ripe he picks it, if he thinks it needs some attention he provides it. And he continues on his way, returning to his hut without knowing whether he has been "walking" or "working." Some time later the cultivated parcel of land will revert to the jungle and cultivation will resume in some other place.

A *hacendado*, or landowner, offered to give a native a machete if he cleared a particular area. He did this so quickly and so well that the hacendado, after giving him the promised machete, offered to give him another if he cleared a space that was just a quarter of the previous area. A really good deal! The native gave him a puzzled look and said: "I have only one right hand, why would I want two machetes?" And he left. He did not want to "progress," but only to live well.

The Andean farmer does not seek to produce the most possible per hectare, or larger produce. He takes pride in the diversity of the varieties he cultivates.

More than once I have seen in Peru – and I am told this is true in Bolivia as well – that when someone wants to buy the entire production without any discount from a poor person, whether an adult or a child, who is selling directly on his or her land, the vendor will say "No." To him or her, selling is not only a commercial act, it is also a human relationship that one has no desire to do without.

For the 85-year-old indigenous Benedicto Torres in Chaupimayo, living well meant rising at five o'clock in the morning and going out to farm his land.

Collectivism. A number of American languages – Quechua, Aymara, Guarani, Mapuche and Mayan languages – use different words to convey the concept of "we" or "us," when speaking with a person from outside the community. One of these words is the "collective I" of the community, while the other includes the person being addressed.

In Peru, major struggles are still being waged in defence of the ayllu, the collective form of organization being fought against by the state.

We referred earlier to what Zibechi showed us about Colombia.

Respect for nature. Unlike "modern" agriculture, which destroys the soil, indigenous agriculture cares for the soil. The indigenous farmer knows that his ancestors lived from it, and that he lives from it as will his sons. Crops are diversified to avoid the spread of blights and absorb distinct nutrients. Crops are rotated to minimize pests and allow mutual nourishment of species.

We know from their remains that terraced farming was practiced by the Incas and pre-Incas in Peru, to prevent erosion. The heirs of those cultures use those terraces when the oppressor state allows it, and they make new terraces. The indigenous people use organic fertilizers. We have mentioned the cultivation of the jungle in imitation of nature and the reversion of those lands to the jungle.

Among all the indigenous peoples, the best produce is provided as an offering to Mother Nature.

Command through obeying. This is a product of the community's mandate. In some communities, after electing their authorities they whip them symbolically to remind them that they are under the rule of the people as a whole.

Serving the public means serving the public, not serving oneself. Often, when someone is appointed to a position, he or she will complain: "I have already served, there are others who still haven't, appoint them," which is also an indication of the principle of rotation of responsibilities. Although the official "laws" prevent it, there are still cases in which a mandate is revoked when the community considers this is necessary.

Consensus. This means a patient search for agreement involving lengthy discussions in which the problematic aspects of the various views expressed are ironed out until an overwhelming majority if not absolute unanimity is achieved. Under this method, the agreement will be implemented by everyone. This is a much more effective process than one in which a majority decides while many remain unconvinced. If the consensus agreement proves to be mistaken, it will be corrected and there will no "guilty ones."

* * *

Of course, even among the indigenous peoples these cultural and ethical roots are being undermined by "modernity," which treats them as outdated: many indigenous use chemical fertilizers, some accept individual ownership of land as progress, and some abandon the land to move to the city and feel superior to those who remain behind.

In their fight to take their destiny into their own hands the indigenous peoples have to accept the use of tools that are foreign to them, such as building political parties that are not characteristic of our culture.

While such parties sometimes serve to promote the struggle, they often divide the communities, in much the same way as religion does, between groups of the select and the rest. We understand that in order to participate in the electoral struggle, the dominant culture forces us to form parties. An example is the Partido Pachacuti in Ecuador. But that party, in supporting Gutiérrez and accommodating some indigenous in positions in a government that was not theirs, divided the Ecuadorian indigenous movement. Today it supports the progressive government of Correa, but it is critical support because, among other things, that government continues to ride roughshod over the indigenous right to prevent mining on their territory.

In Bolivia the indigenous found they had to equip themselves with a political instrument; since they were denied recognition they had to use the MAS. However, the latter, immersed in the party system, limits democracy because, among other things, the people could not directly elect their representatives to the Constituent Assembly and had to vote for the person selected by the MAS party. The Bolivian revolution is a work in progress, and the government of the indigenous Evo Morales acts in reality as an intermediary between the indigenous movement and the system that continues to oppress them. We should bear in mind that the vice-president has championed "Andean capitalism" from the start.

The NGOs are also contradictory tools. On the one hand, they promote the indigenous, while on the other they subject the movement to whoever provides the money, the apparent "leaders" are not always representative, and the NGOs generally practice verticality.

The same things applies to the federations and confederations that have to accommodate the struggle for indigenous demands within the prevailing system, its norms and customs, and this distorts their function.

Undeniable indigenous resurgence

Despite the deterioration of its principles, it is undeniable that the indigenous movement is advancing and gradually and consciously recovering those principles. I refer to our continent but I assume that something similar albeit not as visible is happening on other continents about which I know little.

The reason is that, more than ever before, capitalism is attacking the basic indigenous principles, and this forces us to take a stand in their defence.

We have already referred to the Zapatistas, and we take this opportunity to say that they are the best refutation of the accusation of "exclusive indigenous fundamentalism." On the one hand, they state clearly that "we are proud to be indigenous and we want to be respected as such," while on the other hand they consider themselves brothers of all oppressed Mexicans and of humanity in general. For example, the very first international meeting on the theme of "For Humanity, Against Neoliberalism" was called many years prior to the World Social Forums and was held in the clay of Chiapas.

Today, through "the other campaign," they are coordinating their action with other sectors, indigenous or non-indigenous, that are fighting for the liberation of Mexico and other countries. They coordinate horizontally, they are not "the leadership," and they do not issue orders.

This is the best example but it is not the only one. With all the weaknesses identified above, the indigenous people of Bolivia and Ecuador are making unstoppable advances. The Mapuches in Chile and Argentina are a minority fighting bravely in defence of nature and respect for their identity. In Paraguay the indigenous movement has been the major force behind the Lugo government, while criticizing it for its failure to restore their rights. In Colombia, further to what I said earlier, we recently witnessed the great march on Bogotá of 40,000 indigenous, even though the government is killing the indigenous.

Our brothers and sisters are fighting for the same principles in Guatemala, Venezuela, the United States and Canada and wherever indigenous populations are to be found.

In Peru the struggle was delayed by the government's internal war against Sendero Luminoso (Shining Path) and the Movimiento Revolucionario Tupac Amaru that we suffered for 20 years, which cost the life of 70,000 Peruvians, the majority of them indigenous. In addition many were "disappeared" or jailed, and their organizations smashed.

Since that war ended, the indigenous movement has been rising from the ashes. It is fighting primarily in defense of nature against the destruction caused by mining and petroleum companies that are fiercely defended by the government and the media. It is fighting in defense of the communal organization that is under attack from the state, and in defence of indigenous justice, indigenous medicine, our languages, our agriculture, the sacred coca leaf that the government is attacking under the empire's orders, in defence of art, in defence of indigenous nutrition, in defence of our cosmovision and all other cultural aspects.

There are many battles in the Peruvian highlands, but without a doubt the vanguard is the indigenous population of the jungle, which is the least contaminated, the least "civilized" and which suffers the most discrimination.

Recently they have been fighting in defence of humanity by protecting the forest that is the lungs of the world, aiming their deadly arrows at the government, and demanding that the parliament repeal two anti-indigenous decree laws it has issued.

Return to our roots

If we return to the ethical values of our origins, we will readily understand that the fate of humanity cannot be left to a handful of multinational companies, but must be determined by humanity as a whole. Just as in an indigenous community any problem affecting the collectivity is resolved by it and not an individual, the problem of global warming must be resolved by humanity as a whole and not by a handful of tycoons. It is the collectivity that must agree on whether a mine or factory should open or not.

Naturally, to be able to do this it is necessary to do away with capitalism and ensure that production is in the hands of society as a whole and not controlled by a top-down state as it was under the corrupt bureaucratic system of the Soviet Union, which fell as a result of its own internal rot.

It is the collectivity, not the companies or "the market," that must decide on what "modern" amenities we have to do without if we are to avoid the extinction of our species.

A positive development recently has been the rise of an "ecosocialist" current in the urban population. Unfortunately, a superiority complex in relation to the indigenous, sowed by the dominant capitalist ideology, has inhibited the urban compañeros' understanding of how in reality they still adhere to two of the moral principles – hierarchy and predation – imposed by the colonization, against which the indigenous peoples of America and probably of the entire world have been fighting in practice for more than 500 years.

But the enemy, for its part, is well aware of the importance of the indigenous movement.

In 2000, the CIA noted the existence of a growing threat in Latin America: the rise of "indigenous protest movements."[5] In 1999, a similar report was issued by the Chilean armed forces: the active resistance of the Mapuche people to dispossession from their lands and the destruction of their natural resources by international big business was now a national security issue.

We must return to our original ethical roots, which does not mean returning to lifestyles of the past.

Those in the vanguard of this trend are the indigenous movements, the most outstanding of which is the Zapatistas of Mexico.

Let us build germs of democratic popular power in all possible spheres, in the countryside and cities alike. Let us strengthen the existing ones, cleanse them to the maximum, extend them and spread the word about them.

Let us fight to deepen democracy in all the institutions promoting forms of direct democracy and the right of recall when the social base so wishes. Let us fight for popular election of public officials, not their vertical appointment. The "experts" have the right to convince us about the appropriateness of someone's appointment, but not to appoint that person themselves.

Let us continue to fight capitalism, the essence of which, as we note every day, is the dictatorship of money, on the altar of which it sacrifices humanity, nature and the descendents of the capitalists themselves. And that means we must confront the governments that it uses as its instruments.

I appeal to those fighting in the cities for a new world that they pay attention to those who are in the vanguard of the struggle against the system: the indigenous peoples. They must overcome prejudices of superiority fostered by the oppressors and promoted through consumer society. Unfortunately, I have found that this is not easy, as these prejudices are deeply rooted in the minds of the non-indigenous and even of the indigenous themselves.

I note that these prejudices are unfortunately shared to some degree by the majority of non-indigenous "revolutionaries," who still allow the system to impose its moral principles in their heads.

The sooner the profoundly anti-systemic significance of indigenous struggles is understood, the greater will be the support for those struggles by the non-indigenous.

The sooner they free themselves from the moral domination of capitalism, the closer we will be to winning the new world that we desire.

Another world is still possible, let us continue to build it.

Translator's Notes

1 "Los movimientos en la transición hegemónica." *La Jornada*, March 27, 2009. http://tinyurl.com/pq4k7e.

2 Chomsky on the Obama/Geithner Rescue Plan, http://sacsis.org.za/site/article/121.19.

3 Democracy Now!, "35,000 Protest in London Ahead of G20 Summit." http://www.democracynow.org/2009/3/30/headlines.

4 Soon to appear in English translation as *Mirrors: Stories of Almost Everyone*, http://tinyurl.com/pdlsqf, from which the above translation is taken.

5 Central Intelligence Agency, *Global Trends 2015: A Dialogue About the Future With Nongovernment Experts*. http://tinyurl.com/pfep5c, p.46. See also: http://tinyurl.com/qymymo.

7: BUILDING A CLIMATE EMERGENCY MOVEMENT

*"Environmental devastation will not be stopped in
conference rooms and treaty negotiations:
only mass action can make a difference."*
—Belem Ecosocialist Declaration—

*Real change will only come through the mobilization of broad social forces
with the power and determination to fight and win.*

In Part Eight:

▸ **Only Political Activism and Class Struggle Can Save the Planet**
*Patrick Bond argues that multinational institutions are so weighted
against change that there is no point in trying to reform them: we have
to depend on our own sources of power.*

▸ **Crisis, Challenge and Mass Action** Two leaders of *the Global Justice Ecology Project explain why climate change activists must learn
the lessons of the anti-Vietnam-war movement and mobilize a massive,
powerful and diverse grassroots campaign.*

▸ **How Can We Build an Effective Movement?** *Australian climate
activist Kamala Emanuel's discussion of the strengths and weaknesses
of the 2007 Walk Against Warming illustrates the kind of careful consideration of program and organization that is essential for building a
successful movement.*

▸ **Workers and Climate Change** and **The Three Decisive Social
Forces that Can Stop Climate Change.** *Editorials from Australia's
Green Left Weekly and Britain's Socialist Resistance.*

▸ **Climate Change is a Trade Union Issue.** *A talk by Tony Kearns
of the Communication Workers Union (UK), to the Campaign against
Climate Change's 2008 Trade Union Conference in London.*

▸ **Class Struggle and Ecology** *A discussion document by Liam Mac
Uaid, proposing climate change demands to win support among working people.*

Only Political Activism and Class Struggle Can Save the Planet

Interview with Patrick Bond

Links International Journal of Socialist Renewal, July 5, 2008

What has been the response of the market to the crisis of climate change and what role does carbon trading play?

Multinational corporations are trying to commodify the air, really, and the pollution in the air. They want the right to do that, and they want to codify it with the legal language of contracts and put a price on it and get credit for having already polluted.

And in a sense they're going to get, as the European carbon trading system grants them, further rights to keep polluting. And that's cold, hard cash. They can sell those rights, so that it's not "the polluter pays" principle, it's "the polluter earns."

With the European trading system, many critiques have emerged from within the financial sector about what a crazed market it is. It is a kind of market that you get by creating all sorts of fictional goods, like an apparent reduction in emissions. Well, who's really to judge whether this reduction did really occur in the way that is was argued? You need a very complex regulatory process to find out if that in fact is the case, and whether emissions that would have taken place have been avoided and they should be given credit for it.

It must be determined whether additional emissions have really been mitigated, and what the value of that should be. So it's so hard to measure, and its chaotic to police.

Mainstream environmentalists have such a hang-up about thinking outside their box – because they want to be relevant and maintain ties to the governments and to the UN system – that they're becoming more of a barrier to progress.

It is critical to call some groups on their support for carbon trading as a supposed solution, as it is putting money into the hands of some of the worst polluters and the financiers and hedge funds rather than actually getting the resources we need for a just transition.

Can the UN play a useful role in the campaign to stop runaway climate change?

Fifteen to twenty thousand people protested at the World Conference Against Racism [WCAR in Durban, South Africa, 2001] and over 30,000 at the Summit on Sustainable Development [SSD in Johannesburg, 2001]. Protesters basically said to the UN: "You are now doing more harm than good, when you leave out addressing Zionism, leave out reparations for addressing the impacts of colonialism and Apartheid from the WCAR, and when you infuse the SSD with so much private-public partnership rhetoric that it puts up the world for sale and does nothing for poverty."

The balance of forces on a global scale is so adverse to any progressive change, with neoliberals still dominant and neo-conservatives still being deployed by US President George Bush, like World Bank head Robert Zoellick. There is a neo-con/neo-lib fusion, and a basic acceptance by the global elites that the US can occupy Iraq, for instance.

And that means that, I fear, at the stage we're at of human history, global-scale solutions to reforming these multilateral institutions is an enormous waste of time and energy and a distraction from real activism.

I would say that the changes we need are so dramatic, that laziness and sloth you find in the UN prevents us from getting there. And the US's braking role in this is so powerful, and wouldn't change necessarily with a President Barack Obama.

So we really should be doing much more direct action, and local and international solidarity between groups that take serious campaigning issues such as "Keep the oil in the soil," "Keep the coal in the hole," and "Keep resources in the ground." That way, we really will build a movement, a movement of victims of climate change.

Environmental concerns are often pitted against workers' jobs by governments and the mainstream media. Do you think there is a convergence between workers' rights and environmental sustainability?

There are possibilities to take grievances that are overlapping and interlocking. We need to make the arguments for a just transition away from the really energy-intensive jobs with low pay and high danger, towards a job-safe alternative that could retrain these workers to put together solar hot water heaters.

Sustainable alternatives could receive huge subsidies and be organized in a way that would meet all people's needs. It would require of course big infusions of money, but at least not big infusions of very scarce energy resources.

We have a situation where BHP Billiton has over a thousand workers in its major production cycle, and those workers may be threatened if we succeed in saying the smelters that BHP Billiton runs should be closed.

The reason people are calling for this is because the smelters take 10% of the electricity of the country and only give half a percent of GDP and have not created many jobs. The question is whether we can get a just transition arrangement that would allow those metal workers to instead be making hot water heaters with solar technologies and putting them together in millions of homes.

Those kinds of job creation possibilities would be immense compared to the losses we would have if we shut down that supply of electricity.

If the labour movement says "we want to keep our jobs in the coal mines and in the smelters," we have to have a really frank talk and say "Comrades, couldn't you find an alternative plan, with us, that gives you more jobs with better pay in the renewables sector, for example, in getting solar hot water heaters constructed en masse?"

Right now, it costs about A$1000 for one of these heaters in South Africa. It would really have a big, big impact on people's electricity bills. And to get hot water, for a whole lot of people it would be their first time. Providing solar hot water heaters would be a wonderful new challenge that can unite community and labour if we do it properly.

When we really get the trade unions to think through with us how to protect their workers' jobs and move even more jobs into this sector. That's a formidable potential coalition.

Can you explain the current struggle to de-commodify water and electricity in South Africa?

All of life is a class struggle. The class struggle over who pays what for water and electricity is acute. Suez, a big company from Paris, introduced really diabolical systems for controlling poor people's water in South Africa. The new "buyer politics" involving prepaid meters and low-quality sanitation systems were introduced to control low-income people and limit their access to water. And the same was going on with electricity.

So the resistance has raised slogans like, "Destroy the meters, enjoy the water," or else just going to bypasses and reconnecting people who've been disconnected.

Women in the impoverished Johannesburg township of Soweto are unable to pay [for electricity]. Community groups come round, rip out the electricity meter and they do a bypass with the local electrician working for free, helping to get the electricity free.

That's really a great step forward for advancing people's confidence in fighting for reforms and making the system react. They won some free, basic electricity.

And then the big challenge is to say, how much further change do we have to make? Getting free electricity is important, because people have to be allowed to survive, but really the strategy is not just to make an individual act. Because then success hinges upon whether the electricity company and the sheriff can come in and find the disconnected meter and the electricity still on and do something about it. The task is to find the policy to actually sustain free basic electricity.

Campaigners are saying, "when you hit the hedonistic levels of consumption of water and electricity, then you should really be paying a luxury consumption tax." That would redistribute resources in the system so that poor people would get it.

So in that way you'd decommodify it by providing it to people for free at the low consumption side, and high consumers get nailed with the luxury tax to also encourage conservation – so we don't build more coal-fired power plants or huge dams.

Hopefully, we get both red and green in that struggle and raise the spectre of socialism as a broader way to address these problems.

Some environmentalists promote a user-pays response to climate change, which seeks to charge ordinary people more for basic services to encourage energy efficiency.

This is what divides the ecosocialist movement from the environmentalists who can only see rising prices as a disincentive to consume without any care for the impact that this has on poor people.

Low income automobile users stuck out in the suburbs in British Columbia, Canada, are being hit by the same petrol tax – a carbon tax that applies to petrol. And through no fault of their own – the crazy housing market with all of its capitalist speculation has lead to housing being organized in this way – and through low-paying jobs, they're having to live further away. This makes them more addicted to their cars and they're more vulnerable to this tax.

So taking the class struggle into the climate campaign is so crucial. Not just for equity but to really have the right tactics.

A low-income person is still going to have to drive because public transport doesn't get out to those areas. If you really want to make the gains and raise the idea of actually building a public transport system, it's going to require a much bigger luxury consumption tax on the rich who can afford it, and probably won't even really notice for a while that their prices are going up. We need to get to the point where they do notice and they do stop their hedonistic consumption.

In that case, what is needed to confront climate change?
Well, it's so interesting that even Al Gore can say he's not sure why we haven't seen more direct action at coal-fired electricity generators or coal mines. So if you kind of have a mandate from a major politician to go and do disruptions then it's about time – we all need to do a lot more.

If you think about the high profile autonomous projects around the world that have been considered successful – and stealing water and electricity in

South Africa has been widely celebrated by autonomists – you have to say, well, that works for a little while.

But we really do need a longer term plan that will make the gains we've taken, on the streets and in the communities and in the shop floor, actually real. How can they be turned into good public policy?

There's always a huge danger that, when you fight as a socialist for a reform, that it ends up as a "reformist" reform – it strengthens the system and legitimizes it.

And obviously, no one wants to legitimize capitalism by just adding a bit of free water on top, but the kinds of reforms that socialist activists have in mind are instead "non-reformist" reforms, because they allow more space to struggle and allow you to live another day to make a bigger demand and they give the movement more momentum.

And that the logic that you've built into a reform, like free basic water and free basic electricity, counteracts the internal dynamics and laws of motion of the capitalist system. So such reforms are not about strengthening the system, they're weakening its internal dynamics.

So I think anytime there's a struggle of the working class that establishes very strategic reforms with great muscle, with many members, with many coalition and alliance partners, then we're talking about the possibility of challenging the capitalist system in very serious ways.

And a serious challenge to the capitalist system is what we need now to save the planet. An organized socialist planet is going to be required.

Crisis, Challenge and Mass Action

Anne Petermann and Orin Langelle

Global Justice Ecology Project's mission is to build local, national and international alliances with action to address the common root causes of social injustice, ecological destruction and economic domination. There is no better example of the interrelation of these issues than climate change. For this reason, GJEP has reframed our programs for indigenous rights, protection of forests, and global justice, as well as our work against militarism, economic domination and genetically engineered trees under the umbrella of climate change, since it touches all of these issues.

Climate change may well be humanity's greatest challenge. It is a crisis that must be rapidly addressed if catastrophe is to be averted. Already the impacts are being felt by millions in the world's most vulnerable and marginalized communities. Climate Change is at once a social and environmental justice issue, an ecological issue, and an issue of economic and political domination. As such, it must be addressed through broad and visionary alliances.

To successfully address the climate crisis, we must identify and address the deep root connections that link it to the myriad other crises we face- economic, militarism and war, as well as the intertwined crises of food, water and biodiversity loss. These crises are unified by their common roots in an economic system that encourages banks and corporations to ignore ethical and moral considerations and gamble with the Earth, peoples' lives, and our collective futures in the service of higher profits.

To paraphrase neoliberal economic pioneer Milton Friedman, "the corporation cannot be ethical. Its only responsibility is to make a profit for its shareholders."

Successfully addressing climate change will require a fundamental restructuring of our society that, if thoughtfully done, can lay a new foundation that will simultaneously help us achieve both global justice and ecological balance. What then will the solutions look like? The solutions to the climate crisis will be found in a model that is the opposite of the dominant economic model of incessant and unsustainable growth, oppression and injustice.

Solutions to climate change will not be controlled by corporations. There is no single "silver bullet" solution. Solutions to climate change will be many. They will be small in scale, locally controlled, bioregionally appropriate and socially just. Thousands of such solutions already exist. Opening space for dialogue in communities around the world to uncover, promote and launch these real solutions is key.

At the same time, the large-scale, ecologically and socially devastating corporate-controlled false solutions to climate change that currently dominate the conversation must be eliminated.

Climate justice must become a core part of all of our work. This will require broad and visionary alliances with people and movements around the world to begin the fundamental transformation of society that will enable us to collectively and successfully address the climate crisis.

Global Warming = Global War

> To me the question of the environment is more ominous than that of peace and war... I'm more worried about global warming than I am of any major military conflict. *–Hans Blix, UN Weapons Inspector*

Gross overproduction and overconsumption by and for industrialized countries has resulted in a severely shrinking resource base, as evidenced by pandemic ecological crises, the estimated loss of more than 300 species per day (as a conservative estimate), and by climate change itself. The intensification of the impacts from climate change are further depleting resources such as water and soils and threaten widespread destruction of forests and their biodiversity.

In February 2004, a Pentagon report on global warming was leaked to the press. It predicted that abrupt climate change could bring the planet to the edge of anarchy as countries develop a nuclear threat to defend and secure dwindling food, water and energy supplies. The report went on to say that the threat to global security vastly eclipses that of terrorism, concluding, "disruption and conflict will be endemic features of life. Once again warfare would define human life."

Wars for resources are nothing new. In 1980, Jimmy Carter pronounced the Carter Doctrine, declaring that the U.S. would take any actions necessary to ensure an uninterrupted supply of oil from the Middle East. A report by the World Bank published in 2000 found that countries that produce oil are forty times more likely to be involved in violent conflict.

The World Bank itself is one of the primary engines of global warming, despite the fact that at the 1992 Rio Earth Summit, the Bank was entrusted with promoting and developing renewable energies. According to the Sustainable Energy and Economy Network, since the Rio Earth Summit the World Bank has spent well over $30 billion on fossil fuel exploitation (seventeen times what they spent on renewables). In contrast to the World Bank's "mission" to help address poverty, over 80% of World Bank funded fossil fuels are exported to G8 countries (the eight richest countries in the world).

The World Bank is headed up by former US Trade Representative Robert Zoellick. Zoellick was one of the main architects of the ecologically and socially disastrous North American Free Trade Agreement (NAFTA) and is one of the people behind the Project for a New American Century, the neo-conservative blueprint for American Empire.

The World Bank is now insinuating itself into the global effort to stave off climate change by assuming the role of the world's carbon broker. The World Bank facilitates the global trade in carbon emissions (and profits handsomely through an estimated 13% trading commission). Carbon Trading has been a disaster. Many one-time proponents are now critics. It has resulted in the biggest corporate polluters making windfall profits, while leading to even higher emissions.

This means that the World Bank is directly driving climate change through fossil fuel development at the same time that it is taking a central role in the promotion and implementation of massive-scale, market-based false solutions to climate change-including not only carbon trading, but also carbon offsets like monoculture tree plantations, as well as incinerators, large-scale hydroelectric dams and agrofuels (large-scale unsustainable biofuels).

One of the Bank's newest carbon offset schemes is the Forest Carbon Partnership Facility, which seeks to reduce emissions from deforestation by privatizing remaining tracts of forest for the purpose of "protecting" them as carbon sinks so that companies in the north can use these emissions reductions to avoid reducing their own carbon emissions. The UN is negotiating a similar Reducing Emissions from Deforestation (REDD) proposal.

The International Indigenous Peoples' Forum on Climate Change declared that these reducing emissions from deforestation proposals will:

> result in more violations of Indigenous Peoples' rights. It will increase the violation of our human rights, our rights to our lands, territories and resources, steal our land, cause forced evictions, prevent access and threaten indigenous agricultural practices, destroy biodiversity and culture diversity and cause social conflicts. Under REDD, States and Carbon Traders will take more control over our forests.

The opportunism and irrationality of the climate capitalists cannot be overstated. With the spectre of climate catastrophe looming, oil companies are extracting oil from the tar sands in Alberta, Canada – a process that requires a massive and incredibly toxic strip mining process that includes the destruction of a tract of boreal forest the size of Florida. Extracting the oil from the tar sands is extremely energy intensive and puts out nearly three times the carbon emissions of conventional oil extraction. Not only are tar sands companies ignoring the fact that climate change means we need to be moving away from fossil fuels, not looking for new deposits; they are wantonly destroying vast stretches of intact native forests-which are considered critically important climate stabilizers and one of the keys of the planet eventually recovering from climate change.

Similarly, at the same time that scientists and arctic peoples are raising increasingly urgent alarms about the melting of the arctic regions due to global warming, oil companies are competing to claim the vast oil reserves that lie beneath the melting arctic, while at the same time celebrating that enough ice has melted to allow the opening of the Northwest Passage as a new trade route. There is no consideration paid even to the existing generation, much less future generations.

Disaster capitalism and climate change

Disaster capitalists are seizing on climate change as the newest means to:

▸ expand and consolidate corporate power. Agrofuels, for example, are being promoted through an unprecedented cooperation between oil, biotechnology, agro-industrial and timber corporations.

▸ further entrench centralized energy production by using propaganda and advertising to paint dirty energy "green." Examples of this include:

• *"Clean" coal.* Coal can never be clean. Use of coal, "clean" or not, still means massive-scale mountain-top removal mining or strip mining of indigenous lands. Additionally, "carbon sequestration" technologies, upon which "clean" coal schemes rely, are scientifically unproven.
• *Nuclear power.* Far from being emissions free, nuclear power puts out tremendous greenhouse gas emissions when the entire energy cycle of nuclear power is considered-from the construction of each facility to the mining and enrichment of uranium to the permanent problem of storing the waste.
• *Hydroelectricity.* From the manufacture of the dams themselves, to the methane created through the drowning of vast expanses of land, to the emissions released when water is churned through turbines, dams are yet another example of climate-unfriendly, socially unjust and ecologically destructive energy.

▸ take further control of the commons. Through schemes like the World Bank's Forest Carbon Partnership Facility, the UN's REDD [Reducing Emissions from Deforestation in Developing Countries] and through disaster response-after the Tsunami and Hurricane Katrina, land was taken away from many poor and marginalized people and handed over to developers.

▸ further the commodification of life. An especially egregious example of this is the work of scientific extremists to manufacture entirely synthetic organisms for the production of agrofuels.

▸ prolong the continuation of business as usual.

Among the various profit-making and power centralizing false solutions to climate change being promoted by the disaster capitalists, agrofuels are one of the most disturbing. First came agrofuels manufactured out of food crops like corn. These food-based fuels directly contributed to skyrocketing food prices and escalating rates of starvation, and were quickly and loudly denounced. But besides being a humanitarian disaster, agrofuels have also been proven to have serious impacts on the climate. Corn-based ethanol, for example, requires more fuel to create than is produced. Oil palm derived biodiesel is driving the massive deforestation of Indonesia. The logging and burning of Indonesia's forests each year has made Indonesia the third largest emitter of carbon on the planet. Deforestation is also accelerating in South America due to agrofuels. The rapidly expanding market for soy for both biodiesel and animal feed, coupled with the shift of many soy farmers in the U.S. to corn, due to its high market price (a result of the corn ethanol boom), has led to an acceleration of the destruction of forests in Argentina, Paraguay and Brazil (including in the Amazon) to make room for expanding soy monocultures. Deforestation annually contributes 20% of global greenhouse emissions annually.

The solution, we are now told, is so-called "second generation" agrofuel technologies that do not use food, but rather cellulose such as trees and switchgrass. These, however, will be plagued with the same problems. First, cellulosic agrofuels do nothing to address the question of agricultural land being taken over for production of fuel crops. Second, agrofuels are being used as the excuse to develop and commercialize new and unproven technologies such as the potentially disastrous genetic engineering of trees. GE trees are one of the favoured feedstocks for the future manufacture of cellulosic agrofuels. GE trees threaten to contaminate native forests and indigenous lands with engineered pollen and seeds, leading to devastating, irreversible and unpredictable impacts on forests, wildlife and humans. South Carolina-based ArborGen is developing GE cold-tolerant eucalyptus for deployment in vast plantations throughout the U.S. South. Eucalyptus are notorious for being highly invasive, flammable and water-intensive.

Eliminating corporate-controlled false solutions to climate change such as agrofuels is critical to make room for real, community-controlled solutions to global warming.

The growing global movement for climate justice

> This [international climate negotiation] process has become nothing but developed countries avoiding their responsibilities to cut emissions and pushing the responsibility onto developing countries. [False solutions]... sound very nice but they are trashing our indigenous lands. People are being relocated and even killed; my own people will soon be under water. The money from these projects is blood money. *–Fiu Mata'ese Elisara-Laula of the O Le Siosiomaga Society of Samoa, on the 2007 UN Climate Convention)*

The movement for climate justice grows out of the grassroots and community-based environmental justice movement. Climate change, though often regarded as strictly an environmental issue, has at its core important social justice concerns. Indigenous and rural peoples, women and the poor are already on the front lines of the climate struggle.

According to the UN's Environment and Human Security Group, by 2005 there were already over 20 million environmental refugees-more than refugees from war and political repression combined. By 2010 the group estimates the number could hit 50 million, growing to over 150 million by 2050. In 2007 Christian Aid suggested that nearly a billion people should be permanently displaced by 2050: 250 million by climate change-induced phenomena such as droughts, floods and hurricanes, and 645 million by dams and other development projects.

Some of the same people being threatened by impacts of climate change are also being threatened by proposed "solutions" to climate change. Because in many regions of the world indigenous peoples have been careful stewards of their ancestral lands, these biodiverse and rich lands are now being coveted by the World Bank, corporations and governments. Massive land grabs are taking place to privatize vast expanses of land where legal ownership is unclear or has not been established. These lands are prized for the rich resources they contain, for the development of agrofuel feedstocks or monoculture tree plantations; and for the important role they can play in offsetting carbon emissions.

Both the World Bank's Forest Carbon Partnership Facility, and the UN's Reducing Emissions from Deforestation in Developing Countries (REDD) schemes threaten to relocate resident communities under the guise of protecting the forests so that the carbon they absorb can be used to offset emissions in the North. This *environmental protection = human exclusion* model has been perfected over the years by the likes of Conservation International and the Nature Conservancy. At the World Bank's press conference during the 2007 UN Climate Convention in Bali, Indonesia where Zoellick announced the Bank's Forest Carbon Partnership Facility, The Nature Conservancy pledged $5 million toward the effort.

Contrary to this colonial model, however, one of the steps toward truly addressing climate change must be to give indigenous peoples autonomy and full control over their ancestral lands.

Because of the inherent injustice of REDD and the FCPF, indigenous peoples were joined by people from around the world to stage a loud and angry protest outside of Zoellick's press conference at the UN Climate Convention in Bali. This was, in fact, the most hopeful thing that emerged from the Bali talks where once again the U.S. bullied the rest of the world into accepting "The Bali Roadmap" – a deal with no hard targets for emissions reductions, but rather a vague agreement to talk about potential action on climate change at future meetings.

Social movements, indigenous peoples' organizations and NGOs came together numerous times throughout the UN Climate Convention in Bali to demand real action on climate change, oppose false solutions and to stand up for climate justice. This international effort has continued to grow and expand in the months since the Bali climate talks.

Efforts are now coalescing toward the 2009 UN Climate Conference in Copenhagen. This is where the global climate agreement will be finalized that will succeed the Kyoto Protocol when it expires in 2012. One challenge for the international climate change movement is upping the ante sufficiently over the next two years to force these international climate negotiations to take real, substantial and effective action to address global warming. Ensuring that these negotiations proceed from a climate justice, rather than a corporate capitalist perspective, however, will be a tall order indeed. That widespread direct action will be needed is clear. Coincidentally, Copenhagen climate talks begin on 30 November 2009-the tenth anniversary of the WTO shutdown in Seattle.

Mass action on climate change

> What has been singularly lacking [in the climate change debate] has been any widespread popular campaign. There have been no Seattle-style protests... Politicians respond to pressure. When they have big, angry demonstrations outside their conference centers, it focuses their minds... *–The Guardian (UK)*

The movement against global warming in the United States plays a pivotal role in the global effort to stop climate change. This is because:

▸ With 6% of the world's population, the U.S. emits 25% of the world's carbon emissions. (This, however, does not include the emissions from countries like China and India that directly result from the manufacture of goods for export to the U.S.)

▸ The U.S. military is the largest single emitter of carbon on the planet.

▸ The U.S. and the World Bank (in which the U.S. has de-facto veto decision-making power) dominate the discussion of what to do about global warming with market-based false solutions.

▸ The historic role of the U.S. in the international climate negotiations has been to obstruct any forward progress.

In much the same way that the Seattle protests bolstered the position of the underdog countries in the WTO negotiations, ultimately derailing them, a U.S. mobilization in support of countries fighting for real action on climate change at the international level could help neutralize the obstructive role of the U.S. and its allies by demonstrating that even U.S. citizens are demanding real action.

With the election of Barack Obama, there is a rising sense of possibility in the U.S. and around the world. It is clear, however, that any real change is going to have to come from a mobilized and radicalized grassroots. People are beginning to look back toward the 1960s as a model for organizing and for making the impossible, possible.

In the 1960s and 1970s, the Vietnam War was an omnipresent danger to people in the U.S., Vietnam and around the globe. From the threat of the draft, to the direct threat to life, to the great numbers of dead and wounded soldiers and civilians — with nearly everyone knowing someone who had died in the war-and with the war on the front page of the papers and the lead story of the news nearly every day, there was simply no escape from the direct or indirect impacts of this war. This, of course, had a radicalizing and mobilizing influence. The movement to stop the war became a massive force. When combined with the rising black power and civil rights movements, the militant GI resistance movement, the emerging feminist movement, and of course the overwhelming resistance of the Vietnamese people, the movement became virtually unstoppable.

Today we are seeing a similar situation with climate change. The media bombards us with bad news about the climate as increasingly severe weather-storms, droughts, fires — directly or indirectly impacts growing numbers of people, and we are all sensing that things are not quite as they should be. The parallel between the climate crisis and the 1960s provides us with the possibility of mobilizing a massive, powerful and diverse grassroots movement on climate that takes important lessons from the successes and failures of the 1960s movements.

While raising the militancy of the movement toward international climate negotiations is a crucial component of forward motion on climate change, we must also learn from social movements around the world that are already taking direct action on issues related to climate change. Indigenous peoples in Brazil are taking back their ancestral lands, cutting the non-native and invasive eucalyptus plantations and re-establishing villages. In March 2008, more than 900 women from Via Campesina occupied a eucalyptus plantation and cut down the trees. 800 women and children were violently arrested. Social movements based on small island nations in the Pacific are struggling for the very survival of their peoples. The climate movement must project these voices and stand in solidarity with them. The model of community action at the local level is a key toward solving the climate crisis.

Let's be clear, we cannot buy our way out of this problem. Consuming more "stuff," even energy efficient stuff, is not the answer. Consuming stuff still requires fossil fuels to mine the resources for the stuff, to manufacture the stuff and to transport the stuff.

The myriad solutions to global warming will come, not from the top down, but from communities identifying locally appropriate, equitable and sustainable solutions that are both decentralized and recognize the importance of local control and bioregional distinctions.

The road to a mass-mobilization around the Copenhagen climate talks is being paved by organizations, social movements and indigenous peoples organizations and grassroots activists from all corners of the globe. A unified Call to Action, developed by a group of 100 climate activists from 21 countries has been translated into 18 different languages.

In the U.S., the Mobilization for Climate Justice (www.actforclimatejustice.org/) has formed to organize mass action against climate change and in support of real and just solutions to climate change, beginning with a mobilization around the UN Climate Conference in Copenhagen, Denmark in December 2009.

You can join this process and stand with the growing legions of people around the world who are joining forces to find real solutions to the climate crisis.

> Symbolic resistance must never replace real civil disobedience. You cannot stop war [or climate change-ed.] with a weekend march. We must refuse to comply with the status quo. We be many and they be few and they need us more than we need them. –*Arundhati Roy*

How Can We Build an Effective Movement?

Kamala Emanuel

Green Left Weekly, Nov. 16, 2007

November 11's national Walk Against Warming was an important initiative for the climate change movement. It was smaller than the 100,000 people organizers had hoped for, but the fact that tens of thousands joined the biggest political demonstration of the election period confirms the opinion poll findings that climate change is a grave concern for large numbers of people.

When liberal "conventional wisdom" promotes the view that it is enough to vote for parties with the right policies, it can be difficult to convince people to rally in an election period. It can be harder again to convince the social movement peak bodies – often the ones with the resources and weight to pull off big mobilizations – to call such demonstrations. So the timing of the rallies, two weeks before the election, was to the credit of the organizers and an important way for ordinary people concerned about global warming to demand government action.

Nevertheless, the three key limitations revealed by the rallies pose serious questions for the climate change movement.

The capital city rallies weren't built around clear demands. Posters and fliers carried the slogan "One planet. One climate. Last chance," or modifications of this. But in the absence of clear, concrete demands, the way is open for the manoeuvring of the ALP and Coalition, which can claim to be "against warming" too. If we're not explicit about what needs to be done, we dilute the pressure on them to act.

Linked to this was the decision to invite Labor and Coalition speakers to address the rallies, despite their refusal to commit to the measures necessary to prevent climate disaster. In this, the rally-goers were far in advance of the organizers, heckling and turning their backs on Labor's Peter Garrett in Sydney, and elsewhere giving them a cold reception (compared, for example, to the enthusiastic reception given to Greens speakers such as Bob Brown).

A third shortcoming was the lack of democracy in the organizing of the rallies. Conservation councils in each state organized or, in some instances, co-organized the capital city rallies with other environment peak groups (e.g., Greenpeace in Melbourne). With some exceptions (for example Hobart and in regional centres like Wollongong), meetings were not open to all activists or groups, or were only opened up once all the decisions had been made and the conservation groups were looking for people to spread the word. This restricted discussion and collective decision-making about such issues as which demands and speakers would be best, and reduced the sense of ownership of the event that comes through such democratic participation.

The Sydney rally organizers initially invited Construction, Forestry, Mining and Energy Union mining division secretary Tony Maher – who promotes "clean" coal – to speak at the rally. He was pulled after an email campaign initiated by CFMEU member and Anvil Hill Alliance activist Graham Brown – but this wouldn't have been necessary had the planning taken place in an inclusive way.

Given the urgency of global action to avoid runaway climate change, this is not a campaign we can afford to lose. To be most effective, this movement will need democratic processes and structures, to give participants the benefit of a range of ideas for tactics, demands and priorities, and to ensure the greatest number of people feel empowered to take action together.

It's clear the movement is diverse and needs to be so. There are numerous specific campaigns that must be waged through a combination of measures – in the streets, in direct actions, in the courts. These include the campaigns to stop the Anvil Hill coal mine in the Hunter Valley, halt the expansion of the Newcastle coal export facilities, stop the Gunns' pulp mill and associated native forest logging in Tasmania and many others. They are campaigns on their own, but winning each of them will be essential to reducing greenhouse gas emissions and/or maintaining and increasing the carbon sink (the Earth's ability to absorb the greenhouse gases released into the air).

But as well as supporting these discrete campaigns, we also need to strive for unity across the climate change movement around broader demands, such as for the immediate and deep cuts in greenhouse gas emissions required to keep global warming below at most 1.5° to 2°C and in the longer term to bring the temperature down; for rejecting the non-solutions of nuclear power and "clean coal"; for vast expansion of renewable energy production, alongside efficiency measures; and for an expansion of public transport – which really needs to be free, if it's to be taken up on the scale necessary to get cars off the roads.

To support such campaigns and demands, the movement will need to be independent of the vested interests of the fossil fuel and other greenhouse polluting industries, and their Coalition and Labor lackeys. It will also need to avoid false friends like the nuclear lobby with their cynical attempts to reinvent nuclear power as the solution to climate change. This is not to advocate refusing to work with members of the ALP, or anyone else, to halt climate change. But we do need to oppose attempts to subordinate the tactics and demands we adopt to the electoral interests of the corporate parties that have shown their inclination to put profits ahead of the planet.

In this light, the plans by Melbourne Friends of the Earth to hold a post-election "Where next?" forum for the movement is a welcome initiative. Within the movement, we sorely need such discussions on how to advance this struggle – the efforts of the "greenhouse mafia" of major greenhouse polluters to stymie action that could cut into their profits means that stopping global warming will take a colossal struggle. The left will need to find ways to construct broad alliances to ensure real measures are taken to halt the warming – and that such measures are not only environmentally, but also socially, sustainable.

Workers and Climate Change

Green Left Weekly

Green Left Weekly, April 26, 2008

On May 1, International Workers Day, workers and unionists need to reflect on the greatest challenge facing humanity: global warming.

Workers operate and build the industry that creates greenhouse gases, whether it's mining coal, making cars or clearing forests. We make all the polluting processes work. But we're doing this to satisfy big companies' desire for more profits rather than for social good. If we are to build a sustainable human society, workers are going to have to do it: we hold a key that can unlock this great problem.

Climate change is happening, and accelerating. The US National Oceanic and Atmospheric Administration, in its annual index of greenhouse gas emissions released on April 23, found atmospheric carbon dioxide (CO_2), the primary driver of global climate change, rose 0.6%, or 19 billion tonnes, last year. The primary source of CO_2 is the burning of fossil fuels, which is increasing, the administration scientists reported.

Unions know about the problem, but some, such as the Mining and Energy Division of the Construction, Forestry, Mining and Energy Union (CFMEU), are unfortunately trailing behind the coal lobby supporting a mythical "clean coal" or other inadequate "solutions" that promise a sort of cut-and-come-again resource magic pudding.

In the real world, delaying the shift away from fossil fuel-based energy to clean energy is a dangerous exercise – for all of us. The urgency of the problem can lead some to panic-driven and irrational conclusions.

Some environmentalists are still putting their hopes in an illusion that the captains of industry will, one day (soon), wake up to the enormity of the problem and redirect their capital to sustainable practices. As the science becomes more compelling, these people argue, capital will realize what's at stake and act, even if only out of self interest.

Others, such as Tony Maher of the CFMEU, say "clean coal" is essential to securing jobs in regional Australia. He advises his members they will only have jobs "if coal use – and gas use – becomes a low emission industry here and overseas."

Workers, especially in the coal industry, should not pin their hopes on this desperate fantasy. Coal cannot be made climate-safe – it has to be phased out. This industry is currently Australia's largest export earner, but there are also jobs to be had in building new sustainable energy systems.

There is little chance that the business elite will push for a sustainable economy that protects workers' rights. This is indicated by the carbon-trading schemes currently under discussion, all of which will drastically increase the cost of basic amenities, such as electricity and water, and with no hope of preventing disastrous climate change.

We have a climate emergency, and we need to act now. But we do not have to agree that the current framework is the best way to deal with the global warming challenge.

We do not have to accept mass sackings in the polluting industries. Rather, why not retrain workers for the sustainable energy jobs? We do not have to accept building walls to keep out climate refugees. Let the Pacific and other Islanders in: they have hardly contributed to the global warming problem. We do not have to accept rationing and food shortages while the rich stockpile and profit from the shortages.

Unions have an important role to play in the growing protest movement against global warming. Siding with the coal bosses, such as the Australian Coal Association, delays the inevitable shift away from fossil fuels. It is a short-sighted "fix" which will not sustain jobs and communities into the future.

All union activists should make it their responsibility to support the climate protest movement, to draw their work mates into it, and to get their union leaderships to understand climate change is an emergency.

Workers make the world run, and we can make it run sustainably. This is the only way we'll guarantee our jobs, our livelihoods and our communities. We have a world to win or lose. It is up to us.

██████████████

The Three Decisive Social Forces that Can Stop Climate Change

Socialist Resistance

Socialist Resistance, Summer 2008

The protest against the proposed third runway at Heathrow Airport on 31st May sent a powerful message to Gordon Brown's government: we will not sit idly by and watch while the future of our planet is put at risk. Current plans to expand our airports are cynically irresponsible and fly in the face of the government's professed concerns about climate change.

Of course, carbon emissions do not respect national boundaries. With atmospheric CO_2 concentrations already over 387ppmv, the need for serious global action to radically reduce emissions is more urgent than ever. The Campaign against Climate Change is right to campaign for an effective international treaty.

However, the changes we need to make will not be achieved in UN conference rooms and treaty negotiations alone. They will only be achieved by global mass struggle, by a global mass movement. Building this movement is an urgent task for all ecosocialists, because without it we are destined for a terminal decline into barbarism.

We have already seen the birth of this movement, and its first tentative steps, in the struggles of the indigenous people of the Amazon, in the protests against the refusal of the Bush government to ratify Kyoto, in the demonstrations called around the world to coincide with the UN climate talks, and in thousands of other climate marches, protests, rallies and direct actions.

The Global Climate Campaign was launched by activists in Britain in 2001 in response to Bush's refusal to ratify Kyoto. By 2005, demonstrations were held in 34 countries to coincide with the Montreal climate talks, including a march by 10,000 people in Montreal itself. By the time of the Bali talks in 2007 there were 84 countries taking part. 2007 also saw around 2000 climate demonstrations in all 50 US states as part of the Step it Up campaign.

The task facing ecosocialists now is threefold – to immerse ourselves in the emerging social movement on climate in order to actively build each and every protest; to weld together the diverse and multifaceted strands of this movement into a single powerful force; and to develop, through a wide ranging process of discussion and debate, the strategies that are needed to win.

And there are three social forces that will be decisive in all of these tasks: the indigenous peoples of the South, the organized working class of all countries, and the youth.

Youth and students have already shown their militancy in direct actions against airport expansions and against coal fired power stations. Not only do the young have the biggest stake in protecting the future of the planet, they are also unbowed by the defeats of the past, and are therefore capable of bringing innovative methods of struggle and new waves of radicalism into the movement.

North America's largest manufacturing union, the United Steelworkers, has joined with the Sierra Club, the largest US environmental organization, to launch a strategic Blue-Green alliance under the banner of Good Jobs, A Clean Environment, and A Safer World. This is a clear indication of what is both possible and necessary.

The unions in Britain are also starting to pick up on this issue. In February of this year, three hundred trade unionists met in London for the first ever Campaign against Climate Change Trade Union Conference. Ecosocialists now need to take the climate debate forward at every level within every union, and to win union members in their millions to taking decisive action on climate. Such action may include participation in the mass demonstrations, boycotting biofuels, and preparing and fighting for alternative plans of sustainable and socially useful production.

But at the forefront of this struggle are the indigenous people of the Global South, fighting as they are against incursions into the rainforests by logging companies and agribusiness, and against the biofuels that put corn into car tanks instead of into the mouths of hungry people.

As Bolivian President Evo Morales put it during his speech at the UN General Assembly last September: "The indigenous peoples of Latin America and the world have been called upon by history to convert ourselves into the vanguard of the struggle to defend nature and life."

The indigenous peoples are at the cutting edge of this struggle. Ecosocialists must now follow their lead.

'Climate Change is a Trade Union Issue'

Tony Kearns

Socialist Resistance, Spring 2008

Trade unions have been involved in this issue for quite a number of years. The shop workers' union in 1957 put a motion to the Trade Union Congress calling for boilers, furnaces and motors to be redesigned "to prevent the poisoning of the atmosphere." In 1972 the TUC organized a conference of workers on the issue of the environment. Over thirty-five trade unions attended. In 1990 the TUC passed a motion which raised the enormous danger to the people of the world posed by the effects of global warming.

Some unions are now trying to put their own house in order. The PCS recently held a staff environment open day that was attended by over two hundred members of staff. The PCS now has over eighty environmental reps. I lead an environmental project group in the Communication Workers Union which aims to make all aspects of how we run the union "greener" – for want of a better phrase.

Now there are two types of trade unionists on the issue of the environment but they'll end up as one type of trade unionist. There are those who already believe and are committed to this issue and there are those who don't believe in the effects of global warming or are pretending it isn't happening.

But they will end up believing and getting involved in this cause for one simple reason. As the climate changes and as resources dry up the nature of work and employment will change across the planet. The trade unions that are turning a blind eye now will have to get involved at some stage.

As the nature of what is produced changes that is going to affect workers on a day to day basis as their jobs change or as their jobs vanish or move, around the country or to the other side of the world. Workers on the other side of the world are going to be exploited by the same capitalists who exploit workers in this part of the world. It is a trade union issue because by the nature of what workers do on a day to day basis they are the producers of carbon emissions – not by will but by default. Trade unions and the workers they represent are going to have to get a grip of this.

There's a well-founded criticism that the champions of capitalism's "second eleven" throughout the industrialized world have been the trade unions because of their protectionism when it comes to the creation and protection of jobs at all costs. Sometimes that manifests itself in defending jobs that continue to destroy the environment and add to climate change.

The way I see it is that the environmental movement sprung up out of the new social movements in the 1960s along with things like women's rights, civil rights, gay rights and the anti-nuclear lobby. Funnily enough these are all the issues that trade unions are now taking up. Climate change is now the last issue for trade unions to engage with.

The fact is though that the struggle for the working environment was one of the reasons that trade unions sprung up just after the Industrial Revolution. They struggled for healthy and safe conditions in the workplace. Children were getting maimed and people were being worked to death. It sounds just like what's happening now in the developing world.

For me it's a logical extension to move from wanting to have a safer environment to work in to wanting a safer environment to live on our planet. I don't see how anybody can argue that there's any difference between the day to day work that trade unions do and wanting to ensure that the people we represent go to work in a safe healthy environment. So you can't stand aside and say "we couldn't care less about what type of environment you live in," once they've stepped out of the workplace.

Unions that are ignoring the issue won't be able to do so for much longer for two reasons. Their members at some point are going to demand that they start taking climate change seriously. We did a survey of our young members and asked them "what are the issues that you are concerned about?" We expected them to say "wages, hours and bosses." It wasn't.

Issue number one was housing because due to the ridiculous state of the housing market there's nowhere decent to live. And issue number two for our members under thirty was the environment.

It seems to us that among tomorrow's generation of trade unionists the very narrow idea of trade unionists only being concerned with work is weakening. We can campaign on any issue we want – hours, jobs, conditions – but if we don't have a planet we can live on we are wasting our time.

What are the multi-billion pound companies and the governments we live under going to do when resources get scarce? The film *Mad Max* might look like a documentary in about fifteen years time. There are going to be wars fought over basic resources as they begin to run out. The capitalists aren't just going to say "those environmentalists were right and we were wrong."

I understand the point about what we can do as individuals, things like switching off the stand by on our TV, not using as much water. We can all do these things as individuals but the reason governments and big business rams those suggestions down your throat is because it gets them off the hook.

It stops them doing what needs to be done. While they are lecturing you about switching off lights – which is right – they present that like it is the answer. It's not the answer. It takes up Thatcher's theme that there is no such thing as society, there's no such thing as collectivism, it's all about the individual.

What matters for me as a trade unionist is collective action producing results. On this occasion what's called for is collective action across a broad spectrum of direct action groups, political groups, campaign groups and trade unions coming together to say that "this is the planet we live on and have to make a living on. It's worth fighting for."

My message is that climate change is a trade union issue. If we are really interested in our members we are interested in them twenty four seven and there's no bigger issue for my members than having a planet to live on. The answer is collective action across a broad political spectrum and trade unions are already involved and we are going to get even more involved.

Class Struggle and Ecology

Liam Mac Uaid

August 2008

It is becoming increasingly clear to growing numbers of people that capitalism not only generates war, poverty and insecurity but that it also potentially threatens our survival as a species. As socialists we must explain that only by collective action will we be able to develop solutions to climate change.

The key terrain for this debate in Britain is in the trade unions – but traditionally trade unionists have tended to regard environmentalism as a threat to jobs, and environmentalists distrust the unions because they defend even most polluting industries. The union bureaucracy has always allowed capital free rein to direct production as long as it provided their members with jobs. Union members or leaders rarely question what is produced or how it is produced, and while some unions are now talking of "greening the workplace," the question of the social utility or environmental implications of what is produced are still not a subject of real discussion.

While many environmentalists have taken managerial jobs within the big corporations to "reform them from within" and others continue to advocate pro-capitalist solutions to the environmental crisis, socialists and trade unionists must start thinking about developing alternative plans of production.

Trade unions are not obliged to be defenders of wages and conditions within the confines of capitalism and our comrades are taking a leadership role in developing a trade union network to make the issue of climate change a campaigning priority in the organizations that represent million of workers in Britain. Our activity in the coming years must, as a central priority, aim to make the unions an enthusiastic participant in a mass movement against climate change.

We will never build a mass movement on the basis of arguing for self imposed austerity. The changes we need to make would greatly enhance the quality of life for the vast majority of us. Instead they would release millions of people from the stress of the car and traffic jam by replacing it with free public transport, by significantly shortening the working week, by socializing domestic labour.

We can only solve the problem of climate change through rationally planning what we produce and how we produce it, not by clinging to the anarchy of the market.

Our strategic objective is that the working class resolves capitalism's impending and actual ecological catastrophes in its own interest beginning with collective struggle, mass struggle, and leading, if we are successful in our struggle, to collective planning, to collective control over the resources of the planet. That is the only outcome which will enable humanity to allocate the biosphere's resources not to generating profit for the few but to the satisfaction of real human need.

As we argued in the Socialist Resistance document *Savage Capitalism*:

> Ecosocialists have to start from a class analysis, an analysis that can unite the largest possible number of people to make the rich, not the poor, pay. We support the building of a mass movement, nationally and internationally to impose the types of demand below.
> • For a unilateral reduction of greenhouse gas emissions in Britain of 90% by 2030, with similar reductions in other developed countries;
> • For an international treaty to cap global carbon emissions, not because we think this is an easy option, or even likely to be achieved (this depends on the balance of forces), but because it is necessary and can unite the movements internationally against the failures of the capitalist system;
> • For international rationing of air travel, any market in rations to be made illegal;
> • Opposition to nuclear energy and the building of any new nuclear power stations;
> • For a massive expansion of renewable energy;
> • For subsidies from national and local government: – to replace the use of cars by providing cheap, accessible and frequent public transport – to ensure all new buildings are zero-carbon – to provide insulation, energy conservation, etc. for all homes to make them energy efficient.

On climate change we should campaign around the following transitional and immediate demands which are designed to halt and reverse the global warming process and thus prevent climate chaos and rising sea levels.

These should include a 90% reduction in fossil fuel use by 2050, based on a 6% annual target, monitored by independent scrutiny. The industrialized countries, who have caused the problem, must take the lead in this. The most impoverished peoples are paying the highest price for the actions of the advanced countries. There is no point in asking then to take measures not being taken in the industrialized countries.

This means:

▸ Cancellation of the Third World debt. There is no point on calling on impoverished counties to tackle climate change if they are saddled with debt.

▸ A massive increase in investment in renewable energy including solar, wind, wave, tidal and hydro power (with the exception of destructive mega-dam projects). These should be monitored for anti-social consequences. No nuclear power.

▸ End the productivist throwaway society: production for use and not for profit.

▸ Tough action against industrial and corporate polluters.

▸ Free, or cheap, integrated publicly owned transport systems to provide an alternative to the car.

▸ Nationalization of rail, road freight and bus companies.

▸ Halt airport expansion, restrict flights and end binge flying. Nationalize the airlines.

▸ Redesigned cities to eliminate unnecessary journeys and conserve energy.

▸ Scrap weapons of mass destruction and use the resources for sustainable development and renewable energy.

▸ Massive investment to make homes more energy efficient. Moves towards the collectivization of living spaces.

▸ Nationalization of the supermarkets, localized food production and a big reduction in food miles.

▸ No GM crops for food or fuel.

▸ End the destruction of the rainforests.

▸ Defend the rights of climate change refugees and migrants. Protect those hit by drought, desertification, floods, crop failure and extreme weather conditions.

▸ Renationalize water and protect water reserves. End the pollution of the rivers and the water ways.

8: ECOSOCIALIST RESPONSES TO CAPITALIST ECOCIDE

"Only a genuine socialist mass movement can
counter and defeat the forces that are now pushing
humankind toward the abyss of self-destruction."
–István Mészáros–

Around the world, we are seeing the beginnings of a green-red conver-
gence — environmental activists are turning to Marxism to find tools for
understanding the ecological crisis, and Marxists are concluding that so-
cialism will only succeed if it is based on sound ecological practice.

In Part Nine:

▸ **Making the Greens Redder and the Reds Greener.** *An interview*
on what ecosocialism is and what ecosocialists should do.

▸ **For a Society of Good Ancestors.** *Why has Cuba led the way in the*
fight to save the earth while much richer countries have done nothing?
How can socialists and left greens work together to build a society that
puts the long-term interests of humanity and nature ahead of short-
term profit?

▸ **Climate Change Charter.** *More than most ecosocialist groups,*
Australia's Socialist Alliance has worked to develop a program of
specific proposals for the climate emergency. This second edition of the
SA Climate Charter was published late in 2008.

▸ **The Belem Ecosocialist Declaration.** *Drafted by Danielle Follett,*
Joel Kovel, Michael Löwy and Ian Angus for the Ecosocialist Interna-
tional Network, this declaration was distributed at the World Social Fo-
rum in Belem, Brazil in January 2009.

▸ **Climate Crisis: 21st Century Socialists Must Be Ecosocialists.**
Belgian ecosocialist Daniel Tanuro wrote this essay to persuade Marx-
ists to become ecosocialists. It was adopted at by the International
Committee of the Fourth International in February 2009, as a basis for
international discussion.

Making the Greens Redder
and the Reds Greener

Interview with Ian Angus

Socialist Voice, December 3, 2007
Ian Angus was interviewed by the Greek newspaper Kokkino (Red),
which published a slightly abridged translation.

Let's begin with a large question — what is ecosocialism?

Ecosocialism has grown out of two parallel political trends — the spread of
Marxist ideas in the green movement and the spread of ecological ideas in
the Marxist left. The result is a set of social and political goals, a growing
body of ideas, and a global movement.

Ecosocialism's *goal* is to replace capitalism with a society in which common ownership of the means of production has replaced capitalist ownership, and in which the preservation and restoration of ecosystems will be
central to all activity.

As a *body of ideas*, ecosocialism argues that ecological destruction is not
an accidental feature of capitalism, it is built into the system's DNA. The system's insatiable need to increase profits — what's been called "the ecological
tyranny of the bottom line" — cannot be reformed away.

With that said, it is important to realize ecosocialist thought is not
monolithic — it embodies many different views about theory and practice.
For example, there is an ongoing debate about the view, advanced by some
ecosocialist writers, that social movements have replaced the working class
as the engine of social change.

Finally, ecosocialism is an *anti-capitalist movement* that varies a great
deal from place to place. In the imperialist countries, it is a current within
existing socialist and green-left movements, seeking to win ecology activists
to socialism and to convince socialists of the vital importance of ecological
issues and struggles. We might say that in the global north ecosocialism today focuses on making the Greens redder and the Reds greener.

In the Third World, by contrast, global warming is already a matter of
life and death. People there are fighting environmental destruction — and
the environmental destroyers — on a daily basis. The fights take many forms,
including land occupations, road blockades, and sabotage, as well as more
traditional actions such as petitions, rallies, demonstrations. Such protests
occur daily in dozens of countries.

What we see there is a growing mass pro-ecology movement that incor-
porates socialist ideas — that's especially true in Latin America, where anti-

imperialist governments, with Bolivia and Cuba in the lead, are pressing for strong anticapitalist, pro-environment measures.

A recent letter from Evo Morales to the United Nations illustrates that point and another – that in the fight to save the earth, a vanguard role is being played by indigenous peoples. As Morales said:

> We – the indigenous peoples and humble and honest inhabitants of this planet – believe that the time has come to put a stop to this, in order to rediscover our roots, with respect for Mother Earth; with the Pachamama as we call it in the Andes. Today, the indigenous peoples of Latin America and the world have been called upon by history to convert ourselves into the vanguard of the struggle to defend nature and life.

And he suggested a global political organization to combat global warming:

> We need to create a World Environment Organisation which is binding, and which can discipline the World Trade Organisation, which is propelling us towards barbarism.

That's not just a clever turn of phrase. In that one sentence, Morales says that the environment must be given legal priority over capitalist profits and the neoliberal policies that protect them. That's a profound idea that the left worldwide should adopt and defend.

What is the Ecosocialist International Network?

The Ecosocialist International Network was formed in October 2007, at a meeting in Paris that was attended by ecosocialists from 13 countries. Its main goals are to improve communication and coordination among ecosocialists worldwide, and to organize an ecosocialist conference in Brazil in January 2009, in conjunction with the World Social Forum.

The EIN is a very loose and open organization. Its only organizational structure is a steering committee to plan the Brazil conference. Anyone who supports the broad goals of the ecosocialism is welcome to participate – more information is available on our website, ecosocialistnetwork.org.

How do you respond to socialists who argue that there is no need for specifically "ecosocialist" ideas or activity?

In a certain sense they are correct. Marxism embodies a wealth of profound ecological thought, far more than many green activists realize.

But while concern for ecology was a fundamental part of Marx's thought, and the Bolsheviks were certainly aware of the issue, the sad fact is that the Marxist left ignored this issue for many decades. It's important to correct that – and to do so publicly and explicitly.

Using the word "ecosocialism" is a way of signalling loud and clear that we consider climate change not just as another stick to bash capitalism with, but as a critically important issue, one of the principal problems facing humanity in this century.

But there is more involved. Marxism is not a fixed set of eternal truths – it is a living body of thought, a method of understanding society and a tool for social change. Socialists whose views don't evolve to incorporate new social and scientific insights become irrelevant sectarians – we've seen that happen to many individuals and groups over the years.

Just as Marx and Engels studied and adopted ideas from the scientists of their day – Liebig on soil fertility, Morgan on early societies, Darwin on evolution, and many others – so Marxists today must learn from today's scientists, especially about the biggest issues of the day. Ecosocialism aims to do just that.

Can capitalism solve global warming?

That depends on what you mean by "solve."

Dealing with global warming includes two components – mitigation and adaptation. Mitigation means reducing greenhouse gas emissions so that global warming slows down and eventually reverses. Adaptation means making changes that will enable people to survive in a world where some climate change is inevitable, and where climate chaos is increasingly likely.

In my opinion, capitalism's insatiable need for growth, combined with its massive dependence on fossil fuels as the dominant energy source, means that it is very unlikely that we will see an effective mitigation program from any major capitalist country.

Scientists say that if the average temperature rises more than 2 degrees, dangerous climate change becomes very probable. There is no sign that any of the industrialized countries will implement measures sufficient to stop such a temperature increase – anything they do will be too little, too late.

But if we do not succeed in bringing this system to an end, capitalism will undoubtedly adapt to the new climate. It will do what capitalism always does – it will impose the greatest burdens on the most vulnerable, on poor people and poor nations. Climate refugees will multiply and millions will die. The imperialist powers will fight against the global south, and amongst themselves, to control the world's resources, including not just fuel but also food and other essentials. The most barbaric forms of capitalism will intensify and spread.

In short – yes, capitalism can "solve" global warming, but a capitalist solution will be catastrophic for the great majority of the world's people.

For a Society of Good Ancestors!

Ian Angus

A talk presented in Sydney, Australia in April 2009

The world is getting hotter, and the main cause is greenhouse gas emissions produced by human activity. Enormous damage has already been done, and we will have to live with the consequences of past emissions for decades, perhaps even centuries. Unless we rapidly and drastically cut emissions, the existing damage will turn to catastrophe.

Anyone who denies that is either lying or somehow unaware of the huge mass of compelling scientific evidence.

Many publications regularly publish articles summarizing the scientific evidence and outlining the devastation that we face if action isn't taken quickly. I highly recommend *Green Left Weekly* as a continuing source. I'm not going to repeat what you've undoubtedly read there.

But I do want to draw your attention to an important recent development. Last month, more than 2500 climate scientists met in Copenhagen to discuss the state of scientific knowledge on this subject. And the one message that came through loud and clear was this: it's much worse than we thought.

What were called "worst case scenarios" two years ago by the Intergovernmental Panel on Climate Change actually understated the problem. The final statement issued by the Copenhagen conference declared: "The worst-case IPCC scenario trajectories (or even worse) are being realized ..."

Nicholas Stern, author of the landmark 2006 study, *The Stern Review on the Economics of Climate Change,* now says, "We underestimated the risks ... we underestimated the damage associated with the temperature increases ... and we underestimated the probability of temperature increases."

Seventeen years of failure — with one exception

Later this year, the world's governments will meet, again in Copenhagen, to try to reach a new post-Kyoto climate treaty. Will they meet the challenge of climate change that is much worse than expected?

The politicians' record does not inspire hope.

Seventeen years ago, in June 1992, 172 governments, including 108 heads of state, met at the Earth Summit in Rio de Janeiro.

That meeting produced the United Nations Framework Convention on Climate Change, the first international agreement that aimed "to achieve stabilization of greenhouse gas concentrations in the atmosphere at a low enough level to prevent dangerous anthropogenic interference with the climate system." In particular, the industrialized countries promised to reduce their greenhouse gas emissions below 1990 levels.

Like the Kyoto Accord that followed it, that agreement was a failure. The world's top politicians demonstrated their gross hypocrisy and their indifference to the future of humanity and nature by giving fine speeches and making promises – and then continuing with business as usual.

But there was one exception. In Rio one head of state spoke out strongly, and called for immediate emergency action – and then returned home to support the implementation of practical policies for sustainable, low-emission development.

That head of state was Fidel Castro.

Fidel began his brief remarks to the plenary session of the 1992 Earth Summit with a blunt description of the crisis:

> An important biological species is in danger of disappearing due to the fast and progressive destruction of its natural living conditions: humanity. We have become aware of this problem when it is almost too late to stop it.

He placed the blame for the crisis squarely on the imperialist countries, and he finished with a warning that emergency action was needed: "Tomorrow it will be too late to do what we should have done a long time ago."

After the 1992 Earth Summit, only the Cubans acted on their promises and commitments.

In 1992 Cuba amended its constitution to recognize the importance of "sustainable economic and social development to make human life more rational and to ensure the survival, well-being and security of present and future generations." The amended constitution obligates the provincial and municipal assemblies of People's Power to implement and enforce environmental protections. And it says that "it is the duty of citizens to contribute to the protection of the waters, atmosphere, the conservation of the soil, flora, fauna and nature's entire rich potential."

The Cubans have adopted low-fertilizer agriculture, and encouraged urban farming to reduce the distances food has to travel. They have replaced all of their incandescent light bulbs with fluorescents, and distributed energy efficient rice cookers. They have stepped up reforestation, nearly doubling the island's forested area, to 25% in 2006.

As a result of these and many other projects, in 2006 the World Wildlife Federation concluded that Cuba is the only country in the world that meets the criteria for sustainable development.

By contrast, the countries responsible for the great majority of greenhouse gas emissions followed one of two paths. Some gave lip service to cleaning up their acts, but in practice did little or nothing. Others denied that action was needed and so did little or nothing.

As a result we are now very close to the tomorrow that Fidel spoke of, the tomorrow when it is too late.

Why Cuba?

The World Wildlife Federation deserves credit for its honesty in reporting Cuba's achievements. But the WWF failed to address the next logical question. Why was Cuba the exception? Why could a tiny island republic in the Caribbean do what no other country could do?

And the next question after that is, why have the richest countries in the world not cut their emissions, not developed sustainable economies? Why, despite their enormous physical and scientific resources, has their performance actually gotten worse?

The first question, why Cuba could do it, was answered not long ago by Armando Choy, a leader of the Cuban revolution who has recently headed the drive to clean up Havana Bay. His explanation was very clear and compelling:

> This is possible because our system is socialist in character and commitment, and because the revolution's top leadership acts in the interests of the majority of humanity inhabiting planet earth – not on behalf of narrow individual interests, or even simply Cuba's national interests.

General Choy's comments reminded me of a passage in *Capital*, a paragraph that all by itself refutes the claim that is sometimes made, that Marxism has nothing in common with ecology. Karl Marx wrote:

> Even an entire society, a nation, or all simultaneously existing societies taken together, are not the owners of the earth. They are simply its possessors, its beneficiaries, and have to bequeath it in an improved state to succeeding generations.

I've never known any socialist organization to make this point explicitly, but Marx's words imply that one of the key objectives of the socialism movement must be to build a society in which human beings work consciously to be *Good Ancestors*. We want a society that consciously acts in the long-term interests of humanity and ecosystems, rather than the short-term interests of capital and profit.

That is what the Cubans are doing in practice.

The idea that we must act in the present to build a better world for the future, has been a theme of the Cuban revolutionary movement since Fidel's great 1953 speech, *History Will Absolve Me*. That commitment to future generations is central to what has justly been called the greening of the Cuban revolution.

The Cubans are committed, not just in words but in practice, to being

Good Ancestors, not only to future Cubans, but to future generations around the globe.

Why not capitalism?
But what about the other side of the question? Why do we not see a similar commitment in the ruling classes of Australia, or Canada, or the United States?

If you ask any of them individually, our rulers would undoubtedly say that they want their children and grandchildren to live in a stable and sustainable world. So why do their actions contradict their words? Why do they seem determined, in practice, to leave their children and grandchildren a world of poisoned air and water, a world of floods and droughts and escalating climate disasters? Why have they repeatedly sabotaged international efforts to adopt even half-hearted measures to cut greenhouse gas emissions?

When they do consider or implement responses to the climate crisis, why do they always support solutions that do not work, that cannot possibly work?

Karl Marx had a wonderful phrase for the bosses and their agents – the big shareholders and executives and top managers and the politicians they own – a phrase that explains why they invariably act against the present and future interests of humanity. These people, he said, are "personifications of capital." Regardless of how they behave at home, or with their children, their *social role* is that of capital in human form.

They don't act to stop climate change because the changes needed by the people of this world are directly contrary to the needs of capital.

Capital has no conscience. Capital can't be anyone's ancestor because capital has no children. Capital has only one imperative: it has to grow.

The only reason for using money to buy stock, launch a corporation, build a factory or drill an oil well is to get more money back than you invested. That doesn't always happen, of course – some investments fail to produce profits, and, as we are seeing today, periodically the entire system goes into freefall, wiping out jobs and livelihoods and destroying capital. But that doesn't contradict the fact that the potential for profit, to make capital grow, is a defining feature of capitalism. Without it, the system would rapidly collapse.

As Joel Kovel says, "Capitalism can no more survive limits on growth than a person can live without breathing."

A system of growth and waste
Under capitalism, the only measure of success is how much is sold every day, every week, every year. It doesn't matter that the sales include vast quantities of products that are directly harmful to both humans and nature, or that

many commodities cannot be produced without spreading disease, destroying the forests that produce the oxygen we breathe, demolishing ecosystems, and treating our water, air, and soil as sewers for the disposal of industrial waste. It all contributes to profits, and thus to the growth of capital – and that's what counts.

In *Capital*, Marx wrote that from a capitalist's perspective, raw materials such as metals, minerals, coal, stone, etc. are "furnished by Nature gratis." The wealth of nature doesn't have to be paid for or replaced when it is used – it is there for the taking. If the capitalists had to pay the real cost of that replacing or restoring that wealth, their profits would fall drastically.

That's true not only of raw materials, but also of what are sometimes called "environmental services" – the water and air that have been absorbing capitalism's waste products for centuries. They have been treated as free sewers and free garbage dumps, "furnished by Nature gratis."

That's what the pioneering environmental economist William Kapp

---

Greenhouse gas emissions are not unusual or exceptional. Waste and pollution and ecological destruction are built into the system's DNA.

---

meant nearly 60 years ago, when he wrote, "Capitalism must be regarded as an economy of unpaid costs."

Kapp wrote that capitalism's claims of efficiency and productivity are: "nothing more than an institutionalized cover under which it is possible for private enterprise to shift part of the costs to the shoulders of others and to practice a form of large-scale spoliation which transcends everything the early socialists had in mind when they spoke of the exploitation of man by man." (*The Social Costs of Private Enterprise*, Harvard University Press, 1950)

In short, pollution is not an accident, and it is not a "market failure." It is the way the system works.

How large is the problem? In 1998 the World Resources Institute conducted a major international study of the resource inputs used by corporations in major industrial countries – water, raw materials, fuel, and so on. Then they determined what happened to those inputs. They found that "One half to three quarters of annual resource inputs to industrial economies are returned to the environment as wastes within a year."

Similar numbers are reported by others. As you know, about a billion people live in hunger. And yet, as the head of the United Nations Environmental Program said recently, "Over half of the food produced today is either lost, wasted, or discarded as a result of inefficiency in the human-managed food chain." Inefficiency in this case means that there is no profit to be made by preventing food waste, so waste continues. In addition to exacerbating world hunger, capitalism's gross inefficiency poisons the land and water with food that is harvested but not used.

Capitalism combines an irresistible drive to grow, with an irresistible drive to create waste and pollution. If nothing stops it, capitalism will expand both those processes infinitely.

But the earth is not infinite. The atmosphere and oceans and the forests are very large, but ultimately they are finite, limited resources – and capitalism is now pressing against those limits. The *2006 WWF Living Planet Report* concludes, "The Earth's regenerative capacity can no longer keep up with demand – people are turning resources into waste faster than nature can turn waste back into resources."

My only disagreement with that statement is that it places the blame on "people" as an abstract category. In fact, the devastation is caused by the global capitalist system, and by the tiny class of exploiters that profits from capitalism's continued growth. The great majority of people are victims, not perpetrators.

In particular, capitalist pollution has passed the physical limit of nature's capacity to absorb carbon dioxide and other gases while keeping the earth's temperature steady. As a result, the world is warmer today than it has been for 100,000 years, and the temperature continues to rise.

Greenhouse gas emissions are not unusual or exceptional. Pouring crap into the environment is a fundamental feature of capitalism, and it isn't going to stop so long as capitalism survives. That's why "solutions" like carbon trading have failed so badly and will continue to fail: waste and pollution and ecological destruction are built into the system's DNA.

No matter how carefully the scheme is developed, no matter how many loopholes are identified and plugged, and no matter how sincere the implementers and administrators may be, capitalism's fundamental nature will always prevail.

We've seen that happen with Kyoto's Clean Development Mechanism, under which polluters in rich countries can avoid cutting their own emissions if they invest in equivalent emission-reducing projects in the Third World. A Stanford University study shows that two-thirds or more of the CDM emission reduction credits have not produced any reductions in pollution. The entire system is based on what one observer says are "enough lies to make a sub-prime mortgage pusher blush."

CDM continues not because it is reducing emissions, but because there are profits to be made buying and selling credits. CDM is an attempt to trick the market into doing good in spite of itself, but capitalism's drive for profits wins every time.

Green ecocapitalists

One of the greatest weaknesses of the mainstream environmental movement has been its failure or refusal to identify capitalism as the root problem. Indeed, many of the world's Green Parties, including the one in Canada where I live, openly describe themselves as eco-capitalist, committed to maintaining the profit system.

Of course this puts them in a contradictory position when they face the reality of capitalist ecocide.

In Canada, as you may know, oil companies are engaged in what the British newspaper *The Independent* accurately called "The biggest environmental crime in history," mining the Alberta Tar Sands. If it continues, it will ultimately destroy an area that is nearly the size of Florida, to produce oil by a process that generates three times as much greenhouse gas as normal oil production.

It is also destroying ecosystems, killing animals, fish, and birds, and poisoning the drinking water used by indigenous peoples in that area.

It's obvious that anyone who is serious about protecting the environment and stopping emissions should demand that the Tar Sands be shut down. But when I raised that in a talk not long ago in Vancouver, a Green Party candidate in the audience objected that would be irresponsible, because it would violate the oil companies' contract rights. Obviously, for these ecocapitalists, "capitalism" takes precedence over "eco."

But as capitalist destruction accelerates, and as capitalist politicians continue to stall, or to introduce measures that only benefit the fossil fuel companies, we can expect that many of the most sincere and dedicated greens will begin to question the system itself, not just its worst results.

Greens moving left: Gus Speth

An important case in point, and, I hope, a harbinger of what's to come in green circles – is James Gustave Speth, who is now dean of the Yale University School of Forestry and Environmental Studies. He has spent most of his life trying to save the environment by working inside the system. He was a senior environmental advisor to US President Jimmy Carter, and later to Bill Clinton. In the 1990s he was Administrator of the United Nations Development Programme and Chair of the United Nations Development Group. *Time* magazine called him "the ultimate insider."

Last year, after 40 years working inside the system, Speth published a book called *The Bridge at the Edge of the World: Capitalism, the Environment, and Crossing from Crisis to Stability*. In it, he argues that working inside the system has failed – because the system itself is the cause of environmental destruction.

My conclusion, after much searching and considerable reluctance, is that most environmental deterioration is a result of systemic failures of the capitalism that we have today ... Inherent in the dynamics of capitalism is a powerful drive to earn profits, invest them, innovate, and thus grow the economy, typically at exponential rates ...

That's exactly correct – no Marxist could have said it better. Nor could we improve on Speth's summary of the factors that combine to make contemporary capitalism the enemy of ecology.

An unquestioning society-wide commitment to economic growth at almost any cost; enormous investment in technologies designed with little regard for the environment; powerful corporate interests whose overriding objective is to grow by generating profit, including profit from avoiding the environmental costs they create; markets that systematically fail to recognize environmental costs unless corrected by government; government that is subservient to corporate interests and the growth imperative; rampant consumerism spurred by a worshipping of novelty and by sophisticated advertising; economic activity so large in scale that its impacts alter the fundamental biophysical operations of the planet; all combine to deliver an ever-growing world economy that is undermining the planet's ability to sustain life.

Speth is not a Marxist. He still hopes that governments can reform and control capitalism, eliminating pollution. He's wrong about that, but his analysis of the problem is dead-on, and the fact that it comes from someone who has worked for so long inside the system makes his argument against capitalism credible and powerful.

The socialist movement should welcome and publicize this development, even though Speth and others like him, don't yet take their ideas to the necessary socialist conclusions.

Greens moving left: James Hansen

Similarly, we should be very encouraged that NASA's James Hansen, one of the world's most respected climate scientists, joined in the March 20 demonstration against a planned coal-fired electricity plant in Coventry, England. Hansen is another environmentalist who has worked inside the system for years.

He told the UK *Guardian* that people should first use the "democratic process" by which he means elections. He went on:

What is frustrating people, me included, is that democratic action affects elections but what we get then from political leaders is greenwash.

The democratic process is supposed to be one person one vote, but it turns out that money is talking louder than the votes. So, I'm not surprised that people are getting frustrated.

I think that peaceful demonstration is not out of order, because we're running out of time.

In the same interview, Hansen expressed concern about the approach of the Obama administration:

It's not clear what their intentions are yet, but if they are going to support cap and trade then unfortunately I think that will be another case of green-wash. It's going to take stronger action than that.

Like Speth, Hansen is not a socialist. But he condemns the most wide-ly-promoted market-based "solution," and he calls for demonstrations and protests, so ecosocialists can and must view him as an ally.

Why ECOsocialism?

Which brings me to a question I've been asked many times, including during this visit to Australia. "Why *ecosocialism?*"

Why not just say *socialism?* Marx and Engels were deeply concerned about humanity's relationship to nature, and what we would today call eco-logical ideas are deeply embedded in their writings. In the 1920s, there was a very influential ecology movement in the Soviet Union. So why do we need a new word?

All that is true. But it is also true that during the 20th century socialists forgot or ignored that tradition, supporting (and in some cases implement-ing) approaches to economic growth and development that were grossly harmful to the environment. *Socialist Voice* recently published an interview in which Oswaldo Martinez, the president of the Economic Affairs Commis-sion of Cuba's National Assembly addressed just that question. He said:

The socialism practiced by the countries of the socialist camp replicated the development model of capitalism, in the sense that socialism was conceived as a quantitative result of growth in productive forces. It thus established a purely quantitative competition with capitalism, and development consist-ed in achieving this without taking into account that the capitalist model of development is the structuring of a consumer society that is inconceivable for humanity as a whole.

The planet would not survive. It is impossible to replicate the model of one car for each family, the model of the idyllic North American society, Hollywood etc. – absolutely impossible, and this cannot be the reality for the 250 million inhabitants of the United States, with a huge rearguard of poverty in the rest of the world.

It is therefore necessary to come up with another model of development that is compatible with the environment and has a much more collective way of functioning.

In my view, one good reason for using the word 'ecosocialism' is to signal a clear break with the practices that Martinez describes, practices that were called socialist for 70 years. It is a way of saying that we aim not to create a society based on having more things, but on living better – not quantitative growth, but qualitative change.

Another reason, just as important, is to signal loud and clear that we view ecology and climate change not as just as another stick to bash capitalism with, but as one of the principal problems facing humanity in this century.

Although he has never used the word, so far as I know, one of the strongest defenders of ecosocialist ideas in the world today is Evo Morales, the president of Bolivia, the first indigenous head of state in Latin America.

In a short essay published last November, Evo brilliantly defined the problem, named the villain, and posed the alternative.

> Competition and the thirst for profit without limits of the capitalist system are destroying the planet. Under Capitalism we are not human beings but consumers. Under Capitalism, Mother Earth does not exist, instead there are raw materials. Capitalism is the source of the asymmetries and imbalances in the world. It generates luxury, ostentation and waste for a few, while millions in the world die from hunger in the world.
>
> In the hands of capitalism everything becomes a commodity: the water, the soil, the human genome, the ancestral cultures, justice, ethics, death ... and life itself. Everything, absolutely everything, can be bought and sold and under capitalism. And even "climate change" itself has become a business.
>
> Climate change has placed all humankind before a great choice: to continue in the ways of capitalism and death, or to start down the path of harmony with nature and respect for life.

Slamming on the brakes

Writing in the 1930s when Nazi barbarism was in the rise, the Marxist philosopher and literary critic Walter Benjamin said:

> Marx says that revolutions are the locomotives of world history. But the situation may be quite different. Perhaps revolutions are not the train ride, but the human race grabbing for the emergency brake.

That's a powerful and profound metaphor. Capitalism has been so destructive, and taken us so far down the road to catastrophe, that one of the first tasks facing a socialist government will be to slam on the brakes.

The only choice, the only way forward, is ecosocialism, which I suggest can be defined simply as a socialism that will give top priority to the restoration of ecosystems that capitalism has destroyed, to the reestablishment of agriculture and industry on ecologically sound principles, and to mending what Marx called the metabolic rift, the destructive divide that capitalism has created between humanity and nature.

The fate of the ecological struggle is closely tied to the fortunes of the class struggle as a whole. The long neo-liberal drive to weaken the movements of working people also undermined ecological resistance, isolating it, pushing its leaders and organizations to the right.

But today neo-liberalism is discredited. Its financial and economic structures are in shambles. There is growing recognition that profound economic change is needed.

This is an historic opportunity for ecological activists to join hands with workers, with indigenous activists, with anti-imperialist movements here and around the world, to make ecological transformation a central feature of the economic change that is so clearly needed.

Together we can build a society of Good Ancestors, and cooperatively create a better world for future generations. It won't be easy, and it won't be quick, but together we can make it happen.

Climate Change Charter

Socialist Alliance (Australia)

The fate of advanced human civilization – and perhaps of our species itself – hangs in the balance. Fuelled by human-induced greenhouse gas emissions, global warming is advancing at a pace inconceivable to scientists just a few years ago.

The complete melting in late summers of Arctic sea ice – something that scientists used to predict for the final decades of this century – is now widely expected by 2013-15. As the highly reflective ice is replaced by dark water, much more of the sun's heat is captured. Mean Arctic temperatures in recent years have been as much as 3°C above their long-term averages.

A band of increased warmth 1500km wide stretches south from the Arctic Ocean to cover the main regions of Arctic permafrost. The permafrost is now melting. As it does so, ever-growing volumes of methane gas are bubbling from lakes and swamps.

Given off when plant matter decays in an oxygen-poor environment, methane has a potent greenhouse effect. Though relatively short-lived in the atmosphere the gas, while present, traps heat at around 72 times the rate of carbon dioxide.

Global warming threatens to become self-accelerating as natural "tipping points" are passed, triggering "positive feedbacks" that pour additional carbon from soils and forests into the atmosphere.

After the sea ice, the next tipping point may lie in the forests of the Amazon. Heating up, drying out and burning, its trees and peat lands threaten to let loose a fresh flood of greenhouse gases.

Scientific advances in the last few years have sharply changed the way researchers perceive the climate danger. Earlier computer models of the Earth's climate suggested that if rises in average global temperature could be kept below 2°C above pre-industrial levels, compared to today's figure of 0.8°C, the worst effects of global warming could be avoided.

But new studies warn that there is no level of additional greenhouse gases that we can "safely" release into the atmosphere. Even present levels of warming are highly dangerous, as the swift decline of Arctic sea ice shows.

Moreover, additional warming of at least 0.5°C, the result of greenhouse gases already emitted, is built into the climate system.

To have any hope of avoiding disaster, human society must allot truly massive resources, immediately, to the task of cutting atmospheric greenhouse gases to a point no more than marginally above pre-industrial levels.

The Socialist Alliance acknowledged at its sixth national conference in December that from its present level of just under 390 parts per million (ppm), atmospheric carbon dioxide needs to fall to 300-325ppm. Targets for future emissions must be set at zero, or even negative. And the time-frame? As soon as humanly possible.

Our new position reads:

> Current science indicates that annual emissions reductions of at least 5% will be essential. We propose immediate economy-wide and sector-by-sector planning for all greenhouse gases, to meet these targets on time or before. We must establish mechanisms to review and change these targets as scientific forecasts are updated.

It is true that life on Earth has thrived during long geological ages when temperatures were far above those of the present. But the plants and animals then were very different from today's species, which evolved over millions of years to live on a relatively cool planet.

However, the rate at which global temperatures are now rising appears to be without precedent in the geological record.

Could human beings flourish in the radically impoverished, highly unstable biosphere that business-as-usual emissions are likely to create? Small groups probably would, in a few favourable locations. But civilization as we know it could not survive.

In the boardrooms of huge capitalist corporations, the emerging picture has executives terrified for their profits. Giant polluters like Rio Tinto plead to be exempt from climate change legislation. Big-business media organs conceal the new science, belittle the scientists, and give top billing to ignorant claptrap from denialists and climate sceptics.

And in the government offices, politicians loyal to the corporations frame emissions reduction targets which – like Rudd Labor's 5-15% by 2020 – amount to suicide notes for most of nature and humanity. These miserable targets and Rudd's carbon emissions trading system simply cannot produce the reductions required within 10 years.

Yet the resources needed to avoid climate catastrophe exist – our enormous challenge is to organize a climate action movement strong enough to enforce implementation of a plan for climate sustainability.

Without a plan the movement will be without perspective; without a powerful movement conscious of what it is fighting for, the best climate sustainability plan will never be realized.

This is the understanding with which the Socialist Alliance has produced this second edition of its Climate Change Charter. It outlines the peril we face, and how ordinary concerned people can force history onto the path of climate sustainability.

It's time to stop looking to official Australia for any serious response to global warming. The only force capable of bringing real change to government policy is the climate change movement itself, organizing, protesting, spreading awareness of the drastic seriousness of the crisis and collaborating across the planet.

For the scale and speed of the changes now needed, the best example history offers is the conversion of major economies to wartime production during World War II.

The Socialist Alliance will be doing all it can to help strengthen the movement to make that possible.

Set the greenhouse gas reduction targets that the planet needs

An emissions reduction target will fail to be effective if it still gives us runaway global warming. A target limit for greenhouse gas concentration of 550ppm, accepted by most governments, would produce "at least a 77% chance – and perhaps up to a 99% chance, depending on the climate model used – of a global average temperature rise exceeding 2°." (Sir Nicholas Stern, 2006).

For a safe climate we must aim for a target of 300-325 ppm of atmospheric carbon dioxide. This target is to be achieved as rapidly as possible through immediate and urgent reductions in greenhouse gas emissions with the aim of achieving zero net emissions and then carbon draw-down from the atmosphere. The planet has already warmed by nearly 1°C and even if warming stopped now, there would be extra 0.5°C due to the normal delay in temperature rises.

We need mandatory annual emissions reduction targets of at least 5%. We propose immediate economy-wide and sector-by-sector planning for all greenhouse gases, to meet these targets on time or before. We must establish mechanisms to review and change these targets as scientific forecasts are updated.

Businesses, local councils and government departments should all be required to commit to reducing their overall GHG emissions to zero as part of a national plan.

Negotiate a much stronger treaty after Kyoto

The rich industrial countries are mostly responsible for greenhouse gas emissions, and they must lead the campaign for strong and rapid international climate action. Per head, Australia is one of the highest GHG emitters in the world.

Our government has an obligation to play a leading role in formulating a new international treaty at Copenhagen in 2009 that aims to get all nations to agree to the targets the planet needs.

It is impoverished developing countries like Bangladesh and Kiribati that will be most affected by climate change. Many poor nations will struggle to deal with the symptoms of climate change without massive technical assistance. The rich nations must assist poor nations to develop economic plans that avoid high-pollution industries and encourage the use of renewable energy.

This assistance is just part of repaying our ecological debt.

Australia must also accept some of the environmental refugees to be displaced by rising sea levels, especially from the Asia-Pacific region.

Attack energy inefficiency — aim for zero waste

One of the easiest ways to reduce GHGs is by increasing efficiency and reducing waste. More efficient appliances, insulating homes, better recycling, improved and more efficient public transport, producing locally-produced goods – these are some of the simple but effective changes that are possible right now.

But these changes will not happen fast enough if they're left to the individual consumer's response to appeals to save energy, and to the "sticks and carrots" approach of energy price hikes and tax rebates.

To begin the transition to sustainability, we must set energy efficiency as a national goal, and then develop targets, standards, regulations and national and local campaigns to achieve it.

In Venezuela and Cuba the goal of eliminating incandescent light bulbs was achieved by having teams of volunteers install free government-supplied, low-energy replacement bulbs. This is the sort of initiative that's need-

---

*The resources needed to avoid climate catastrophe
exist – our enormous challenge is to organize a
climate action movement strong enough to enforce
implementation of a plan for climate sustainability.*

---

ed to make Australia's 5.5 million homes energy efficient.

Governments committed to energy efficiency should have sustainable energy household conversion plans, with annual targets for solar power and heating installation compulsory for energy utilities. These plans would build on and promote the various community initiatives dedicated to goals like creating "zero emission" housing, schools and other facilities.

They would require the same approach from business, with systematic energy audits and set compliance deadlines. Firms that don't upgrade to low emissions technology and processes would have to close or be taken over.

They would also monitor and establish strict standards for the energy use of business products. Businesses that operate in a market-based capitalist economy concentrate on selling products, and are unlikely to implement climate-friendly techniques unless strong regulations are introduced.

Integral to the plan would be the phasing out of the $9 billion in fossil fuel subsidies to energy-hungry industries like aluminium refining. Industries that are heavy users of energy would be required to obtain their energy needs from sustainable sources.

All products require energy to be manufactured. Waste of energy and resources are built into the entire economy. More profits are made from designing products not to last, and pollution produced along the way goes on to become someone else's problem. Even traditional recycling largely ignores manufacturing waste and assumes that relatively few products can be reused or recycled at the end of their lives. Most consumer products – with all the energy and raw materials that have gone into their production – one way or another become landfill.

In a zero waste economy, products are designed so that they can be repaired, re-used and disassembled for recycling. We must start to require manufacturers to take back their used products (cars, TVs, computers, etc.) and re-use the components.

Governments and the coal industry are spending millions of dollars researching "clean coal" technology. This costly and unproven technology endeavours to capture carbon dioxide from coal burning and then bury it underground, where it would remain a potential threat to future generations.

Coal burning now accounts for around 36% of Australia's GHG emissions; mining and handling coal adds even more. A plan for phasing out coal mining and export must be developed, and this must involve creating new jobs for miners in sustainable industries. Transitional assistance should be offered to help developing countries like India source their energy needs from renewables. No new coal mines or coal-fired power plants should be approved.

The nuclear lobby began its push for the expansion of uranium mining well before the impacts of global warming were fully known. It then decided to use concerns about climate change to promote the nuclear agenda.

Expanding the nuclear cycle will not solve climate change. The time needed for approval and construction of nuclear reactors is much too long to reduce achieve the necessary reduction in emissions within the next 15-20 years. Huge amounts of energy and water are used in uranium mining and power generation, and the development of nuclear technology risks further nuclear weapons proliferation.

The dangers inherent in the long-term storage of nuclear waste remain present, and the risk of disastrous accidents such as occurred at Chernobyl can never be discounted.

Aboriginal communities have resisted the expansion of uranium mining and the dumping of nuclear waste on their traditional lands. Their right to have a say over whether mining can take place on their lands, must be restored.

100% renewable energy by 2020

Australia could meet its basic energy needs from a combination of non-fossil fuel sources like solar, wind, biomass derived from agricultural wastes, tidal and geothermal (hot rocks beneath the Earth's surface).

Countries like Spain and Denmark already produce more than 20% of their energy from solar and wind power. Australia should set a target of having all of its electricity generated by renewable energy by 2020.

While massive government subsidies continue to be given to dirty fuels like brown coal, research into renewable energy technologies is not given adequate funds.

This lack of serious research and development funding for renewable energy means that the fossil fuel and nuclear industries can delay any change towards sustainability. It hampers the rapid development of renewable technologies with reduced unit costs that would enable them to compete with their cheaper polluting products.

The quickest way to guarantee that renewables are taken up at the speed needed to limit GHG increases is not to leave this job to the market and private industry – even "green" industry – but to create an adequately funded, publicly-owned renewable energy network.

The Socialist Alliance calls for the creation of a Sustainable Energy Authority to drive this effort, and the overall conversion to energy sustainability.

Towards a new agricultural model —
encourage organic farming, protect the forests

Agriculture accounts for 16% of Australia's greenhouse gas emissions. Our current agricultural practices – based on highly mechanized planting and harvesting of single crops and on artificial fertilizers – consume huge quantities of fossil fuels. This not only creates pollution, but when fossil fuel supplies start to diminish, food security along with the climate will be threatened.

Australia must start a transition to carbon-neutral and organic farming. The use of naturally arid areas to grow water-intensive crops, such as rice and cotton, must end.

Existing farming communities should be encouraged with income, resources and training to make the transition to organic agriculture.

Food production should be decentralized and localized to reduce the energy needed to transport and refrigerate foods. The Socialist Alliance supports the growth of urban agriculture, especially as many cities are built on our most fertile lands.

All organic waste, including green waste and sewage, should be composted and the methane gas by-product harnessed for use as an energy source. This avoids methane gas escaping into the atmosphere from landfills, which currently occurs.

Land clearing and outdated forestry practices such as old-growth logging are the biggest cause of greenhouse gas emissions in Tasmania, and account for 6% of national GHG emissions. Moreover, native forests that have not been logged store up to three times more carbon than forests that have been logged.

To increase this "carbon sink" capacity, extensive programs of native-forest planting must be initiated, as well as programs to increase the capacity of soils to capture carbon.

Carbon in the form of finely divided particles of charcoal, or "biochar," is extraordinarily persistent in soils. In the Amazon basin in Brazil, indigenous peoples practised a slash-and-char economy that involved burying charcoal to create, over time, rich black soils known as "terra preta." Some of these soils have been found to be thousands of years old.

Biochar is produced through a process known as low-temperature pyrolysis, in which plant matter is heated to 350-500 degrees Celsius in an oxygen-poor environment. The plant matter undergoes reactions that release further heat, maintaining the process. Various gases are given off, some of which can be condensed to form a liquid biofuel, while others can be burnt to produce electricity.

As much as 50 per cent of the original plant matter remains in the form of biochar, which in turn can be used to scrub carbon dioxide and oxides of nitrogen from the flue gases. The result is to make the biochar a rich nitrogen fertilizer.

Experiments in Western Australia show that when buried in soils, biochar dramatically increases yields of wheat. The porous grains of carbon also improve retention of water and of plant nutrients.

It has been estimated that by the end of the century, as much as 9.5 billion tons of carbon – more than currently emitted globally through the burning of fossil fuels – could be buried each year by adding biochar to soils. Not only could global warming eventually be reversed, but the impact on food production would be enormous.

Although biochar production can be based on forestry waste and crop residues, in Australia a better source of plant matter would be mallee species currently grown as windbreaks on grain farms. Mallee can be harvested every three to five years. As global warming makes marginal grain areas too dry for cropping, mallee cultivation could be substituted.

In large areas of central Queensland land cleared for cattle-raising could be put back under its original tree cover of fast-growing brigalow. This could then be harvested for pyrolysis.

As well as being used for carbon sequestration and soil improvement, biochar could provide an emissions-neutral substitute for coal in metals smelting.

Creating a large biochar industry would require the designing and mass production of small pyrolysis plants. These would be sited every 50 km or so in appropriate regions. The impact on rural employment – and on job prospects for displaced coal miners – would be obvious.

Make public transport free, frequent, accessible and reliable

Transport is responsible for 14% of Australia's greenhouse gas emissions, a share that is still increasing. Road transport accounts for around 90% of that share. A transport system where cars carry 80% of people to work and trucks carry 60% of goods is not only highly inefficient, but it creates huge volumes of GHG emissions.

To reverse this trend we have to put public transport at the centre of our urban development plans.

Although trains are 40 times more energy efficient than cars, we won't reduce or stop using cars and trucks unless there's huge investment in public and rail freight transport to make it a real option for commuters and industry.

A successful public transport system will have reliable, frequent services available to everyone within 10 minutes walk of a service, especially in outer metropolitan regions. It will have to be a publicly owned, integrated system of heavy rail, light rail, ferry and bus services.

But we need to make it more attractive to users. To accelerate the switch to public transport it has to be free. That's what transport authorities have always done when they really need to move large numbers of people quickly, as in the 2000 Sydney Olympics. It's what has happened in the Belgian city of Hasselt: within a year of introducing free bus fares, patronage increased by 870%.

Most people think that this proposal would cost a vast amount of money. However, this reaction fails to measure the total (economic, social and environmental) cost and benefit of public transport against the total cost and benefit of continuing to shift people and goods by private car and truck.

On that scale, public transport wins hands down. For every 10% switch from car and truck and into public transport, the costs of air pollution, greenhouse gas emission, car accidents, traffic congestion, motor vehicle waste disposal, noise pollution and road maintenance would drop by at least $1.4 billion. Free and frequent public transport combined with policies that stimulate cycling and walking is the only serious approach to curbing greenhouse gas emissions in the transport sector.

Carbon trading schemes won't solve the crisis

Mainstream political debate on global warming is dominated by discussion of emissions trading systems [ETS]. These involve "capping" national GHG emissions at a target level and issuing permits or licences to polluting industries that aim at restricting the volume of carbon dioxide they emit, by requiring polluters to pay for these licences. The Rudd Government proposes that such a system, its carbon Pollution Reduction Scheme, will commence in 2010.

These schemes are riddled with loopholes. In theory, the total amount of carbon that can be released is reduced each year, the price of carbon rises and those who don't make the change to carbon-saving technologies pay the price. In practice, the schemes are very difficult if not impossible to police and the price of carbon is set far too low to force business to abandon its polluting practices quickly enough to have anything like the impact on overall emissions that is needed.

For example, the CSIRO has calculated that carbon would have to trade between $350 and $575 a tonne to produce the (inadequate) level of carbon emission reductions targeted in the Stern Review. In early 2009 the carbon price in the European ETS had fallen to $20 a tonne.

Carbon credits are also given out for "carbon offsets," such as planting a forest plantation somewhere, even if the plantation would have gone ahead anyway or if another forest was cut down in order to plant it! These credits permit companies to carry on polluting, while continuing to profit.

If the credits are given out by governments instead of being sold or auctioned, and if the caps are too lenient, industries suffer no penalties and can keep polluting as usual – which is what has happened with the European

Union's scheme over the last two years.

No solution without public ownership and democratic control

The principle of "polluter pays" means that the polluting companies should be directed to clean up the mess they have made. Individual consumers do use polluting products but they are rarely responsible for the decisions that result in the pollution occurring: it is the big industries that must bear the costs.

The first measure to ensure a just solution is to take over industries that will not stop polluting, and place them under public ownership and scrutiny. In this way, those operations that are essential can be identified and kept (and cleaned up) while non-essential aspects can be scaled back or shut down. The profits that these public enterprises will still make can be re-invested in further programs.

Private power companies have a vested interest in making us all use more energy, whereas what is really needed is less use of energy and clean power targets that can be met with renewable sources.

But Australian governments have continually privatized public utilities, handing vital infrastructure over to the private sector. Public ownership and control over the vital area of energy generation and distribution is essential to bring this sector under an overall plan for greenhouse gas reduction and environmental sustainability.

Guarantee jobs, involve workers
in the fight for a liveable environment

As old industries die, their workers are normally thrown on the scrap heap of unemployment. For example, as oil prices rise and cars become too expensive, the fossil-fuel based auto industry may well shrink to a boutique luxury service and masses of workers lose their jobs.

The same can be said for unsustainable agriculture, coal mining and similar industries. A plan for a transition to a sustainable and just economy is therefore essential. These workers would become the driving force and moral guarantor of the new sustainable society, and not left behind with the de-commissioned machinery.

Workers are critical to identifying and eliminating waste and pollution in the workplace, closing down old industries and opening new ones. The transition also needs government-funded "climate action brigades" – teams of people who can provide practical assistance and resources to assist households and communities improve their energy efficiency.

Socialist Alliance proposes a massive program of converting energy infrastructure that will demand a large number of workers, requiring extensive redeployment and training. We will also need an expansion of free public education to provide sufficient numbers of skilled professionals to achieve the necessary research and development goals.

Working people and their unions can also show the way to sustainability to the rest of society by producing model projects, like high standard, carbon neutral, sustainable housing – proof that the combination of appropriate technology with workers' skills will be key in the transition.

Change the system, not the climate!

None of what we have outlined is going to happen unless it is fought for by an informed and mobilized community. In the words of climate scientist James Hansen:

> The alternative scenario is feasible, but it is not being pursued. Our best hope? The public must become informed and get angry.

Australia's fossil fuel industries won't accept these measures. For years they funded climate sceptics to produce reports that threw doubt on the reality and severity of the problem. The former Howard Government was their faithful servant, by trying to undermine the Kyoto protocol and by refusing to take action that would reduce the profits of the coal, aluminium, electricity and forestry industries.

Now, faced with overwhelming community concern, organizations like the Business Council of Australia are concerned to preserve their members' polluting capital for as long as possible behind a new thin coat of greenwash as they pressure (successfully) the Rudd government to implement GHG reduction targets so inadequate that they have been condemned by Ross Garnaut's, the government's chief adviser on the issue.

Despite its strident criticism of Howard's denialism, the ALP is almost as much the creature of the big polluters as the Coalition, fixated on "clean coal" and allowing more uranium mining. It proposes targets for emissions reductions by 2050 that would mean Australia emitting 6-10 times (per person) the Earth's estimated capacity to absorb carbon, and lead inevitably to catastrophic climate change.

Both major parties cynically claim to be protecting jobs, despite the decline in working conditions in some industries (e.g. speed-ups and health and safety declines in coal mining), and job losses in others (e.g. forestry).

The Socialist Alliance says that the planet and future generations are more important than corporate profits.

By knowingly spreading disinformation, standing over elected governments and resisting change despite the risks to all people and our planet, these corporations have lost the right to control the resources they are wasting.

The community cannot afford vested interests like theirs to continue to determine policy. To replace their control of policy will require a movement that is independent of either of the major parties, but is strong enough to put pressure on whichever party is in government.

Just as previous mass movements forced the Australian government to withdraw from the war in Vietnam and stop plans to dam Tasmania's Franklin River, so the movement to avert climate catastrophe must mean more than just voting for change. The campaign must also happen in the streets, workplaces, schools and universities to win wide public support for the changes that need to be made.

Creating those changes also means challenging the capitalist market, which has failed to protect future generations and can no longer be allowed to stop us from averting climatic disaster. The measures outlined above are not only absolutely necessary to prevent global warming getting out of control, they also lay the basis for a society that is sustainable on an ongoing basis, because they subordinate production to human and environmental imperatives.

The Socialist Alliance 10-point climate action plan

1. Implement immediate emission reduction targets with the aim of reducing net emissions to zero as soon as practicable, with a goal of achieving 100% of power from renewable sources by 2020. Introduce annual reduction targets of at least 5% to ensure that these targets are met.

2. Initiate further international treaty negotiations aimed at getting all countries to agree to these targets. Prioritize cutting rich industrial nations' emissions, and supply aid to poorer countries to assist them in harnessing renewable sources of energy for industrial development.

3. Start the transition to a zero-waste economy. End industrial energy waste by legislation. Improve or ban wasteful consumer products. Engage workers in industry, with the appropriate technical experts, to redesign products and jobs sustainably.

4. Require the fitting of all feasible energy efficiency measures to existing houses and subsidies owner-occupiers for the costs. Allow renters to use the same system. Install photovoltaic solar panels and solar hot water heaters on home roofs, subsidized or owned by the electricity authority. Give commercial buildings a deadline to meet six-star energy standards within two years, and 10-star standards within 10 years.

5. Bring all power industries under public ownership and democratic control. Begin phasing out coal mining and coal-fired power immediately. Provide guaranteed jobs and retraining on full pay for coal mining and power-station communities, with new sustainable industries being built in their areas and paid redundancies offered. Run the maximum possible base-load power from existing natural gas and/or hydro power stations

instead of coal only as an interim measure until renewable energy is available. Coal to be used only for predicted energy peaks in the short term.

6. Bring the whole car industry under public control. Re-tool this industry to manufacture wind turbines, public transport vehicles and infrastructure, solar hot water, solar photovoltaic cells. Subsidize the conversion of private cars to electric power.

7. Accelerate the construction of wind farms in suitable areas. Boost research into all renewable energy sources. Build pilot solar-thermal and geothermal plants now. Create localized power grids.

8. Stop logging old-growth forests and begin an urgent program of re-forestation and protecting biodiversity to ensure a robust biosystem that can survive the stress of climate change and provide an increased carbon sink.

9. Phase out industrial farming based on fertilizers, pesticides and fuel sourced from petroleum. Work with farmers and their organizations to make food production sustainable and carbon negative. Restrict farming areas to ensure that riverine, forest and other indigenous ecosystems return to healthy states. Encourage new farming practices including organic and urban farming. This process must allow for security of food supplies, and guarantee full employment and retraining for rural communities.

10. Make all urban and regional public transport free and upgrade services to enable all urban residents to use it for regular commuting. Nationalize and upgrade interstate train and ferry services to provide real alternatives to air travel. Priorities rail freight. All rail, light rail and interstate freight to be electrified or to run on biofuels from waste where possible. Encourage bicycle use through more cycleways, and better facilities for cyclists. Implement free or very cheap bicycle rental networks.

The Belem Ecosocialist Declaration

Ecosocialist International Network

> The world is suffering from a fever due to climate change, and the disease is
> the capitalist development model.
> — Evo Morales, president of Bolivia, September 2007

Humanity's choice

Humanity today faces a stark choice: ecosocialism or barbarism.

We need no more proof of the barbarity of capitalism, the parasitical system that exploits humanity and nature alike. Its sole motor is the imperative toward profit and thus the need for constant growth. It wastefully creates unnecessary products, squandering the environment's limited resources and returning to it only toxins and pollutants. Under capitalism, the only measure of success is how much more is sold every day, every week, every year – involving the creation of vast quantities of products that are directly harmful to both humans and nature, commodities that cannot be produced without spreading disease, destroying the forests that produce the oxygen we breathe, demolishing ecosystems, and treating our water, air and soil like sewers for the disposal of industrial waste.

Capitalism's need for growth exists on every level, from the individual enterprise to the system as a whole. The insatiable hunger of corporations is facilitated by imperialist expansion in search of ever greater access to natural resources, cheap labour and new markets. Capitalism has always been ecologically destructive, but in our lifetimes these assaults on the earth have accelerated. Quantitative change is giving way to qualitative transformation, bringing the world to a tipping point, to the edge of disaster. A growing body of scientific research has identified many ways in which small temperature increases could trigger irreversible, runaway effects – such as rapid melting of the Greenland ice sheet or the release of methane buried in permafrost and beneath the ocean – that would make catastrophic climate change inevitable.

Left unchecked, global warming will have devastating effects on human, animal and plant life. Crop yields will drop drastically, leading to famine on a broad scale. Hundreds of millions of people will be displaced by droughts in some areas and by rising ocean levels in others. Chaotic, unpredictable weather will become the norm. Air, water and soil will be poisoned. Epidemics of malaria, cholera and even deadlier diseases will hit the poorest and most vulnerable members of every society.

The impact of the ecological crisis is felt most severely by those whose lives have already been ravaged by imperialism in Asia, Africa, and Latin

America, and indigenous peoples everywhere are especially vulnerable. Environmental destruction and climate change constitute an act of aggression by the rich against the poor.

Ecological devastation, resulting from the insatiable need to increase profits, is not an accidental feature of capitalism: it is built into the system's DNA and cannot be reformed away. Profit-oriented production only considers a short-term horizon in its investment decisions, and cannot take into account the long-term health and stability of the environment. Infinite economic expansion is incompatible with finite and fragile ecosystems, but the capitalist economic system cannot tolerate limits on growth; its constant need to expand will subvert any limits that might be imposed in the name of "sustainable development." Thus the inherently unstable capitalist system cannot regulate its own activity, much less overcome the crises caused by its chaotic and parasitical growth, because to do so would require setting limits upon accumulation – an unacceptable option for a system predicated upon the rule: Grow or Die!

If capitalism remains the dominant social order, the best we can expect is unbearable climate conditions, an intensification of social crises and the spread of the most barbaric forms of class rule, as the imperialist powers fight among themselves and with the global south for continued control of the world's diminishing resources.

At worst, human life may not survive.

Capitalist Strategies for Change

There is no lack of proposed strategies for contending with ecological ruin, including the crisis of global warming looming as a result of the reckless increase of atmospheric carbon dioxide. The great majority of these strategies share one common feature: they are devised by and on behalf of the dominant global system, capitalism.

It is no surprise that the dominant global system which is responsible for the ecological crisis also sets the terms of the debate about this crisis, for capital commands the means of production of knowledge, as much as that of atmospheric carbon dioxide. Accordingly, its politicians, bureaucrats, economists and professors send forth an endless stream of proposals, all variations on the theme that the world's ecological damage can be repaired without disruption of market mechanisms and of the system of accumulation that commands the world economy.

But a person cannot serve two masters – the integrity of the earth and the profitability of capitalism. One must be abandoned, and history leaves little question about the allegiances of the vast majority of policy-makers. There is every reason, therefore, to radically doubt the capacity of established measures to check the slide to ecological catastrophe.

And indeed, beyond a cosmetic veneer, the reforms over the past thirty-five years have been a monstrous failure. Isolated improvements do of course occur, but they are inevitably overwhelmed and swept away by the ruthless expansion of the system and the chaotic character of its production.

One example demonstrates the failure: in the first four years of the 21st Century, global carbon emissions were nearly three times as great per annum as those of the decade of the 1990s, despite the appearance of the Kyoto Protocols in 1997.

Kyoto employs two devices: the "Cap and Trade" system of trading pollution credits to achieve certain reductions in emissions, and projects in the global south – the so-called "Clean Development Mechanisms" – to offset emissions in the highly industrialized nations. These instruments all rely upon market mechanisms, which means, first of all, that atmospheric carbon dioxide becomes a commodity under the control of the same interests that created global warming. Polluters are not compelled to reduce their carbon

---

*Environmental destruction and climate change
constitute an act of aggression by the rich
against the poor*

---

emissions, but allowed to use their power over money to control the carbon market for their own ends, which include the devastating exploration for yet more carbon-based fuels. Nor is there a limit to the amount of emission credits which can be issued by compliant governments.

Since verification and evaluation of results are impossible, the Kyoto regime is not only incapable of controlling emissions. It also provides ample opportunities for evasion and fraud of all kinds. As even the *Wall Street Journal* put it in March, 2007, emissions trading "would make money for some very large corporations, but don't believe for a minute that this charade would do much about global warming."

The Bali climate meetings in 2007 opened the way for even greater abuses in the period ahead. Bali avoided any mention of the goals for drastic carbon reduction put forth by the best climate science (90% by 2050); it abandoned the peoples of the global south to the mercy of capital by giving jurisdiction over the process to the World Bank; and made offsetting of carbon pollution even easier.

In order to affirm and sustain our human future, a revolutionary transformation is needed, where all particular struggles take part in a greater struggle against capital itself. This larger struggle cannot remain merely negative and anti-capitalist. It must announce and build a different kind of society, and this is ecosocialism.

The Ecosocialist Alternative

The ecosocialist movement aims to stop and to reverse the disastrous process of global warming in particular and of capitalist ecocide in general, and to construct a radical and practical alternative to the capitalist system. Ecosocialism is grounded in a transformed economy founded on the non-monetary values of social justice and ecological balance. It criticizes both capitalist "market ecology" and productivist socialism which ignored the earth's equilibrium and limits. It redefines the path and goal of socialism within an ecological and democratic framework.

Ecosocialism involves a revolutionary social transformation, which will imply the limitation of growth and the transformation of needs by a profound shift away from quantitative and toward qualitative economic criteria, an emphasis on use-value instead of exchange-value.

These aims require both democratic decision-making in the economic sphere, enabling society to collectively define its goals of investment and production, and the collectivization of the means of production. Only collec-

---

If capitalism remains the dominant social order,
the best we can expect is unbearable climate conditions,
an intensification of social crises and the spread of the
most barbaric forms of class rule

---

tive decision-making and ownership of production can offer the longer-term perspective that is necessary for the balance and sustainability of our social and natural systems.

The rejection of productivism and the shift away from quantitative and toward qualitative economic criteria involve rethinking the nature and goals of production and economic activity in general. Essential creative, non-productive and reproductive human activities, such as householding, child-rearing, care, child and adult education, and the arts, will be key values in an ecosocialist economy.

Clean air and water and fertile soil, as well as universal access to chemical-free food and renewable, non-polluting energy sources, are basic human and natural rights defended by ecosocialism. Far from being "despotic," collective policy-making on the local, regional, national and international levels amounts to society's exercise of communal freedom and responsibility. This freedom of decision constitutes a liberation from the alienating economic "laws" of the growth-oriented capitalist system.

To avoid global warming and other dangers threatening human and ecological survival, entire sectors of industry and agriculture must be suppressed, reduced, or restructured and others must be developed, while providing full employment for all. Such a radical transformation is impossible without collective control of the means of production and democratic planning of production and exchange. Democratic decisions on investment and technological development must replace control by capitalist enterprises, investors and banks, in order to serve the long-term horizon of society's and nature's common good.

The most oppressed elements of human society, the poor and indigenous peoples, must take full part in the ecosocialist revolution, in order to revitalize ecologically sustainable traditions and give voice to those whom the capitalist system cannot hear. Because the peoples of the global south and the poor in general are the first victims of capitalist destruction, their struggles and demands will help define the contours of the ecologically and economically sustainable society in creation. Similarly, gender equality is integral to ecosocialism, and women's movements have been among the most active and vocal opponents of capitalist oppression. Other potential agents of ecosocialist revolutionary change exist in all societies.

Such a process cannot begin without a revolutionary transformation of social and political structures based on the active support, by the majority of the population, of an ecosocialist program. The struggle of labour – workers, farmers, the landless and the unemployed – for social justice is inseparable from the struggle for environmental justice. Capitalism, socially and ecologically exploitative and polluting, is the enemy of nature and of labour alike.

Ecosocialism proposes radical transformations in:

▸ the energy system, by replacing carbon-based fuels and biofuels with clean sources of power under community control: wind, geothermal, wave, and above all, solar power.

▸ the transportation system, by drastically reducing the use of private trucks and cars, replacing them with free and efficient public transportation;

▸ present patterns of production, consumption, and building, which are based on waste, inbuilt obsolescence, competition and pollution, by producing only sustainable and recyclable goods and developing green architecture;

▸ food production and distribution, by defending local food sovereignty as far as this is possible, eliminating polluting industrial agribusinesses, creating sustainable agro-ecosystems and working actively to renew soil fertility.

To theorize and to work toward realizing the goal of green socialism does not mean that we should not also fight for concrete and urgent reforms right now. Without any illusions about "clean capitalism," we must work to impose on the powers that be – governments, corporations, international institutions – some elementary but essential immediate changes:

> ▸ drastic and enforceable reduction in the emission of greenhouse gases,
> ▸ development of clean energy sources,
> ▸ provision of an extensive free public transportation system,
> ▸ progressive replacement of trucks by trains,
> ▸ creation of pollution clean-up programs,
> ▸ elimination of nuclear energy, and war spending.

These and similar demands are at the heart of the agenda of the Global Justice movement and the World Social Forums, which have promoted, since Seattle in 1999, the convergence of social and environmental movements in a common struggle against the capitalist system.

Environmental devastation will not be stopped in conference rooms and treaty negotiations: only mass action can make a difference. Urban and rural workers, peoples of the global south and indigenous peoples everywhere are at the forefront of this struggle against environmental and social injustice, fighting exploitative and polluting multinationals, poisonous and disenfranchising agribusinesses, invasive genetically modified seeds, biofuels that only aggravate the current food crisis. We must further these social-environmental movements and build solidarity between anticapitalist ecological mobilizations in the North and the South.

This Ecosocialist Declaration is a call to action. The entrenched ruling classes are powerful, yet the capitalist system reveals itself every day more financially and ideologically bankrupt, unable to overcome the economic, ecological, social, food and other crises it engenders. And the forces of radical opposition are alive and vital. On all levels, local, regional and international, we are fighting to create an alternative system based in social and ecological justice.

Climate Crisis: 21st Century Socialists Must Be Ecosocialists

Daniel Tanuro / Fourth International

Published in French, February 2009. Translation by Ian Angus.

I. The Climate Threat: Causes, Responsibilities, Social and Ecological Impacts

1. Climate change is an unprecedented reality

Climate change is a fact. In the 20th century, the Earth's average surface temperature rose 0.6°C, sea level went up between 10 and 20 centimetres, glaciers retreated significantly almost everywhere, the violence of North Atlantic hurricanes increased, and extreme weather phenomena such as storms, floods and droughts, were recorded in unprecedented numbers.

This is not a matter of cyclical variations (such as, for example, the El Nino phenomenon) but of profound, long-term changes that reflect an important overall imbalance of the climate system. The driving force underlying this imbalance – the rise in average surface temperature – is unprecedented for at least 1300 years. It is strongly correlated with another phenomenon, this one unprecedented for 800,000 years: an increase in the concentration of atmospheric carbon, in the form of carbon dioxide and methane – two gases whose contribution to the greenhouse effect was confirmed by physics long ago.

The conclusion that the major cause of global warming is the rise in greenhouse gas emissions is over 90% certain: it is no longer the subject of credible debate on the scientific level. It is well established that the present global warming is unprecedented and differs radically from other periods of global warming that the Earth has experienced. In past inter-glacial periods, natural variations in the Earth's position relative to the Sun or in solar activity caused global warming, which on one hand promoted the development of life and on the other reduced the absorption of CO_2 by the oceans, and these two factors in turn led to a rise in the concentration of CO_2 in the atmosphere, which further accentuated global warming. Today the chain of causality has been reversed: natural factors explain only a very limited part (approximately 5 to 10 percent) of global warming; most of the present rise results directly from a very rapid increase in the atmospheric concentrations of CO_2 and methane, resulting from human activity. In other words: previously climate warming caused the increase in the greenhouse effect, today the increase in the greenhouse effect is causing climate change.

2. The expression "climate change" is misleading: we are confronted with a brutal swing, irreversible on the human time-scale.

The expression "climate change" is misleading: it implies gradual modification, but what we face is a brutal and accelerating shift. It results from three types of economic activities that increase atmospheric concentrations of greenhouse gases:

(a) Forests, natural meadows, soil and peat bogs retain carbon in the form of organic matter. This carbon is freed by deforestation, the transformation of natural meadows into cultivated land, the draining of wetlands, and bad cultivation methods. Moreover, the excessive use of artificial nitrate-based fertilizers (17.9 percent of emissions) causes emissions of nitrous oxide, another greenhouse gas.

(b) Any combustion produces carbon dioxide (CO_2) emissions, but there is a great difference between CO_2 that comes from biomass combustion, and CO_2 that comes from burning fossil fuels (coal, oil, natural gas). The first is recycled without any problem by the ecosystems (green plants and oceans) which continuously absorb and emit CO_2 (the "carbon cycle"). The second, in contrast, can only be recycled to a limited degree because it exceeds the ecosystems' absorption capacity. For two centuries the burning of fossil fuels has injected important quantities of CO_2 (56.6 percent of emissions) into the atmosphere, rapidly and continuously.

(c) Some industrial processes emit greenhouse gases (fluorinated gases) that don't exist in nature.

Carbon is present naturally in the atmosphere only in very weak concentrations. It is precisely for this reason that human activities can have such an impact on the climate system. Today we are sending twice as much greenhouse gas into the atmosphere as nature can absorb. The excess accumulates, leading to an increase in greenhouse gases and therefore of temperature, and the accumulation tends to accelerate as global warming increases. The principal mechanism of global warming can thus be summed up as saturation of the carbon cycle by emissions of gas originating from human activities.

This warming is irreversible on a human timescale. Even if atmospheric concentrations of greenhouse gases were stabilized immediately, global warming would continue for nearly a thousand years, because the enormous masses of ocean water take a very long time to reach temperature equilibrium. If concentrations are not stabilized, the mechanism will inevitably speed up dramatically, unleashing extremely dangerous phenomena such as the disintegration of the polar icecaps or the release of the enormous quantities of methane contained in frozen ground (permafrost) and possibly also in the depths of the oceans.

It would be a dangerous error to gamble on the possibility that reserves of coal, oil and gas will be exhausted in time to protect humanity from these major risks. In fact, proven fossil fuel reserves (in particular of coal) are more than sufficient to cause uncontrollable acceleration. If that happens, the Earth will likely return to conditions that it has not known for 65 million years and that humanity has consequently never experienced: a world without ice, where sea level is about a hundred metres higher than at present.

3. The climate upheaval is not due to human activity in general but to the form this activity has taken since the capitalist Industrial Revolution.

The climate upheaval is not due to human activity in general, as the media and the IPCC reports say, but rather to the form of this activity since the capitalist Industrial Revolution, in particular to the burning of fossil fuels. The fundamental cause is the capitalist and productivist logic of accumulation, whose historical centre of gravity is located in the imperialist metropolises.

The economic take-off of the Industrial Revolution could not have occurred on a large scale without coal, but it would be simplistic to impute climate change to "progress" in general. In fact, new possibilities for renewable energy appeared fairly quickly; if they had been exploited, they would have made possible both reasonable development and a protected environment. There is a glaring contrast between the long-continuing lack of interest in the photovoltaic effect which was discovered in 1839, and the immediate infatuation of capitalist and non-capitalist countries with atomic fission. The nuclear industry would not have been possible without large-scale public investment, authorized in spite of the technology's terrible dangers. Solar energy has never benefited from such interest.

As capitalism developed, big energy groups acquired the decisive economic weight that enabled them to shape the energy system to reflect their interests. The power of these groups results not only from the fact that energy is essential to any economic activity and that energy requires long-term investments, but also from the fact that the limited character of fossil fuel deposits and the possibility of their private appropriation makes monopoly prices possible, allowing the companies to reap large superprofits in the form of energy rent.

In particular, the key role of oil as an abundant and cheap source of liquid fuel with high energy content has enabled the increasingly concentrated and centralized capital that controls this sector to occupy a strategic position, in the economy and in politics. Together with the coal companies, the electricity industry and the major sectors that depend on oil (automobile, shipbuilding and aeronautics, petrochemicals), the oil multinationals systematically blocked the development of alternative energy resources, technologies and models of distribution, while encouraging overconsumption and limiting progress in energy efficiency, in systems and products.

To understand the mechanisms of climate change, our analysis must also take into account the general tendency of capitalism towards concentration and centralization, the ceaseless replacement of living labour by dead labour, technical standardization, and the overproduction of mass consumer goods for the world market. In particular, after the Second World War, this tendency resulted in the manufacture of millions of individual cars, which, while "pulling" the long wave of growth in the post-war decades, contributed to an explosive rise in the use of fossil fuels, and therefore of emissions.

More recently, neoliberal capitalist globalization, massive export of capital to the emerging countries, lean production for the world market, the dismantling of public transport (in particular rail), and the spectacular increase in air and maritime transport have given fresh impetus to this process.

4. The countries of "really existing socialism" also bear a heavy responsibility: renouncing the world revolution, they aped productivism and copied capitalist technologies.

No analysis of climate change can ignore the responsibility of countries that tried to embark on a non-capitalist road. Mainly as a result of bureaucratic degeneration, these countries returned to productivism and took the waste of natural resources, in particular energy, to unprecedented levels.

Tsarist Russia was a backward country. After the war, the revolution and the civil war, it would not have been possible to get it back on its feet without fossil fuels. This partly explains the absence of forward thinking by Soviet theorists on the inevitable fate of a system based on non-renewable sources, but other factors were involved (cf. section 4 below). What seems certain is that the economic development of the USSR could have made it possible to explore other choices, but the Stalinist dictatorship and the degeneration of "socialism in one country" blocked that road.

By abandoning the perspective of world revolution, by counting on peaceful coexistence with imperialism in the hope of safeguarding its own privileges, by stifling creative thought, the Stalinist bureaucracy chose both to follow in the military-driven technological footsteps of the developed capitalist countries, and to imitate the capitalist energy system, which was specifically designed to meet the needs of capital. This logic culminated under Khrushchev in the illusion of catching up with and overtaking the USA. It led in particular to the senseless development of nuclear energy, which was to lead to the catastrophe of Chernobyl.

The bureaucratic system of material incentives to managers, with bonuses based on the amount of material consumed, was a specific driver of waste. The resulting energy system was even more polluting and wasteful than the capitalist model it aimed to emulate, and even less efficient.

Lastly, contempt for the needs for the masses, their exclusion from political decisions and the determination to maintain them in a state of social atomization led to largely irrational choices in a whole series of fields (town and country planning, architecture, town planning, not to mention the forced collectivization of agriculture). These choices aggravated the waste of resources and the energy inefficiency of the whole system, not to mention leading to serious consequences in other domains, in particular pollution and public health.

As a result, after the Second World War, the CO_2 emissions of the USSR and parts of Eastern Europe comprised a significant share of world emissions. A comparison between the annual per capita carbon gas emissions in these countries with those in the developed capitalist countries in the same period clearly shows the responsibility of "really existing socialism" for the disruption of the climate. Just before the fall of the Berlin Wall, for example, annual per capita CO_2 emissions came to 20.7 tons in Czechoslovakia and 22 tons in the GDR. The comparable figures in the USA, Canada and Australia – the biggest emitters of CO_2 in the developed capitalist world – were 18.9, 16.2 and 15 tons, despite their considerably higher per capita GNP levels.

5. Climate change has catastrophic consequences for humanity and ecosystems.

Climate change has catastrophic consequences for humanity and ecosystems. There is no doubt that the negative effects will be greater than the positive effects, even for a limited rise in temperature. According to the IPCC:[1]

▸ Any temperature increase between +1°C and +5°C will intensify droughts in subtropical regions and in semi-arid tropical areas. Over +2°C, millions more people will be subjected to coastal floods each year. From +3°C, approximately 30% of coastal wetlands will be lost.

▸ Already, global warming is reducing the harvests of small farmers and the catches of fisher folk who produce the means of subsistence for local populations. From +1°C in tropical regions, it is anticipated that productivity losses of some cereals will increase, and from +3.5°C, a loss of productivity for all cereals. In the temperate regions (high latitudes), productivity will increase for some cereals from +1°C, then an increasingly general decrease in productivity will occur from +3.5°C.

▸ Already, health systems are facing additional workloads due to malnutrition, diarrhoea, cardio-respiratory and infectious diseases, caused by climate change. Increased morbidity and mortality are already being experienced during heat waves, floods and droughts, as is the expansion of regions affected by certain disease vectors (anopheles that transmit malaria, ticks that transmit Lyme's disease...). What's more, burning fossil fuels contributes to air pollution, in particular the fine particles that are a major cause of the extremely worrying increase in respiratory diseases such as asthma.

▸ From +1°C, it is estimated that 30 percent of animal and plant species will face increased risk of extinction. A rise of +5°C will cause significant extinctions of species in all regions of the world. These projections are all the more alarming in that other factors such as land use and chemical pollution are already contributing to a wave of extinction greater and more rapid than the Earth experienced 60 million years ago, when the dinosaurs disappeared. Over and above the important aesthetic, emotional and cultural effects of these extinctions, the radical reduction in species constitutes a serious threat to human life, because biodiversity determines the capacity of ecosystems to adapt. This is particularly true of cultivated ecosystems, because the amount of diversity determines the availability of plants that can be selected for their resistance to climate changes.

▸ From approximately +2.5°C, between 15 and 40 percent of terrestrial ecosystems will start to emit more CO_2 than they absorb. When that happens, carbon cycle saturation will accelerate, and we may face uncontrollable "runaway climate change."

On a human level, according to some projections, the number of victims of various disasters, diseases and shortages tends to increase more and more quickly as temperatures rise. For a rise of +3.25°C compared to the pre-industrial period, which is approximately the mid-range of IPCC projections, coastal floods will affect 100 to 150 million victims between now and 2050, famines up to 600 million and malaria 300 million, while water shortages will affect up to 3.5 billion more.

These estimates obviously involve high degrees of uncertainty, and they are subject to social factors that can increase or reduce them to some degree, especially if global warming is limited. But it is nevertheless true that, with no change in policy, the scale of the threat is considerable.

6. The peoples of the South, the principal victims of climate change, are already paying a heavy price.

Between 2000 and 2004, the world experienced an average of 326 climate disasters a year, affecting a total of 262 million people – nearly three times as many as between 1980 and 1984. More than 200 million of those victims lived in non-OECD countries that have only a marginal responsibility for increased greenhouse gas emissions. In the developing countries, one out of every 19 people was affected by a climate disaster, compared to one out of 1500 in the OECD countries – 79 times more.[2]

Without effective action, this climate injustice will accentuate dramatically. The United Nations Development Programme says that climate change will prevent even its manifestly insufficient "Millennium Objectives" from being achieved. Catastrophic climate change will likely plunge some of the poorest countries into a spiral of social and economic decline, with no way out. For example, the vast majority of the hundreds of millions of human beings threatened by the rise in the level of the oceans are located in China (30 million), India (30 million), Bangladesh (15-20 million), Egypt (10 million) and in deltas such as the Niger and Mekong (10 million) If the oceans rise one metre, a quarter of the population of Vietnam will have to move.

Increased food insecurity is another glaring illustration of climate injustice. Some experts say that by 2080 agricultural production in the developed countries could increase 8%, while production in developing countries will fall 9%. Latin America and Africa would be affected most, with production falling by more than 12%, perhaps as much as 15%. The IPCC says that in parts of sub-Saharan Africa and Asia, the productivity of non-irrigated agriculture could be cut in half. Consequences are likely to include greater dependence on capitalist agribusiness, more domination by latifundists, increased poverty and famine affecting small farmers, rural migration and environmental degradation.

7. The example of Hurricane Katrina shows that the workers and poor people of the developed countries are also at risk.

Hurricane Katrina, which struck New Orleans in September 2005, showed that the poorest sectors of the working class in developed countries are little better equipped to face climate change than the masses in countries dominated by imperialism: they live in the areas most exposed to disasters, they have no way to escape – or they are afraid to do so from fear of being unable to return and losing everything – and their property is under-insured or not insured at all.

Katrina killed 1500 people and displaced 780,000 more. 750,000 had no insurance. 28% of New Orleans' total population and 35% of its African-American population lived in poverty, compared to 12% and 25% of the U.S. as a whole. Poor neighbourhoods were the most affected: the flooded districts were 75% Black.

Because public authorities did not organize evacuation, 138,000 of the city's 480,000 inhabitants were trapped without drinking water, electricity or telephones. They waited more than five days before aid came. The vast majority were poor workers, unemployed, poor children, and elderly people without resources.

This balance sheet is inseparable from the class, imperialist and racist policies of the US ruling class in general and the Bush administration in particular. From 2003, to finance the "war on terror," Washington systematically slashed the budget of the department charged with maintaining the levees; in 2005, it received barely a sixth of the resources it requested. This arrogant and brutal policy continued after the disaster, through a rebuilding strategy that drove the poor out of the city and through attacks on workers' social gains, in particular, abolition of the minimum wage.

This balance sheet is also inseparable from other social inequalities that characterize capitalist society, above all those imposed on women. It is no accident that African-American women and their children paid the heaviest price in New Orleans. Women are in the front line because they account for 80% of the 1.3 billion people who live below the poverty line. And, because of their specific oppression, women are affected in specific ways. For example, in the least developed countries, climate changes necessitate collecting more wood for heating and reduced income from agricultural work, tasks carried out mainly by women. In more developed countries, precarious employment, part-time work and low wages particularly affect women; as a result they have less ability to protect themselves against the effects of climate change. In both cases, single mothers, especially young women, are affected most severely.

II. Saving the Climate:
Physical and Human Constraints

8. Climate change is a matter of extreme urgency. Even very radical and rapid reduction of greenhouse gas emissions is unlikely to keep us from crossing the danger threshold.

According to the IPCC, if current emissions trends continue until 2100,the Earth's average surface temperature will increase by 1.1° and 6.4°C over the 1990 level. The size of this range results from uncertainties about the models themselves on one hand, and about the various possible scenarios of social and economic development on the other..

The fact that temperature increases between 1990 and 2006 were at the top end of the range of projections, leads to the conclusion that unless changes are made humanity is likely to face temperature increases of +4.5°C or more in the short term, compared to the end of the 18th century.

That would involve a change in living conditions at least as great as the change between now and the last Ice Age, 20,000 years ago – but instead of taking millennia, this change could occur in a few centuries, or even less. Such rapid change seriously reduces the possibilities of adaptation, for both human societies and ecosystems.

In 1996, the EU, basing itself on then-current estimates of the "dangerous change" threshold, set a maximum 2°C increase as its climate policy objective. Since then, these estimates have been reduced: experts now place the threshold at about 1.7°C. Even at that level the risks are high, especially in regard to biodiversity, ocean levels, and agricultural productivity in tropical and subtropical countries.

The average surface temperature of the Earth has increased 0.7°C since the pre-industrial period and a further 0.6°C is probably already in the pipeline. Consequently, room for manoeuvre to save the climate is extremely narrow. The situation must be considered critical.

Greenhouse gases stay in the atmosphere for long periods, approximately 150 years for CO_2. This means that temperatures can only be stabilized by reducing emissions, – and since the target level is low, the reduction must be rapid and severe.

The most radical scenarios considered in the fourth assessment report (2007) involved atmospheric concentrations of CO_2 between 350 and 400 parts per million (ppm), or 445-490 ppm of CO_2 equivalents.[3] This would require (a) reductions in annual global emissions that begin in 2015 at the latest, leading to (b) a 50% to 85% reduction in total emissions by 2050.

The developed countries, which have been burning fossil fuels for more than two hundred years, are responsible for more than 70% of climate change – so the reductions required of developed countries and of countries dominated by imperialism must reflect their different historic responsibilities for climate change. The former should reduce emissions by 80% to 95% by 2050, beginning with a 25% to 40% cut by 2020. For the latter, the IPCC calls for emission cuts that "deviate substantially compared to the baseline" between now and 2020, and between now and 2050 for Africa.[4]

CO_2 is an inevitable product of any kind of combustion and the burning of fossil fuels provides 80% of the world's energy, so these objectives represent a colossal challenge. They require nothing less than near-total abandonment of fossil fuels in less than a century, which requires a profound social and economic transformation.

Even if these objectives were achieved, the rise in temperature would still slightly exceed 2°C: according to the IPCC, the increase will range between 2.0° and 2.4°C over approximately a millennium. In other words, it appears impossible to avoid crossing the danger threshold. Only one rational conclusion is possible: the most extreme reduction targets are needed, not as a vague "aspirational goal" but as an absolute necessity.

9. The targets are all the more imperative, because the IPCC's reports underestimate some drivers of climate change.

To properly appreciate the immensity of the challenge, it is important to understand that the IPCC's conclusions rest on conservative assumptions. Simple prudence dictates that we must base our actions on most pessimistic projections, and regard them as the minimum required.

This stems from two facts in particular:

a) The IPCC underestimates non-linear phenomena. One of the principal causes of uncertainty in climate projections is the great complexity of non-linear phenomena such as the possible disintegration of the icecaps of Greenland and the Antarctic. Simple ice melting is a continuous process, but the disintegration of icecaps progresses by leaps, and it has so far not been possible to model it. This no doubt helps to explain why the observed rise in ocean levels was 3 millimetres a year between 1990 and 2006, 60% percent more than the models projected. The ice accumulated in Greenland and the Antarctic would, if it all melted, increase ocean levels by about 6 metres and 60 metres respectively. According to some specialists, atmospheric CO_2 concentration is in the process of crossing the qualitative threshold that led to the formation of the Antarctic icecap 35 million years ago – but in the other direction! As a result, sudden partial collapse is possible in the short or medium term, and that could increase ocean levels by several metres in less than a century. This is one of the most serious threats posed by climate change in the short and medium term.

b) The IPCC overestimates the downward trend in the carbon intensity of the economy. Producing one unit of GDP requires a certain quantity of fossil energy, therefore a certain volume of emissions. Studies show that the energy intensity and the carbon intensity of the economy have decreased fairly steadily since the Industrial Revolution.[5] If this tendency continues, less effort would be necessary to reduce emissions than if the intensity were stationary, or increased. The work of the IPCC is based on this assumption.

However, that assumption is contradicted by recent reality: since 2000 carbon intensity has risen compared to forecasts. This results in particular from massive capital investments in China and India, leading to the construction of many coal-fired power stations that produce cheap electricity and cheap products for the Western market. Some estimates say that 17% of the increase in world emissions since 2000 results from the rise in the carbon intensity of the economy – in other words, from using more polluting technologies.

10. The only structural strategy is reduction in emissions at source. Priority must be given to reducing emissions produced by burning fossil fuels.

In theory, there are three ways to mitigate climate change: protection and expansion of carbon sinks, capture and geological sequestration of CO_2, and reduction of emissions at the source. Only emissions reduction offers a structural solution.

Deforestation is the second greatest cause of greenhouse gas emissions, so we can avoid making the problem worse by protecting existing forests. But it is not a structural solution, because, (a) mature forests emit as much carbon (by respiring) as they absorb (by photosynthesis) and (b) as we have seen, after a certain point global warming causes forests to emit more than they absorb.

Growing trees absorb more carbon than they emit, so planting trees can be a means of fighting against climate change under some social and ecological conditions. But it is not a structural solution either, because (a) expansion of forests is limited by the space available and (b) the carbon absorbed is released when trees are felled (or, depending on how the wood is used, some time later).

"Carbon Capture and Sequestration" (CCS) involves separating CO_2 as it comes out of polluting factories, and then injecting it into deep airtight geological reservoirs. The possible sequestration sites seem to have a great deal of capacity. Enthusiasm for CCS reflects the fact that it would allow continuing exploitation of coal reserves, which are much larger than reserves of oil and gas. However, it is clear that CCS is not a structural solution either: the reservoirs have necessarily finite capacity and only CO_2 emitted by large enterprises can be captured.

This leaves reduction of greenhouse gas emissions at source as the only structural answer to carbon cycle saturation. Reduction strategies exist for all the gases concerned, but radical reduction of CO_2 emissions caused by burning fossil fuels constitutes the strategic axis of the rescue of the climate because burning fossil fuels is the main cause of global warming, because CO_2 is by far the most important greenhouse gas, and because the lifespan of CO_2 in the atmosphere is relatively long.

In addition to these technical arguments, it should be stressed that, from a social perspective, emissions from automobile or air transport cannot be considered equivalent to methane emissions produced by rice cultivation or the non-fossil CO_2 emissions produced by the slash-and-burn agriculture practised by forest-based indigenous peoples.

11. Absolute reduction of energy consumption in developed countries is a prerequisite for a transition to renewable energy and for rescuing the climate.

A radical reduction of fossil CO_2 emissions will require two simultaneous processes: replacement of fossil energy by renewable energy, and reduced energy consumption.

The technical potential of solar energy in its various forms (wind farms, solar thermal, solar photovoltaic, hydraulic, marine) is equivalent to between 7 and 10 times current global energy consumption.[6] Progress in scientific research and technique could increase that very considerably in coming decades. Total decarbonizing of the world economy without recourse to nuclear power is thus not just a dream, and in itself does not require a sharp retreat in human development or in our emancipation from heavy, repetitive or dangerous work.

However, this enormous technical potential does not mean that renewable sources can simply replace fossil sources, while nothing else changes. In fact:

(a) solar energy is diffuse,

(b) it comes in various shapes and forms, more or less usable, in various parts of the world, and,

(c) most of these forms are intermittent, so their use requires the development of storage systems, using new vectors and ad hoc infrastructures.

That means that the transition to renewable energy requires construction of a new international energy system, decentralized, diversified, economical, oriented to maximum efficiency, and based solely on the exploitation of solar potential. This will be a gigantic undertaking, requiring major investments. What's more, it will require energy that, at least in the first phases of the transition, must be mainly of fossil origin and therefore a source of additional emissions, or nuclear and therefore a source of unacceptable ecological, social and political dangers (see below).

As we have seen, to prevent the temperature from rising much above 2°C, world emissions must start falling no later than 2015. That means that supplementary emissions generated by the transition must be offset elsewhere. Concretely, the urgency and seriousness of the climate crisis are so great that a transition to renewable energy, in the present state of our knowledge, only offers a way out if it is strictly counterbalanced by a drastic reduction in energy consumption in the countries that use the most energy per capita. That in its turn implies a reduction – not proportionate but nevertheless considerable – of exchanges of matter, that is, of material production and consumption.

The fight against climate change thus decisively confirms more general environmental conclusions about the unsustainability of the increasingly rapid rate at which capitalism is taking resources from the natural environment without allowing the time necessary for their renewal.

12. Energy consumption in the developed countries must be drastically reduced. This process can involve not only the maintenance of past conquests but also social progress.

Reduced energy consumption mainly concerns the developed capitalist countries, where there is substantial potential for reduction of emissions by energy economies. This is confirmed by differences between countries: for example, an inhabitant of the USA consumes, on average, the equivalent of 8 tons of oil a year, while an inhabitant of Switzerland with a comparable standard of living consumes 4 tons.

Although very high, current estimates of the potential for energy reduction are substantially underestimated. In particular, they do not consider most of the structural characteristics which make capitalist society a machine for wasting energy and resources:

- ‣ the tendency to overproduction and overconsumption,
- ‣ useless or harmful production (advertising, arms manufacturing, etc.),
- ‣ separate production of heat and electricity,
- ‣ inefficient use of energy by machinery of all kinds, massive transfers of production to emerging countries that produce mainly for developed capitalist countries,
- ‣ hyper-development of transport to enable "just-in-time production" for the world market,
- ‣ accelerated product obsolescence, aberrations of destruction/reconstruction due to wars,
- ‣ absurd capitalist use of space (urban sprawl, industrial parks, etc.),
- ‣ not to mention the frenzy for material possessions by the rich and compulsive consumption as compensation for mass social alienation.

It is technically feasible to cut energy use in half in the EU and Japan and to 25% of present levels in the USA. Given the concrete mechanisms of the system's massive built-in energy waste, the least we can say is that such a change is compatible not only with preserving existing social conquests, but that the change will produce additional social gains, if we make the right political choices.

13. The climate cannot be saved without the participation of the South. The right to development of the peoples of the South must therefore be based on clean technologies.

It is no longer true that even the most drastic changes in the developed countries alone can save the climate. In just a few years, some participation by the countries dominated by imperialism, especially the big emerging countries, has become essential. IPCC estimates, calculated on the basis of differentiated historical responsibilities, stipulate that these countries must "deviate substantially in relation to the scenario of reference" by 2020 (2050 for Africa).

Emissions reductions of 15% to 30% compared to the "business as usual" scenario, are possible through a combination of forest protection and improved energy efficiency. But, apart from social strategies, realization of the fundamental right to social and economic development requires a massive transfer of clean technologies, so that these countries can escape economic development based on fossil fuels.

14. It is not enough to fight against climate change: it is necessary to adapt to changes that are now inevitable. This is a major challenge for the people of the South.

The effects of climate change are already being felt, and not even extremely radical and rapid reduction of greenhouse gas emissions will prevent all climate change. Any action strategy must therefore include both mitigation of the phenomenon itself and adaptation to effects that have become inevitable – and it must do so on a world scale, taking into account the varying historical responsibilities and capacities of each country.

In general terms, mitigation and adaptation are linked: if mitigation is strong and rapid, less adaptation is required, and vice versa. If the temperature rises more than 2°C above the pre-industrial level, adaptation will be increasingly problematic and expensive, and after a certain point it will be impossible to prevent ecological disasters on a very large scale, including catastrophes with hundreds of millions of human victims.

Adaptation doesn't just involve construction or reinforcement of protective infrastructure (barriers against floods or rising water levels, storm havens, drainage systems, etc.), and expanded emergency services. Climate change affects all aspects of social life and all ecosystems, and is likely to affect them even more in the future. Adaptation measures must therefore be implemented in very many fields: management of water resources, town and

---

Over and above technical concerns,
the most important adaptation measure is drastic
reduction of poverty and social inequality

---

country planning, agriculture, forestry, public health, environmental policy (safeguarding wetlands and mangroves, in particular), dietary habits, insurance against risks, etc.

Adaptation is a major challenge for countries dominated by imperialism, where the effects of climate change are already being sharply felt. The developed countries, those mainly responsible for climate change, are already investing massively in adaptation at home but it is also their responsibility to finance the adaptation of the less developed countries. The UNDP estimates that this will require a North-South financial transfer of $86 billion dollars a year starting in 2015.

Over and above technical concerns, the most important adaptation measure is drastic reduction of poverty and social inequality. Indeed, capacity for adaptation is directly linked to resources, social rights and the effectiveness of social safety nets. Adaptation is a particularly important challenge for women in the poorest countries, and thus for society as a whole, because women's work provides some 80% of food production.

15. Population levels are related to the evolution of the climate, but they
are not a cause of climate change. It is desirable that the demographic

transition continue, but population control measures are not an answer to the climate challenge.

The size of the world's population is obviously a factor in determining the path to climate stabilization. If there are six billion people, cutting emissions in half means limiting emissions to 0.5 tons of carbon a person per year; if there are nine billion, and everything else is equal, annual emissions will need to be reduced to approximately 0.25 tons per person. But such global calculations conceal the fact that a country like the USA, with just 5% of the world's population, consumes 25% of energy resources and produces a quarter of all greenhouse gas emissions.

The developed countries emit between eight and twenty times more CO_2 per person than the countries dominated by imperialism. In the years 1950 to 1990:

(a) population increases in the so-called "developing" countries contributed significantly less to the increase in CO_2 emissions than increased consumption in the developed countries;

(b) if population growth in the countries of the South had stopped in 1950 but CO_2 emissions had risen to Northern levels, global warming would be much more serious than it is now; and

(c) if per capita emissions in the North had matched Southern levels, global warming would definitely be less serious it is, even in the absence of any policy of population control.

Thus population growth in developing countries is not the main cause, or even a major cause of climate change. Population growth, first in the developed countries and then in the countries dominated by imperialism, is itself a product of the mode of production and consumption that was created during the Industrial Revolution. Relative overpopulation is a major feature of this system, which permanently needs a "reserve army."

It is clear from IPCC reports that this system threatens us with climate catastrophe, so the system should be confronted without delay. This is the only way to meet the challenge of global warming within the very short timescale that we have available, while respecting human rights, especially women's rights.

The demographic transition [the trend to lower birth rates], which is largely underway in the developing countries, is progressing more quickly than predicted. For many environmental reasons, it is desirable that the transition continue. That requires social progress, the development of social safety nets, providing health information to women and guaranteeing their right to control their own fertility, including the right to safe abortions. Necessarily, this is a long-term process. Short of resorting to unimaginable barbarism, no population control program can be an effective response to the climate crisis.

III. The Capitalist Response

16. Capitalist lobbying has cost us 30 years in the battle for the climate.

Scientific warnings about the risk of global warming were first issued in 1957. Ever since it was established in 1958, the Observatory of Mauna Loa (Hawaii) has confirmed the accelerating accumulation of greenhouse gases in the atmosphere, but we had to wait more than 20 years for the United Nations to convene the first World Conference on the climate (Geneva 1979) and more than 30 years for the Intergovernmental Panel on Climate Change (IPCC) to be established. Two years later the IPCC released its first assessment report (Geneva, 1990): its conclusions have been confirmed by the IPCC's three subsequent reports.

At the Rio Earth Summit in 1992, a first symbolic step towards implementing the international action recommended by the IPCC was taken when 154 countries signed the United Nations Framework Convention on Climate Change (UNFCCC). It included the important principle of "common but differentiated responsibilities," and set an "ultimate objective" – "to achieve ... stabilization of greenhouse gas concentrations in the atmosphere at a level that would prevent dangerous anthropogenic interference with the climate system." But no target level was specified: the document merely expressed hope that states would voluntarily reduce their emissions to 1990 levels by 2000. It wasn't until 1997 – forty years after the first scientific warnings– that concrete objectives were set in the Kyoto Protocol.

The extremely slow spread of awareness of the danger could be explained in the early period by uncertainty and by the very long-term nature of the effects of climate change. But after that, a key role was played by capitalist lobbyists. In fact, beginning in the 1980s, representatives of the sectors of US capital most linked to fossil fuels created and liberally financed lobbying structures that literally purchased sceptical scientists, journalists and political representatives in order to prevent the growing consensus among climatologists from winning over decision makers and public opinion.

Sometimes playing on science, sometimes playing on distrust of it, sometimes stressing the sacrifices required by the Kyoto Protocol, sometimes its insignificance, these lobbyists made every effort to systematically portray the reality of climate change as a dubious and disputed hypothesis, or even an apocalyptic religious fad or an international plot against the American way of life.

By their multi-pronged campaign, the lobbyists won hegemonic influence over U.S. politicians at all levels. Given the dominant role of the USA as *the* imperialist superpower, this hegemony enabled them (a) to exert decisive influence at key moments in international climate negotiations (the conference in The Hague, 2000); and, (b) to provide the arguments used by many capitalist forces on the international scene.

Eventually, the "Inconvenient Truth" asserted itself, including in the American ruling class. But lobbying allowed the multinationals to gain 30 years of fossil energy, and made humanity lose 30 years.

17. The Kyoto Protocol, the only binding international treaty to date, isn't just totally inadequate: the carbon market it established increases social and climate injustice.

The first attempt by governments to provide a comprehensive response to climate change, the Kyoto Protocol (1997), calls on the industrialised countries to reduce their emissions by 5.2% compared to 1990 during the period 2008-2012. It is obvious that the treaty is totally insufficient. A 5.2% reduction does not put the developed countries on a path towards the 25% to 40% cut required by 2020 or to 80% to 95% by 2050. The USA's non-ratification means that the effective reduction would be only 1.7%. The objectives are weakened even further by the fact that the Protocol treats temporary increases in the absorption of carbon by the forests as equivalent to structural reductions in emissions. What's more, emissions from air and maritime transport (2% of total emissions) are not included.

The reduction quotas assigned to states are still further softened by three "flexibility mechanisms" – the Clean Development Mechanism (CDM), Joint Implementation (JI) and Emissions Trading. Trading allows companies in the developed countries which exceed their reduction targets to sell permits to emit tons of carbon.

CDM (and JI as well) allow developed countries to replace part of their targets by investments in reducing emissions in the countries of the South and Far East. These investments generate tradable "emission credits" (or certified rights). All this is presented as proof that the climate can be saved by capitalist means, by creating a market for trading emission rights and credits. In fact, many of the rights and credits don't reflect any structural reduction – and more than 50% of the CDM credits of the CDM don't involve any real reduction in emissions at all.

As for trading, experience since 2005 with the ETS system implemented by the European Union shows that, in practice, that "cap and trade" systems involve reduction objectives (caps) that are set to meet the needs of corporate profits, and that the biggest polluters reap enormous superprofits which they are not even required to invest in clean technologies.

In these ways, the Protocol is part of the global offensive of the ruling classes against working people, of the imperialists' offensive against the countries they dominate, and of the capitalist battle for the appropriation and the commodification of natural resources:

‣ Instead of reducing their own emissions, the imperialist countries can acquire carbon credits cheaply while crippling the ability of developing countries to reduce theirs in future.

▸ CDM and JI, linked to the trading system, allow multinationals to open new markets by investing in developing or transitional countries and to intensify their blackmail of working people.

▸ Developing a carbon market opened a new field of activity for the International Monetary Fund and the World Bank. The foundation thus established for carbon neo-colonialism, involving distribution of emission quotas between countries on the basis of the volume of greenhouse gases emitted in 1990, locks in unequal North-South development.

▸ Privatization and commodification of the right to emit carbon, along with the appropriation of the ecosystems that can absorb it, constitute a capitalist takeover of the Earth's carbon cycle, and potentially the total appropriation of the biosphere that regulates this cycle.

▸ Kyoto does not take into account the steps that big developing countries were already taking in this direction. So Kyoto gives the ruling classes of the rich countries a convenient pretext for burning fossil fuels and destroying forests for as long as possible, in the name of development.

At the same time, the Protocol includes a number of regulatory measures:

▸ it sets targets and deadlines for reducing emissions; it establishes penalties for non-compliance.

▸ it specifies that flexibility mechanisms can only be used as a "complement" to domestic measures; investments in nuclear energy are not eligible for CDM credits.

▸ credits from investments in forest sinks are limited, even banned by some states.

The continuing opposition of capitalist lobbyists to these measures reflects the essential antagonism between the physical measures needed to stabilise the climate, on the one hand, and the logic of profit accumulation on the other.

18. While sharpening inter-imperialist rivalry, the reality of climate change and the challenge of obtaining energy are forcing the ruling classes to consider a global response to climate change.

Faced with the extent and growing strength of the scientific consensus, with increasingly obvious impacts of global warming, and under the pressure of public opinion, the ruling classes are now considering a binding strategy that would be more ambitious and more long-term than the Kyoto Protocol.

The fact that this turn started earlier in Europe and Japan than in the United States reflects the specific situation of the three big capitalist blocs.

Japan and the EU seek to reduce their intense energy dependence by improving energy efficiency and diversifying their sources of supply. They hope to win competitive advantage in the carbon market that is taking shape, in the "green" technology market, and in the market for nuclear power in particular. On the other hand, the oil and coal sectors have an extremely strong position in the structure of US capitalism, which moreover has built a geostrategic alliance with the oil monarchies of the Gulf.

The European Union is in the forefront. After the summit in The Hague (2000) it played a leading role in the implementation of the Kyoto Protocol, without the United States, in the negotiation of the Marrakech Agreements. In 2005 the European Emission Trading System was launched, an experience which will probably be used as model for a future world market in emissions rights. The same year, at the G8 summit, Tony Blair for the first time called for reducing global emissions by 50% by 2050; that proposal was adopted at the Hokkaido/Toyako G8 summit in 2008.

In this context, the position of the United States and its allies in climate negotiations became increasingly untenable. While the Bush administration continued to reject mandatory reductions and firm deadlines, and challenged the differentiated treatment of imperialist countries and those dominated by imperialism, a growing number of sectors of big US capital came out in favour of a quota policy for emissions. Four factors motivated this progressive shift:

(a) fear that the cost of inaction exceeds the cost of action in the long term;

(b) belief that a planned reduction of emissions is inevitable, so it is better to prepare and organize according to global rules;

(c) fear that the climate policy of the EU and Japan will give a significant advantage to competitors in "green" technologies;

(d) the evidence, from the EU experience, of the benefits of "cap and trade" coupled with CDM.

This realignment in the US ruling class resulted in many initiatives by companies, employers' federations, municipalities and states. Little by little, climate change sceptics lost influence, to the point that eight bills of varying importance, favouring emission quotas, were tabled in the House of Representatives. This shift found its way, to varying degrees, into the programmes of the two candidates to succeed Bush.

A parallel evolution took place among the ruling classes of the big emergent countries, in particular China, Brazil, South Africa, Mexico and, to a lesser extent, India. Initially, the bourgeoisies of these countries were content to affirm their right to development and to put the entire responsibility for the action to save the climate on the developed countries. The acceleration and concrete socio-economic impacts of climate change, the increased importance of climate and energy policy to imperialism in general, and the deep concern of the people in some countries, made this position untenable.

Nor could they ignore two facts that are impossible to avoid: that global warming is affecting the countries dominated by imperialism most severely, and that stabilization at a level that isn't dangerous for humanity is impossible without some participation of these countries in the effort to reduce emissions. Faced with the need to accept collaboration with the world effort in principle, the ruling classes of the big emergent countries are preparing for tough negotiations with imperialism over terms, with the aim of defending their own capitalist interests. Some governments (China, Mexico) took the initiative by unilaterally setting their own emission reduction targets, so as to avoid, as much as possible, having more unfavourable terms imposed by the imperialist powers.

Broadly speaking, change is promoted in all countries by the prospect of growing tensions over oil and gas supplies, due to the depletion of reserves. Beyond the ups and downs caused by cyclical changes and speculation, this tension will tend to keep oil prices high, leading to increases in the prices of other fossil fuels and biofuels, and consequently of agricultural products.

All of these factors explain why the U.S. administration's position was outflanked at the Bali conference in December 2007, leading to the relative unblocking of the negotiations for a new international treaty to succeed the Kyoto protocol.

19. The capitalist policies being developed for 2012-2050 are even more neo-liberal than Kyoto; they suggest a rise in the average surface temperature of 2.8° to 4°C, possibly more. This is a major crime against humanity and the natural world.

The "Bali road map" adopted referred explicitly to the quantified targets in the IPCC 2007 report (see above, point 8). The ink was not yet dry when the G8 decided in favour of a 50% reduction of global emissions by 2050, without mentioning either the upper end of the range of overall reduction proposed by the IPCC (85%), or the proposed reduction objective for developed countries (80% to 95% by 2050), or the intermediate targets for these countries (25% to 40% by 2020), or the need for absolute reductions in global emissions to begin by 2015.

At the beginning of 2008, the European Commission proposed to member states and the European Parliament a "climate-energy package" involving a 20% reduction in emissions, 20% gains in energy efficiency, and 20% renewable energy. including 10% use of biofuels in transport, by 2020.

This "package" is lower than the IPCC's recommendations and incompatible with the objective of a maximum rise of 2°C which the Council adopted in March 1996.[7]

In autumn 2008, in the context of the "financial crisis" triggered by the subprime mortgage crash and the capitalist recession, several member states (notably Italy, Poland and the Czech Republic) and several industrial sectors (automobile, iron and steel) challenged the goals and methodology of the "package." In December 2008 the Council decided to retain the symbolic 20-20-20 formula, but it is now essentially just a facade. The bosses won on two key points: free emission rights for sectors that are "exposed to international competition" and for coal-fired power stations in new member states, and massive outsourcing to developing countries through the CDM – in non-ETS sectors (building, transportation, agriculture, etc.) nearly 70% of reductions can be located in the South.

A similar process is taking shape in the United States. Barack Obama's "energy-climate" programme envisages reducing emissions by 80% between now and 2050. The objective seems impressive but it barely meets the low end of the range proposed by the IPCC for the developed countries, while, given its emission levels, the USA should be at the high end of the range. By 2020, Obama has promised to return US emissions to the 1990 level, implying a 20% reduction from present levels. Once again, this seems impressive but it is actually much less than the IPCC recommendations, and less than the reduction the USA would have been obligated to meet by 2012 if it had ratified the Kyoto Protocol.

Obama has also announced a "cap-and-trade system" in which emission rights will be auctioned and proceeds used to finance reform of the energy system, and programmes to mitigate the cost of this reform for the most disadvantaged social layers.

As in Europe, we can expect that US employers will exert maximum pressure on this project and that they will obtain satisfaction in the name of competitiveness. As a result the social cost of the "energy-climate" policy will rise, and its ecological effectiveness will decline. Similarly, as in Europe, opportunities for American companies to purchase CDM credits instead of reducing emissions will increase as the climate targets become more ambitious and restrictive. The proposed Dingell-Boucher Bill, for example, allows companies to buy enough carbon credits to defer any emissions reduction until 2029.

The climate-energy policy proposed by Barack Obama during his presidential campaign is a key element of a policy that aims to safeguard the declining hegemony of US imperialism. The turn away from the policies of the Bush administration is characterized by the following points in particular:

(a) a desire for energy independence from Middle East oil and the unstable regimes of the region;

(b) development of a range of alternative solutions, mainly coal, biofuels, nuclear power and energy efficiency;

(c) acceptance of the need for binding quantified targets for reductions in US emissions as a prerequisite for playing a leadership role in negotiating an international climate agreement involving the big emergent countries;

(d) a quest for an alliance with the EU against the emerging countries, on the issue of those countries' role in the climate effort, and with the emerging countries against the EU on other issues, such as energy technology;

(e) massive support for US capital in the area of so-called low-carbon energy technology.

20. For capitalism, saving the climate amounts to squaring the circle. Incapable of solving the difficulty, it will try to win time by plunging headlong into new technology, coupled with market expansion.

Start reducing global emissions by 2015, cut emissions in developed countries by 80% to 95 percent in just over forty years, radically reduce energy needs, carry out a massive transfer of clean technology to the developing countries and finance the necessary adaptation – for these conditions to be fulfilled in a productivist system amounts to squaring the circle.

Incapable of solving the problem, capitalism is trying to postpone it by driving forward with technological changes that rest mainly on the following elements:

(a) Exploitation of the large known coal reserves (approximately 200 years worth at the current rate of extraction) as an increasingly important source of energy for electrical production, through development of Carbon Capture and Sequestration technology, and also for the production of alternative fuels for the transport sector.

(b) Massive development of biofuels, both first generation (sugar-based ethanol, vegetable oil-based diesel) and second generation (cellulose-based ethanol) for the transport sector, involving large-scale changes in land use, particular in more productive tropical and subtropical regions, and increased use of genetic engineering.

(c) Development of deep offshore oilfields and exploitation of non-conventional reserves such as heavy oil, tar sands and oil shale.

(d) Exploitation of potential energy savings by increased energy efficiency, primarily in electricity and manufacturing, areas in which there is considerable potential for emission reductions in emerging and transition countries, but also in the construction and transport sectors. But capitalism's ability to exploit this potential is limited by effective demand.

(e) Combined development of nuclear, wind and solar (thermal and photovoltaic) power. De facto treatment of nuclear power as renewable energy, leading to a significant increase in the number of nuclear power stations and the development of new nuclear technologies such as fourth generation power stations and super-breeders that can extend the life of known uranium reserves (approximately 60 years with current technology).

(f) Maximum use of carbon sinks (tree plantations, protection of existing forests and wetlands, low carbon agriculture), use of waste as an energy source.

Implementation of such technological responses will require creation of a market that can set a single worldwide price for carbon, an agreement that quantifies the trade-off between increases in absorption and reductions in emissions, trade agreements that establish norms and quotas (including personal tradable quotas, if necessary), taxes and incentives, mechanisms for measurement and reporting, etc. It also and especially requires a new international treaty that is even more neo-liberal than the Kyoto Protocol, involving the imperialist countries, the emergent countries and the rest of the world, fixing the contribution of each in the global effort and allowing maximum outsourcing of emission reductions from the developed capitalist countries to the developing countries.

This outsourcing is a key component of capitalist climate policy. Imperialism's goal is to reduce the cost of the energy transition as much as possible while using the countries dominated by imperialism as sources of biofuel and cheap carbon credits. These can be generated either by preserving existing forests, or by planting new trees, or, above all, by "clean" investments in renewable energy or energy efficiency. The effort thus fits into the general offensive of imperialism against developing countries, as conducted by the IMF, the World Bank and the WTO, but implementation is complicated by the realignment of global power relations resulting from rise of the large emerging countries.

While giving lip service to the idea that climate change is "the greatest market failure" (Nicholas Stern), the capitalist response, which is based on more markets and therefore more goods, tends to reverse the priority completely: instead of reducing energy consumption while satisfying real human needs, renewable energy and improvements in energy efficiency are used to open new opportunities for capitalist accumulation, which requires more energy. Emission reduction is subordinated to the imperatives of profit. In practice, the goal of increasing the percentage of energy from renewable sources supplants the goal of reducing total greenhouse gas emissions.

21. In addition to being completely inadequate for climate stabilization, the capitalist response has other ecological consequences that are extremely threatening for humanity.

The nuclear option carries a major threat to human survival. The question of waste remains unresolved, the risk of radioactive leaks is impossible to eliminate completely, and the danger of proliferation of nuclear weapons – and therefore of actual use of these weapons – is inseparable from the technology. It should be added that nuclear technology is a technically irrational choice: it is an inefficient way to protect the climate, and it is incompatible with the needed energy revolution. The energy efficiency of a nuclear plant, at 30%, is lower than a gas-fired power station; its carbon footprint is mediocre across the production chain and can only worsen as it resorts to using less and less rich deposits of uranium; known reserves of ore are limited, equal to about 60 years of consumption with today's technology.

A response to climate change based on nuclear power is completely impractical: given the number of power stations which would have to be built (one per week for 50 years), the time needed to build them and the cost, all-nuclear power is impossible. Nuclear technology which now accounts for 2.7% of world power consumption and 17% of global energy consumption, can never meet more than a fraction of human needs. Finally, the focus of alternative energy must be renewable energy and efficiency delivered by a radically decentralized energy system, which is completely incompatible with the ultra-centralization required for a nuclear system.

That's also true for the costly ITER research project on nuclear fusion, a particularly useless project, in view of humanity's good fortune in benefiting from a danger-free nuclear power station that costs nothing, will function for about 4.5 billion years, and which recycles its own waste: the Sun.

Although biofuels cover only a negligible fraction of energy needs in transportation, they have already amply demonstrated their perverse effects. Inevitably, the logic of production for profit leads in practice to the production of ethanol and biodiesel for market demand being given priority over the satisfaction of the basic right to food, before the rights of indigenous communities and before protection of the environment. Here also, technical irrationality rears its head, because in most cases biofuel production uses more energy than it delivers. The transition to second generation biofuels does not, in itself, eliminate the shortcomings. Even if sufficiently strict rules block conversion of agricultural land to the production of cellulose-based ethanol, the demand from the transport industries is great enough that enormous areas of non-agricultural land – or water – will be converted to intensive monoculture, with all the consequences that flow from pesticide pollution and destruction of biodiversity.

The critique of biofuels applies, *mutatis mutandis*, to non-conventional oil resources: the exploitation of heavy oils, tar sands and oil shales requires enormous energy use and a great waste of other resources, especially water – and the environmental impact is particularly severe. Moreover, in many cases, the deposits are located in areas inhabited by indigenous communities whose rights are threatened.

Given the urgency of the situation, and for social reasons, CCS could be an acceptable transitional measure as part of a quick exit strategy for fossil fuels: it could, in particular, make it possible to plan the redeployment of miners. But that isn't what's planned today. CCS is, rather, a new capitalist attempt to push back physical limits without concern for consequences. Governments talk about "clean coal," but it is a myth if we take into account the difficulty of mining itself, dust pollution, the health consequences and the ecological impact of coal mines.

The fight against climate change is likely to give a major boost to genetic engineering, leading to a qualitative increase in the risk inherent to this technology. For example, the production of genetically modified trees (fast growing Genetically Modified Organisms to increase the capacity of carbon sinks, low lignin or high cellulose GMOs, etc.) increase the risks of allergies. But the biggest threat could come from genetic engineering to produce second generation biofuels, by developing genetically modified bacteria and microalgae that multiply the danger of dissemination and hybridization.

22. The capitalist response involves redoubled attacks against workers, poor peasants, women, indigenous communities and the poor in general, as well as a widening of social inequality.

Whatever "energy mix" is chosen, energy prices will increase, hitting working people in two ways: in their direct energy needs, and in the consumer goods they need, since the bosses will pass on their energy costs to consumers.

Since energy is a component of constant capital, energy price increases will press down the rate of profit, leading employers to intensify their attacks on wages, indexation, social gains and, in general, give them more incentive to use all possible means to increase the rate of exploitation.

Already, we find that the world carbon market gives capitalists new means of exacerbating competition between workers. Workers face a new form of blackmail over jobs and investment, aimed either at forcing them to bend to the neo-liberal dictates of the multinationals, or to manipulate them into supporting protectionist measures or subsidies to business. At the

---

The world carbon market gives capitalists new means of exacerbating competition between workers

---

same time, the various incentives and other market instruments designed to expand the market for renewable energy and to improve energy efficiency benefit not only employers but also the affluent middle classes, the wage-earning petty bourgeoisie and the higher strata of the proletariat, aggravating inequality in income distribution, access to mobility, etc.

The introduction – still only hypothetical – of personal tradable carbon quotas would further intensify this tendency to inequality, creating a market in which the poor would sell their quotas in order to purchase consumer goods.

In the countries dominated by imperialism, capitalist climate policy gives a new impulse to the separation of producers from their traditional means of production – above all from the land – leading either to the poor leaving rural areas or their transformation into rural proletarians in biofuel plantations, oil holdings etc., or their displacement to less productive land, or entry into the tourist industry. All of these involve reduced autonomy and degradation of living conditions for large numbers of people (in particular for women, who play key roles in food production) as well as increased attacks against indigenous communities and their rights.

23. Unable to create the social conditions for structural emissions reduction, the capitalist governments of the developed countries are using the fight against climate change as a pretext for imposing austerity.

For the bourgeoisie, the claim that climate change is "caused by humanity" comes at just the right moment for them to try to justify austerity and sacrifice in the name of science, and just when growing awareness of the threat of global warming creates favourable conditions for promoting the "green products" sector of the economy. But, by blaming a product of the capitalist Industrial Revolution on "humanity," bourgeois propaganda contributes to morbid and irrational trends that combine misanthropy, fatalism, individualistic cynicism and reactionary nostalgia.

The most dangerous result of this deliberately orchestrated confusion is a strengthening of Malthusian and neo-Malthusian ideas that blame the ecological crisis mainly or exclusively on population growth and thus on the poor, since they have more children than the rich – and thus on developing countries, where women's fertility is generally higher than in developed countries. Once draped in religious views, today these ideas are packaged with pseudo-science that misuses concepts from scientific ecology (such as "carrying capacity") to treat social relations as products of unchanging human nature. Some of these campaigns are supported by scientists whose work in ecology actually expresses a priori bourgeois prejudices, as can be seen clearly in the case of the so-called "tragedy of the commons."

Ultra-reactionary political currents try to use fear of climate change to win wider support for their hate campaigns against immigrants, asylum seekers, against women's right to control over their bodies, and against aid to developing countries. Religious sects and reactionary religious currents integrate the climate threat into end-of-the-world theology that preaches submission to the established order.

There is a real danger that the predictable failure of its climate policies will ultimately lead capitalism to opt for strong regimes and *dirigiste* policies to mobilize all available resources as it does in times of war. Such a policy would inevitably involve renewed attacks on social and democratic rights.

24. The capitalist response to the climate challenge increases the risk of wars over resources.

In the countries that are most vulnerable to capitalist globalization and structural adjustment, the impacts of climate change increase the probability of crises leading to chaotic situations, such as armed conflicts between warlords. By aggravating shortages in regions that are already under intense water stress, climate change increases the importance of control over water resources and creates the conditions for water wars between states. But the greatest danger could result from heightened competition for ownership not only of declining fossil energy resources, but also of new energy resources. The climate-energy challenge is thus part of the broader context of gradual transition from a bipolar world (imperialism vs countries dominated by imperialism) under US hegemony, to a tripolar world (imperialism vs emergent countries vs least developed countries) in which the battle for imperialist leadership rages.

IV. Build a Movement to Fight Climate Change

25. The fight against climate change will not be won by some combination of lobbying, spectacular actions and media campaigns to promote changes in individual consumer behaviour, but by mass mobilization.

The fight for the climate is political; it requires above all the building of a powerful social movement. The fight can be won, as is shown by the example of Australia, where mass mobilization (150,000 demonstrators in November 2007) led to a first partial success: the defeat of a conservative government that supported George W. Bush's policies, and the ratification of the Kyoto Protocol by the new government. In the face of climate emergency and the criminal policies of capitalist governments, we must work in every country to build of a powerful and united mass movement, coordinated globally, following the "single issue campaign" example of previous mobilizations against war and the arms race.

The goal of this movement is not to propose complex policies, but to force governments to accept, at a minimum, the IPCC's most prudent recommendations, and to respect the principles of "common but differentiated responsibilities," of social and democratic rights, and of the right to lives worthy of the word "human." We must defend this goal against currents that seek to lower the emissions reduction targets in the name of realism, but also against those who denounce them as inadequate, (We try to win the latter group to our side by demanding "at a minimum" respect for the IPCC's "most prudent" recommendations.) Our goal is to take advantage of the IPCC's legitimacy as a basis for the broadest possible unity of action, while at the same time exposing the duplicity of governments that vote for the IPCC

"Summaries for Policymakers" in international climate conferences but ignore them in practice.

The difficulties of building mass actions in defence of the climate, reflect the nature of climate change, in particular its relatively slow pace at present, as well as the spatial and temporal gap between causes and effects. There is thus much work to be done to disseminate scientific information on global warming and its impacts. This effort must particularly target activist groups within the various social movements and left-wing political currents. These groups can play a decisive role: only they can identify concrete links between the global climate threat and specific social problems, particular at the local level, and on that basis work out strategies for combining social struggles with the fight to save the climate. Building the movement must be conceived of as building a network of social resistance activities on different terrains, with coordinated activity and occasional united demonstrations organized around a common minimum platform. The creation of climate committees, united fronts or coalitions, within the framework of the Global Climate Campaign will facilitate the building of such a network.

26. Within the climate movement, we need to build a left current that links the fight for the climate to social justice.

The necessary transformation is so great that it cannot happen without the mobilization and active involvement of the exploited and oppressed who constitute the vast majority of the population. Capitalism's anti-social and anti-environmental policies offer them nothing: it reinforces imperialist domination and capitalist competition and violence, and intensifies exploitation, oppression, social inequality, competition between workers, violations of rights and the private appropriation of resources.

In particular, capitalist policies provide no answer to the major challenge of ensuring jobs, wages and social gains for the millions of workers now employed in the sectors that emit the most greenhouse gas, such as the oil, coal, cement, glass, iron and steel industries, as well as transportation. A policy that ignores that can only encounter legitimate social resistance. Instead of promoting awareness of the climate danger, it may push sections of the population into the arms of climate change sceptics. This is a particular danger among people who are severely affected by the rising cost of energy and where the social weight of small employers (farming, fishing, trucking) could encourage violent reactions among desperate businesses, exerting strong pressure on governments.

The big environmental NGOs try to press governments into more radical action on the climate, without realizing that radical action targeting climate alone leads to attacks on the exploited and oppressed. This is a dead end. We favour a combined fight for the climate and for social justice. Within the broad movement, we work for the constitution of a left current that links both dimensions and consequently argues against solutions based on market mechanisms (carbon pricing, bonuses and tax incentives for renewable energy, trading in emission rights, etc.), accumulation, neo-colonial domination and the headlong drive into purely technological solutions. The left current seeks to bring together left wing forces in the trade-union, ecologist, global justice, feminist, and third-worldist movements, the de-growth left, members of radical left organizations, thoughtful scientists, etc. It contributes to the building of the broad movement, in practical and political terms, by supporting every initiative that advances the idea of an alternative climate policy.

27. The social movements must make defending the climate an important part of their programmes and struggles.

Within the perspective of building broad mobilizations rooted in existing struggles, we must work to ensure that defence of the climate becomes a major concern of social movements, so that it finds concrete expression in their demands on all fronts. For example:

(a) *The fight for peace.* The production and the use of weapons is unacceptable madness in view of climate change which itself may be an additional cause of conflicts.

(b) *The fight against poverty, for the right to development and to social protection.* Capacity for adaptation to climate change is directly proportional to the level of resources and development. Social inequality increases vulnerability and hinders energy change.

(c) *Women's struggles.* The need for adaptation to climate change particularly reinforces the importance and urgency of women's specific demands for equal rights, for social care of children, against the double work day, for the right to abortion and contraception.

(d) *The fight for jobs.* Vast numbers of jobs can be created by slashing energy consumption, redeveloping the land and cities, protecting biodiversity, and developing public transportation and renewable substitutes for fossil fuels.

(e) *The fight for access to land, water and natural resources, and for organic peasant agriculture.* Rural communities that practise labour-intensive organic agriculture can play a leading role in increasing the capacity of carbon sinks and reducing greenhouse gas emissions in the agricultural sector.

(f) *The fight against the globalization and liberalization of agricultural markets.* As well as causing the ruin of rural populations, famine, rural migration and/or plundering of ecosystems, the liberalization of agricultural markets is also an important source of emissions, both direct (transportation of products for export) and indirect.

(g) *The fight for the right of asylum.* The increasing number of environmental and climate refugees makes freedom of movement essential and the only humane response.

(h) *Struggles for indigenous communities' rights.* Their knowledge of and interaction with ecosystems, especially forests, gives these communities a unique role in preserving and expanding carbon sinks.

(i) *The fight against work "flexibility" and insecurity, and against the lengthening of the working day.* Staggered and flexible working hours, and capitalist pressure to increase labour mobility, force workers to use cars. "Just in time" production is a major cause of greenhouse gas emissions in the transport sector. A general reduction of work-time is a prerequisite for the development, on a mass scale, of alternative models of consumption and leisure.

(j) *The fight against privatization, for public provision of high-quality transportation, energy and water.* Only free, publicly-provided mass transit can guarantee everyone the right to mobility and reduce transportation emissions. Privatization of electricity production increases the complexity of managing intermittent renewable sources to the network. Only non-profit state enterprises can meet the challenge of completely eliminating housing sector emissions in two or three decades. For personal, non-exchangeable water and energy quotas, provided free and determined by social priorities, combined with rapidly rising rates for overuse, and absolute ceilings on consumption.

28. Climate change poses a crucial challenge for the trade union left, one that requires going beyond the struggle for the redistribution of wealth.

The leaders of the major international trade-union confederations are generally willing to support capitalist climate policies, subject to negotiation of favourable terms. This is often concretized in proposals for a "Green New Deal" based on the illusion that the development of green technology will reduce unemployment and initiate a new long wave of capitalist prosperity and expansion. The social-environmental impact of a sustained capitalist revival are ignored. On the contrary, the trade-union bureaucrats strongly support capitalist productivism and profitability, and the dominant elements of capitalist climate policy: government aid to "green" companies, "ecological taxes," Clean Development Mechanism, carbon trading, even support for nuclear energy and biofuels. This co-management policy is likely to result in the trade union movement, especially in the developed countries, being seen as co-responsible for climate disasters and their impact on poor people in poor countries. It can only sow divisions between workers on the international level, and between sectors within countries.

In view of the importance of the climate and energy challenge, it is essential that the trade-union left seize opportunities to make it a central element of its fight to change the labour movement's direction. This will be difficult since, strategically speaking, the struggle is incompatible with new economic growth, even so-called "green growth." Rather, it aims for reduced energy consumption, for suppression of useless or harmful production, for

---

The trade union left must free itself from
a narrow focus on redistribution of wealth,
must contest the very concept of wealth
and the way that wealth is produced

---

retraining workers employed in those sectors, etc. This is a considerable obstacle, an illustration of how workers are chained to the capitalist mode of production, and depend on it in their daily live.

This obstacle can only be overcome by challenging capitalist ownership through such demands as:

(a) Put activities that are decisive both for saving the climate and for satisfying fundamental human needs under public control – in the first place, expropriate without compensation the capitalist companies that control the extraction, conversion and distribution of energy.

(b) Establish public ownership and financing, and international sharing, of research – and its results – into alternative technologies, especially renewable energy and energy efficiency;

(c) Initiate local, regional, national, and global plans for a transition to a society without fossil fuels, in which as far as possible production and consumption are colocated and in which the workers in the fossil fuel industry receive retraining with no loss of wages and benefits, under workers' control.

To meet this challenge, the trade union left must free itself from a narrow focus on redistribution of wealth, must contest the very concept of wealth and the way that wealth is produced – in other words, the very foundations of the capitalist mode of production. Only in that way can we free the resources of imagination and creativity needed to mobilize workers around concrete objectives. This approach increases the importance of demands such as reduced working time including reduction of work, no loss of wages and proportional hiring of new workers, and workers' control over work intensity, production, energy, etc.

29. Massive transfer of clean technologies to the countries dominated by imperialism, and the financing of adaptation to the effects of climate change in these countries, requires debt cancellation and the establishment of special funds, created by a substantial tax on capitalist profits. These must be democratically controlled by the people and their social organisations.

Since participation by the countries dominated by imperialism is essential, saving the climate requires global sharing of resources and knowledge. It must include:

(a) cancellation of the Third world debt and return to the peoples of the assets that Southern dictators have hidden in Western banks;

(b) lifting of banking secrecy, abolition of tax havens, inheritance taxes, a tax on capital speculation etc;

(c) a substantial increase in spending by the imperialist countries on development assistance;

(d) the creation, in addition to aid from individual countries, of a single global fund for adaptation to the inevitable effects of climate change in developing countries and for transfer of clean technologies to the public sectors of these countries, with no financial conditions;

(e) financing this fund through taxes on the profits and superprofits of the sectors most responsible for climate change – in particular, oil, coal, automobiles, and electrical production;

(f) abolition of patents in health care, and in the technologies that enable essential consumer goods and services (transport, light industry, water and energy, communications) so that all the world's people can have access to basic goods;

(g) financial compensation, administered by the affected populations, for countries of the South that refrain from exploiting their fossil fuel resources.

However, wealth transfer from the North is not, by itself, enough to resolve the climate challenge in the South. The capitalist model of development, which subordinates the economies of the countries of the South to the imperatives of accumulation, in a framework of the global production and exchange, is completely incompatible with the necessary 15% to 30% reduction in emissions by 2020 (2050 for Africa). That objective can only be achieved by endogenous development that responds to the needs of the great mass of the population, and that is therefore linked to land reform that supports peasant agriculture and to reorientation of production to the domestic market.

Reconciling the right to human development and saving the climate therefore requires action against the local ruling classes, who use the right to development as a pretext to reject any limits on burning fossil fuels, to plunder natural resources, to appropriate the forests, to act as intermediaries in the carbon credits market, to produce biofuels and to export agricultural, food and industrial products at low prices to the developed countries. To prevent them from intensifying this socially and ecologically damaging development model, the financial resources and technological means that are offered to the countries of the South must be democratically controlled by the people of these countries and their social movements. In this respect, the fight against climate change confirms the theory of permanent revolution in the colonial and semi-colonial countries.

30. The response to climate change must combine all major ecological challenges, for a perspective of really sustainable development.

The history of capitalism is marked by environmental crises that were "solved" without an overall ecological vision, by implementing the partial technological responses that the profit imperative allowed. Only later did the new technology's harmful environmental effects become evident. Total destruction of European forests was avoided by coal mining which became a major cause of climate change. Soil exhaustion was avoided by massive use of fertilisers, today a source of greenhouse gases and a cause of both pollution and of excess nutrients in water. The growth of the hole in the ozone layer was slowed down by using refrigerant gases that contribute significantly to the greenhouse effect. Etc. etc.

Repeating this "sorcerer's apprentice" approach with the climate/energy crisis risks even more dangerous consequences. That's particularly true of the increased use of nuclear power and genetically modified organisms. Opposing these technologies is one of the most important tasks before the left. They must be condemned as symbols of the madness of capitalism's drive for growth, as examples of its absurd attempts to jump over its own head to maintain the profit system no matter what.

More generally, the climate challenge encompasses all environmental issues, so our response must be equally broad. In particular, we must support:

(a) Defence of rainforest, including for the rights of the indigenous communities that depend on its resources (carbon sinks);

(b) Defence of biodiversity;

(c) Rational public management of water resources;

(d) Opposition to the poisoning of the biosphere by the approximately 100,000 different petrochemical-based compounds that do not exist in nature and thus often cannot be naturally broken down;

(e) Elimination of gases that destroy stratospheric ozone and their replacement by ecologically safe substances;

(f) Opposition to air pollution and its impact on human health (asthma, cardiovascular diseases) and ecosystems (acidification, tropospheric ozone).

31. We must expose the gap between the capitalists' plans and the scientists' recommendations. The social movements must build links with critical scientists, and question the ownership of knowledge and the social role of research.

Government claims that their capitalist and liberal climate policies are based on "science" must be challenged. To do this, we expose the vast gulf that separates those governments' declared goals from the IPCC's most conservative conclusions. We need to understand and support the key elements of climate science, while criticizing the conservative ideological and social assumptions that most scientists still accept. The left needs to connect with scientists, invite them to share their expertise with social movements, challenge them on their political positions, urge them to speak out on the contradictions between the rational global approaches that are needed and the compartmentalisation of science that capitalism imposes. The important role that scientific expertise plays in developing climate policy means that relations between social movements and critical and humanistic researchers, laboratories and associations are very important.

Within that context, we need to develop a more general analysis of the role of science and research in the fight for socially just solutions to the climate crisis. We do not reject technological solutions, or the idea of development and progress. On the contrary, we argue that scientific and technical research must be freed from capital's grip, so that they can be massively and rapidly focused on genuinely sustainable development of renewable energy sources, on progress in energy efficiency and on rational resource management. To achieve this, we demand massive public financing of research, an end to contracts that tie universities to industry and financial capital, and democratic setting of research priorities according to the need for a socially just transition to an ecologically sustainable society.

32. We oppose efforts to put the blame on individuals, while favouring socially responsible behaviour towards energy use.

The left opposes guilt-laden government propaganda that attributes blame for global warming and responsibility for saving the climate to individual behaviour, to every person in every class. Such arguments cover up social inequality and capitalism's responsibility, diverting attention from the profound structural changes that are needed.

But that doesn't mean that the left can avoid the question of individual behaviour, or refuse to support any attempt to change consumer behaviour. Quite the contrary.

It is an illusion to believe that the climate can be saved by a "cultural contagion" movement against overconsumption. In the absence of structural change, such a campaign can only mean the adoption of monastic life-styles by some individuals, a step that is unlikely to be contagious. But it is also irrational to bet on hypothetical revolutionary breakthroughs in science as a way of avoiding the problem of overconsumption and the individual behaviour it entails. The urgency of climate change imposes on us a need, here and now, to make decisions based on existing technology and scientific knowledge. Abstract faith in progress, the belief that we will be saved by a technological deus ex machina can only justify inaction – the proponents of cultural contagion are at least doing something to save the climate.

Instead of counterposing structural changes in production to action that focuses on consumption, the left must view the latter as a way to underline the need for the former. In the first place, awareness of the seriousness of

---

Within the limits of what is socially possible, elementary ethics requires anyone whose basic needs are satisfied to act in a manner that avoids contributing to climate change

---

global warming and its impacts is inconsistent with behaviour that displays flagrant and cynical disregard for the environment: within the limits of what is socially possible, elementary ethics requires anyone whose basic needs are satisfied to act in a manner that avoids contributing to climate change. As well, alternative social practices, and democratic campaigns and mobilizations, that challenge productivism and consumerism, even on a limited basis, can play important positive roles in building collective awareness that structural changes are needed in production.

So we support democratic campaigns and actions against advertising pollution, capitalist appropriation of public spaces, waste of natural resources, ubiquitous automobiles, the explosive expansion of air transport, products produced by destroying rainforests, etc.

33. *When emergencies occur, we must support peoples' disaster relief.*

Climate change considerably increases the risk of droughts, floods, landslides and other disasters that particularly hit workers and the poor. In developing countries, such disasters can become catastrophic. In such cases, we must prepare to intervene with the social movements in two ways: by demanding that governments live up to their responsibilities, and by supporting, in association with activists around the world, direct, popular and solidarity-based aid programs that are managed by local populations and their organizations. Experience with natural disasters has shown that such peoples' aid programs deliver help more quickly and at lower cost, and that the aid is more directly geared to the real needs of the poor. What's more, they promote the emergence of new forms of social action that challenge the established order.

V. Open the Way to the Ecosocialist Alternative

34. Governments' inability to do what's necessary to save the climate is rooted in fundamental features of capitalism.

Competition drives each owner of capital to replace workers by machines which, by increasing labour productivity, can generate super profits above the average profit, and thus win competitive advantage. This race for technological rent, which accelerates as technology develops, intensifies the system's tendency to overproduction, and therefore overconsumption. Overproduction and overconsumption inevitably involve increases in the volume of material production. This in its turn requires on one hand increased use of resources (including energy), and production of more waste on the other. Tendencies such as "dematerialization" [reduced use of material inputs in manufacturing], more efficient use of resources, and recycling waste can slow this process, but not prevent it. Stationary capitalism is a contradiction in terms: since capitalism's aim is to produce value – meaning, in general and abstract form, exchange values – the system, as Marx wrote, knows no limit other than capital itself.

This is the context for analyzing climate change. For some 200 years, the system has appropriated abundant fossil energy resources from the natural environment, treating energy as an inexpensive part of constant capital. An invisible waste product of this productive consumption, carbon dioxide, has accumulated in the atmosphere to the point where emissions are now twice as great the ecosystems' ability to absorb them.

We would logically expect that over long periods there would be a strong correlation between the volume of CO_2 emissions and the long waves of capitalist expansion and stagnation. Thus the "thirty glorious years" of post-war expansion, powered by automobiles and other mass consumer goods coincides with emissions increases so great that the concentration of greenhouse gases in the air have brought us near to large-scale climate catastrophe. After a slight decline and stabilization in the 1970s and 1980s, emissions began rising again, now driven by globalization of capitalist production and transportation, by China's transformation into the workshop of the world, and by the debt-fuelled U.S. economic recovery.

Global warming and the ultimately inevitable exhaustion of fossil fuels appear as physical obstacles, as limits that the system faces but cannot understand or draw the necessary conclusions from. Climate change provides another demonstration of the fact that the capitalist system, because it requires unlimited accumulation of value leading to accelerated capital circulation, cannot adapt itself to physical limits and environmental rhythms.

35. Climate change takes the crisis of contemporary capitalism to an unprecedented global level, and contributes to making it a major systemic crisis, a crisis of civilisation.

Global warming confirms in physical terms the political judgment that revolutionary Marxists came to more than 60 year ago: the objective conditions for a non-capitalist society are not only ripe, they have begun to rot. The climate crisis is the most vivid and all-encompassing demonstration of this decay. Still not eliminated, still not replaced by a non-productivist system, the "third age of capitalism" has pushed humanity towards irreversible and extremely serious degradation of the environment that threatens the living conditions of hundreds of millions people.

If radical measures that can stop this process are not taken soon, humanity will face multiple large-scale catastrophes with incalculable social and political consequences.

In economic terms, the brutal austerity policy pursued during the long recession in the early 1970s led to an unprecedented situation that continued for 25 years: the rate of profit recovered but the rate of capital accumulation did not, while mass unemployment remained, poverty grew, and inequalities expanded explosively. The prolonged inability of the system to initiate a new period of growth demonstrates its historical exhaustion, and ultimately reflects the increasing difficulty of offsetting the tendency of the average rate of profit to fall by increasing the rate of exploitation, and the contradictions which result from that for the realization of surplus-value.

In social terms, capitalism escaped the Great Depression by crushing the workers' movement, by fascism and war, at the cost of permanent inflation and an irreversible climate imbalance. To open a new historical period of prosperity, capitalist society will have to experience an "exogenous shock" at least as drastic as that of the 1930s. The recession initiated by the subprime crisis indicates that, despite the defeats of the workers' movement, the conditions for a new long wave of expansion are not present.

In environmental terms, even if the spread of clean technology is accelerated by massive government aid to business (that is, a new transfer of wealth from labour to capital), a long period of capitalist growth similar to the post-war boom would inevitably involve years of increased consumption of fossil fuel, and thus therefore an expansion of greenhouse gas emissions that would be more than sufficient to trigger climate catastrophes.

In short, the fight against climate change poses a fundamental choice between civilizations: capitalist productivism at the expense of the environment and the majority of society, versus a non-capitalist alternative.

36. The climate and social crises can only be resolved jointly and structurally, by breaking with the logic of capital accumulation, by replacing the production of commodities with production of useful goods (use values).

Climate stabilization at a level consistent with the precautionary principle requires that global emissions begin to fall no later than 2015 and drop between 50% and 85% by 2050, and still further by the end of the century. This has to be done without nuclear power, without massive production of biofuels for world markets and with only limited use of Carbon Capture and Sequestration.

With what we know today, as we have seen, this can only be done by significantly reducing energy consumption and by the introduction of renewable energy. Increases in energy efficiency and decreases in the economy's fossil fuel intensity are not enough. Quite apart from the socially and politically decisive question of rebalancing resource use (North-South, North-North, South-South) some reduction in material production is needed.

But capitalism is fundamentally productivist. It satisfies social needs, even in its own market-distorted way, only when the exploited and oppressed force it, by their struggles, to drop crumbs from the table of accumulation. In this system, decreased material production and consumption can only happen temporarily, during overproduction crises that aggravate social crises, poverty, unemployment, and the growth of inequality.

This means that the climate challenge makes the anti-capitalist alternative a matter of objective urgency. It rules out any strategy based on participation in bourgeois institutions in the hope that gradual transformation is possible. Indeed, the only way to break out of the spiral of accumulation, which is incompatible with saving the climate, is to replace the production of commodities for the accumulation of (potentially unlimited) wealth with the production of use values for the satisfaction of (necessarily limited) human needs. Structural changes in production (including transportation) are therefore essential. Only such changes can create a material basis for changes in consumption. They require not only massive transfers of wealth from capital to labour, but also challenges to capitalist property rights. Both aspects come together in the demand for nationalisation without compensation of the entire credit sector (banks and insurance) which has major strategic importance. The fight against climate change thus offers an opportunity to return to the method of the transitional programme: on one hand by reasserting humanity's need for non-capitalist solutions, and on the other hand by providing the basis for an integrated series of concrete demands that, taken together, are incompatible with the normal operation of the capitalist system.

The exact demands can vary greatly from country to country and from region to region, depending on the particular level of development, social structures, ecosystem characteristics, specific energy concerns, etc. Broadly speaking, their transitional character flows from their being seen as offering effective solutions to both the ecological/climate crisis and the social crisis. Job creation in socially useful areas, the right to energy and housing, free public transport, opposition to pollution and its health impacts, responsible use of marine resources, forests and lakes – all of these are key areas in which proposals can be advanced for emission reductions, rational management of energy and material resources, reduced social inequality, increased democratic rights and resistance to commodification.

As this shows, questions of ecological/climate efficiency and emissions reduction are not side issues. On the contrary, they require particular emphasis, because the fight against global warming is a global issue with major social implications, and because anti-capitalist methods are more effective against climate change than capitalist methods, a fact that can only deepen the system's crisis of legitimacy as it faces a challenge whose importance it cannot deny.

37. The very fact that it is a gigantic global problem that must be solved quickly to head off still more serious disasters, means that climate change offers an exceptional opportunity to argue for anti-capitalist alternatives, in eminently practical, rational and immediate terms.

Climate change, and the colossal scale of action need in a very short time (two generations), can produce complex reactions among broad masses of people: denunciation and disbelief, cynicism, exacerbation of the alienation produced by the insecurity of life in late capitalist society. These sentiments can be used and manipulated not only by bourgeois governments, but also by mystical movements that offer irrational and eschatological [end of the world] pseudo-solutions. They can also be exploited by reactionary currents that attribute the environmental crisis to "human nature" and propose potentially barbaric neo-Malthusian solutions. The danger of reactionary responses is particularly serious when the class struggle is at a low ebb, dominated by defensive struggles in which environmental issues are seen as irrelevant.

But it would be wrong to conclude from this difficult situation that we should limit ourselves to very immediate demands, or, worse, that we can ignore the question in the hope that tomorrow will be a better day. On the contrary, in this situation we need to boldly combine agitation around immediate demands with broad anti-capitalist propaganda that is clear, direct, radical and comprehensive. This is both necessary and possible: necessary because it is the only way to respond to the objective ecological and social aspects of the challenge, and thus to demonstrate that we offer a way out; and possible because climate change, by its very nature as a gigantic global problem that must be solved quickly to head off still more serious disasters, offers an exceptional opportunity to argue for anti-capitalist alternatives, in eminently practical, rational and immediate terms.

Indeed, because this is an urgent matter, it is possible to appeal directly to the ethical awareness, conscience and reason of broad masses of people on fundamental questions such as the need, regardless of cost, to implement all appropriate means to fight climate change; to treat air, water, land, genetic resources, solar radiation, and energy in general as humanity's common property; to redistribute wealth and expand the public sector in order to mobilize every available means. It is possible to do this with great authority, basing ourselves thoughtfully on the expert scientific analyses that can help legitimize the anti-capitalist alternative.

The crisis of the socialist movement, including the very negative ecological balance sheet of "really existing socialism" cannot be ignored; it weighs down the ability of the exploited and oppressed to resist and counterattack. By responding effectively to the possibilities offered by climate change to promote anti-capitalist views that are rooted in a comprehensive ecological and social perspective, revolutionary Marxists can help rebuild the international workers' movement around a struggle of great social – even civilizational – importance.

38. Carbon cycle saturation and the deletion of non-renewable resources mean that, unlike in the past, the emancipation of the working class is impossible without taking natural constraints into account.

By itself, opposition to growth does not address societal or civilizational needs, nor is it a strategy for broad mobilization for social change – especially not if it just means cutting the Gross Domestic Product, a measure that includes only the quantity of wealth, ignoring qualitative human and ecological needs. Reducing physical production and consumption is necessary in the short-term to save the climate, because capitalism has taken humanity so far down a dead end street.

But such a reduction doesn't prejudge future possibilities of development: it is just one aspect of the necessary transition to a low carbon economy. To avoid provoking reactionary responses, that quantitative measure must be accompanied by qualitative measures: redistribution of wealth, reduced working time and public sector development. If these steps are taken, then, so long as it targets useless or dangerous products, reduced material production is compatible with increased wellbeing, wealth and quality of life for the immense majority of humanity, through social investment in education, health, culture, community life, public transport, land use, and free essential services.

Capitalism and the growth of material production and consumption are inseparable, but growth is an effect, not a cause. It is the production of value, the abstract form of exchange values (commodities), that results in a permanent tendency to unlimited accumulation of wealth on one side, and permanent expansion of poverty on the other. Climate policies that ignore this dual reality are almost certainly doomed to fail. The crucial factor and principle lever of the anti-capitalist alternative is thus still what the socialist movement has always depended on: mobilization of the exploited and oppressed against a system that is based on the race for profit, on private ownership of the means of production, on the production of commodities, on competition and on the wages system. But these no longer fully define the alternative. Carbon cycle saturation constitutes the most obvious and com-

---

Socialism must be judged not only by its contribution to satisfying human needs but also by its environmental sustainability

---

prehensive proof that unlike in the past, the emancipation of the working class is impossible without taking into account major natural constraints: limited resource reserves that cannot be renewed in historical time, the time needed to replenish renewable resources, the laws of thermodynamics, the laws and rhythms that govern ecosystems and biological cycles.

Lenin's brief definition – socialism is soviets plus electricity – is thus obsolete: we must also ask whether the electricity is produced from renewable or fossil energies, in what quantities, and with what environmental impacts.

To pose a comprehensive alternative to the dual ecological and social challenge – which is really a single ecosocial challenge – the socialist movement must answer these questions. It is not enough to say that socialism must incorporate ecological concerns, that socialists must consider ecological issues, develop ecological demands and support mobilizations in defence of the environment. The real challenge is to integrate socialism into the overall ecology of the terrestrial super-ecosystem – which means that socialism must be judged not only by its contribution to satisfying human needs but also by its environmental sustainability. Furthermore socialists must accept that complexity, unknown factors and the ever-changing nature of the biosphere add a degree of unavoidable uncertainty to the entire project.

Integrating socialism into ecology involves a cultural revolution in the socialist movement. This is essential if we are to overcome the compartmentalised, utilitarian and linear view that nature is just the physical platform from which humanity operates, the store from which it draws the resources needed to produce its social existence and the rubbish dump in which it stores the waste from this activity. In reality, nature is simultaneously the platform, the store, the dump – *and* all the living processes that, using the external supply of solar energy, constantly circulate and reorganize matter between all of these functions. So wastes and their disposal must be compatible, in both quantity and quality, with the ecosystems' capacities and recycling rhythms, so that the delicate biosphere's smooth operation is not compromised. That smooth operation depends on the number and the diversity of the participants, as well as on the quality and complexity of the multiple chains of activity that link them. In the final analysis the balance of many processes determines whether nature can provide the resources humanity needs.

In this context, the concept of "human control over nature," so full of positivist confidence, must be abandoned. From now on, the only socialism that is really possible is one that satisfies real human needs (i.e. needs freed from market alienation), democratically determined by human beings themselves, while always carefully taking into account the environmental impact of these needs and of the ways they are met.

39. Marx's major ecological error is not that he regarded nature as an unlimited reservoir of resources, but that he did not extend to energy the concept of "rational regulation of exchanges," which he had applied to soil.

In the 19th century, Liebig's work on soil exhaustion due to the breakdown of the nutrient cycle caused by urbanization and the internationalization of agricultural markets led Marx to postulate that, since labour necessarily mediates between human beings and nature, the breakdown could only be overcome if exchanges of matter between humanity and the environment were rationally regulated.

This idea that the "metabolism" between society and nature is historically determined and that mankind, because it produces its social existence consciously, must assume responsibility for rational regulation of material exchanges between humans and the Earth, is remarkably relevant today: it rivals the best modern analyses of the world's ecological problems. It shows that Marx, despite some ambiguous formulations in his work, was not ignorant of natural cycles and was aware that the finite environment consists of finite resources.

Concerning rational management of soil, this awareness was expressed powerfully in programmatic terms: it was the need to restore the nutrient cycle that led Marx and Engels to argue for abolition of the separation between town and country, a position that was as important in their eyes as the related argument for abolishing the separation between manual and intellectual work.

So Marx's major ecological error was not that he regarded nature as an unlimited reserve of resources, but that he didn't apply to energy the concept of rational regulation of material exchanges that he himself developed in regard to soil.

In his analysis of the Industrial Revolution, Marx did not see that the transition from wood to coal involved a shift from renewable to non-renewable energy, and that exploitation of the latter would inevitably come into conflict with the need for rational regulation of the exchange of carbon between society and its environment. While they clearly saw capitalism's tendency to exhaust the only two sources of all wealth – "the Earth and the workers" – an analysis that let them brilliantly anticipate the dynamic that would unite big industry and capitalist agriculture in simultaneously impoverishing urban workers, rural workers and the soil's fertility, the authors of the *Communist Manifesto* did not foresee that capitalism's use of non-renewable fossil fuels would inevitably lead humanity into an energy cul-de-sac.

The materialist conception of history does not exempt technology from the principle that all human activities are socially and historically determined. Marx himself violently denounced the class character of capitalist mechanization. However, his failure to understand the importance of the transition from wood to coal caused him to leave the class character of energy sources unexplored.

Since the very same steam engines were used to transform the chemical energy of wood and coal into mechanical energy and heat, a failure to see the differences between the two sources of energy had no practical consequences in Marx's time. But the situation changed with oil, and even more with nuclear energy, and that means we must take a clear position: either we view some energy sources as non-neutral and reject their associated technologies; or we view all energy sources as neutral and conclude that using the associated technologies is not in itself inappropriate. If we take the latter position, we are contradicting the thesis we started with, that technology is historically and socially determined. That allows the technocratic position that Marx pushed out the door to return through the window.

Marx's successors bear major responsibility for the fact that the concept of "rational regulation of material exchange between humanity and nature" and the related issue of the separation between town and country was forgotten in the 20th century. At the end of the 19th century, the invention of synthetic fertilisers seemed to have solved the problem of soil fertility, a key component of the ecological discussion in Capital. However, no Marxist author asked whether this solution was compatible with the "rational regulation of the exchange of matter" between humanity and nature. More importantly, none of them, including the revolutionaries, used the concepts that Marx had applied to soil fertility to evaluate the burning of fossil fuels and the plundering of other non-renewable resources from the perspective of "social metabolism."

The causes of this astonishing failure remain to be analyzed in detail. Russia's backwardness, the Stalinist counter-revolution, social-democratic productivism and a lack of interest in the evolution of natural science on the part of many 20th century Marxists – all of these played a part. But so too did exaggerated optimism, an irrational hope that science and technology would always find a way to escape capitalism's ecological dead ends. The radical challenge that climate change poses to this faith in progress is the most important reason why Marxists, since the 1970s, have had considerable difficulty in responding to environmental challenges. That is why the integration of socialism and ecology is a fundamental precondition for the restoration of Marxism's revolutionary vitality.

40. The energy question is central to any alternative. The perspective of "solar communism" extends Marx's concept of "social metabolism," deepening it and drawing new conclusions from it. It justifies using the new concept of "ecosocialism."

The energy question is central to the climate crisis and to any alternative. It is therefore essential that Marxists avoid the ambiguities and the dead ends of their predecessors, including Marx himself, in this regard. The concept of an energy system – defined as the mode of production considered from perspective of energy transformation – allows us to say that the capitalist system is characterized by:

(a) the near-total appropriation of energy sources, of conversion and transmission, and their transformation into commodities (including the commodification of the labour power placed at the disposal of the employers by human converters).

(b) the preponderant use of fossil fuels that generate both profits and greenhouse gases.

(c) the centralization and concentration of capitalist ownership of energy resources and converters, leading to increased centralization of the system itself.

(d) inefficient use of energy and high levels of waste, resulting mainly from the drive for profit, but also from the system's centralized structure, the geographical separation of production from markets, from useless production, from the lack of inter-sector economic planning, and from excessive mechanization.

(e) the globalization of supply, military protection of access to energy resources and imperialist control of the producer countries.

(f) the formation of increasingly inter-connected and centralized networks.

(g) the establishment around fossil fuels, mainly oil, of a powerful energy-industrial complex that includes the automobile aeronautical, shipbuilding and petrochemical industries.

(h) the increasing integration of agribusiness into this complex through production of fertilisers and biofuels, and the extension of genetic engineering.

(i) the tendency, inherent in the logic of accumulation of capital, to ceaselessly increase supply and demand, which is particularly expressed in energy by the spread of nuclear technology.

From the energy perspective, the socialist transformation of society requires the destruction of this centralized system, which is anarchic, wasteful, inefficient, capital-intensive, based on non-renewable fuels, and designed to support the overproduction of commodities. It must be replaced by a system that is decentralized, planned, economical, efficient, makes full use of human labour, is based exclusively on solar energy and is designed to support the production of necessary, durable, recyclable and reusable use-values. This transformation will affect not only the production of energy in a narrow sense but the entire industrial system, as well as agriculture, transportation, leisure activities and land use.

The energy/climate challenge leads us to consider the socialist revolution as involving not only the destruction of bourgeois state power, the creation of a proletarian state which immediately starts to wither away and the progressive introduction of workers' control, but also as the beginning of

---

The integration of socialism and ecology is a fundamental precondition for the restoration of Marxism's revolutionary vitality

---

a process of destruction of the old system of capitalist production and its replacement by a system that uses other technologies and other industrial processes to serve democratically decided goals.

This extremely profound historical upheaval can only be based on the victory of socialist revolutions on a world scale, when the abolition of the principal inequalities of development has made it possible to guarantee everyone the basic right to an existence worthy of the word "human." It assumes in particular every country has achieved food and energy autonomy. Far from involving stagnation or an end of development, it requires major progress in science and technology, and the social ability to implement those advances under democratic control, with everyone's active participation in a culture of prudent management of the biosphere. Indigenous communities can make an invaluable contribution to building that culture.

Revolutionary Marxism has long argued that, once basic human needs are satisfied, the qualitative development of human beings would take precedence over the quantitative growth of things. That view comes from Marx, who argued that true wealth involves free time, social relations and understanding the world. The perspective of solar communism is a logical continuation of that non-productivist vision, an extension that deepens it and draws new conclusions about demands, tasks and programme.

This deepening justifies using the new word "ecosocialism." As a concentrated expression of the common struggle against capitalism's exploitation of human beings and destruction of natural resources, ecosocialism does not proceed from some fantasy about idealistically establishing harmony between humanity and nature, but rather from the concrete need to manage the material exchanges between society and nature, following sound ecological principles – that is, in a manner that is to the greatest possible degree compatible with the proper functioning of ecosystems.

Notes

1 IPCC, *Summary for Policy Makers*, 2007. Note that the temperature variations here are based on 1999 and so must be increased by $0.7°C$ in order to indicate change from pre-industrial times.

2 UNDP, *World Report on Human Development*, 2007/2008

3 CO2 equivalents take into account all greenhouse gases, as if they were all CO2.

4 A "substantial deviation" involves a variation of 15% to 30% from the baseline.

5 Energy intensity and carbon intensity designate respectively the quantity of energy consumed and the quantity of carbon emitted in the form of gas in order to produce one unit of GDP.

6 We might add geothermic energy, the only non-solar energy source, but its potential is marginal.

7 The objective would be raised to 30% if an international agreement includes comparable reductions by other industrialised countries and signification participation by the emerging countries. That would still remain at the low end of the range recommended by experts.

Some suggestions for further reading

Books

Paul Burkett. *Marx and Nature: A Red and Green Perspective.* (St. Martin's Press, 1999) <us.macmillan.com/marxandnature>

John Bellamy Foster. *Marx's Ecology: Materialism and Nature* (Monthly Review Press, 2000) <www.monthlyreview.org/books/index.php>

John Bellamy Foster. *The Ecological Revolution.* (Monthly Review Press 2009) <www.monthlyreview.org/books/index.php>

Dave Holmes, Terry Townsend, John Bellamy Foster. *Change the System not the Climate!* (Resistance Books, 2007) <www.resistancebooks.com/>

Jonathan Hughes. *Ecology and Historical Materialism.* (Cambridge University Press, 2000) <www.cambridge.org/>

Jane Kelly & Sheila Malone. *Ecosocialism or Barbarism.* (Socialist Resistance, 2007) <resistancebooks.blogspot.com/>

Joel Kovel. *The Enemy of Nature: The End of Capitalism or the End of the World?* (Zed Books, 2007) <www.zedbooks.co.uk>

Larry Lohmann. *Carbon Trading: A Critical Dialogue on Climate Change, Privatisation and Power.* <www.carbontradewatch.org>

Jonathan Neale. *Stop Global Warming: Change the World.* (Bookmarks, 2008) <www.bookmarks.uk.com>

Kevin Smith. The Carbon Neutral Myth: Offset Indulgences For Your Climate Sins. (Carbon Trade Watch, 2007) <www.carbontradewatch.org>

David Spratt & Philip Sutton. *Climate Code Red* (Scribe, 2008) <www.scribepublications.com.au>

Derek Wall. *Babylon and Beyond: The Economics of Anti-Capitalist, Anti-Globalist and Radical Green Movements.* (Pluto Press 2005) <www.plutobooks.com/>

Websites and Blogs

Another Green World <another-green-world.blogspot.com/>

Campaign against Climate Change <www.campaigncc.org/>

Carbon Trade Watch <www.carbontradewatch.org/>

Climate Ark Climate Change and Global Warming Portal <climateark.org/>

Climate Change Social Change <climatechangesocialchange.wordpress.com/>

Climate Code Red <climatecodered.blogspot.com>

more...

The Corner House <www.thecornerhouse.org.uk/>

Durban Group for Climate Justice <www.carbontradewatch.org/durban/>

Ecosocialist International Network <ecosocialistnetwork.org/>

Europe Solidaire sans Frontières <www.europe-solidaire.org>

Global Justice Ecology Project <www.globaljusticeecology.org/>

Indigenous Environmental Network <www.ienearth.org/>

Joel Kovel <www.joelkovel.org/>

Left Click <leftclickblog.blogspot.com>

Liam Mac Uaid <liammacuaid.wordpress.com/>

Marxists Internet Archive <www.marxists.org/>

Marxsite <www.marxsite.com>

Mobilization for Climate Justice <www.actforclimatejustice.org>

New Economics Foundation <www.neweconomics.org/>

RealClimate Climate Science from Climate Scientists
    <www.realclimate.org/>

Socialist Alliance (Australia) <www.socialist-alliance.org/>

Stop Climate Chaos <www.stopclimatechaos.org>

Magazines, Newspapers, Journals

Climate and Capitalism <www.climateandcapitalism.com>

Green Left Weekly <www.greenleft.org.au/>

International Socialist Review <www.isreview.org/>

International Viewpoint <www.internationalviewpoint.org/>

La Lucha Indígena <www.luchaindigena.com/>

Links: International Journal of Socialist Renewal <links.org.au/>

Monthly Review <monthlyreview.org/>

MRzine <mrzine.monthlyreview.org>

Socialist Resistance <socialistresistance.org/>

Socialist Voice <www.socialistvoice.ca>

Socialist Worker <socialistworker.org>

Zmag <www.zmag.org>

Printed in the United States
152075LV00002B/9/P